Sports Extra

Sports Extra

CLASSICS OF SPORTS REPORTING

Edited by STANLEY FRANK

NEW YORK

A. S. BARNES & COMPANY

CONTENTS

---

v

Contents

Contents

The Age of Reason

Contents

Foreword

I T HAS BEEN SAID that much of the best and most arresting
writing to be found in American newspapers appears on
the sport pages, a thesis we do not intend to stress or sub-
stantiate. The only purpose of this book is to present representative specimens of sportswriting that have inspired highly
favorable and flattering acceptance of the men who report
sport as competent craftsmen in their special field.

This, admittedly, is not an authoritative anthology of all
the outstanding sport stories written in the last fifty, or even
five, years. The literature of sport is so extensive that it is
manifestly impossible to include in one volume all the men
who merit recognition. Of necessity, the list has been re-
stricted to one typical piece by a comparative handful of name
writers who are known nationally. This arbitrary arrange-
ment has eliminated many deserving brothers in the lodge
and the complete exclusion of writers on small-town papers
where, for all anyone knows, the Lardners, Runyons and
Peglers of the 1950's may be flourishing.

A book twice the length of this one would, perforce, over-
look many stories considered "classics" by the readers, writers
and their close relatives. By definition, any story not con-

tained herein automatically will be raised to classic eminence for at least two days.

Not all the selections belong in the realm of pure literature. The boys had no time to compose a piece for the ages: it is, indeed, a wonder that the syntax is relatively unscrambled and the English is reasonably good. The majority of these stories was written in a huge, outdoor psychopathic ward with anywhere from 30- to 100,000 inmates screaming insanely and the copy desk demanding a lead for the next edition, and damn' quick, too. Much of the copy was fed in short "takes," or paragraphs, to telegraph instruments clattering insistently and it was written in the white heat of excitement on eighteen crowded, precarious inches of wooden benches and tables under frightful conditions—rain, cold, heat and the critical attention of insects that fly or crawl or have the power of speech.

Several stories of historical and technical value were, unfortunately, unobtainable; old newspaper files are incomplete and faded clippings of memorable events crumbled to dust at the touch of the hand. With the exception of the first two selections, all material was taken directly from American newspapers. The exceptions (Hazlitt's essay on Cavanagh the Fives-Player and Marquand's introduction to Donald Barr Chidsey's "John The Great") were used for two reasons: (1) They are distinguished pieces of writing; (2) they establish the philosophic approach to sport this book endeavors to achieve.

We like to believe a few lines from Hazlitt's sentimental tribute to Cavanagh is justification—if it is needed—for publishing this book at this time of world crisis: "...It may be said that there are things of more importance than striking a ball against a wall—there are things indeed that make more noise and do as little good, such as making war and peace, making speeches and answering them, making verses and blotting them, making money and throwing it away...."

Another purpose of this collection is to chart the subtle changes in America's attitude toward sport and the men who play games for pleasure and/or profit. We have attempted to underscore this transformation by arranging the selections in chronological order and, at the same time, to highlight the attending changes in the technique of sportswriting.

The claim has been made that in normal times the average American male adult's chief interest, apart from his family and the business of making a living, is wrapped up in sport. Most generalizations are false—including this one—but it is an even-money shot that such a sweeping induction is not an outrageous overstatement.

Until the 1920's, the general public regarded professional athletes as crude, muscular muggs engaged in activities hardly worthy of attention from gentlemen of breeding and culture. Amateurs were accepted with more tolerance, but it was founded essentially on the snob appeal of the social sports, and even the football players of the Ivy League were looked upon as strange species in the human zoo.

The crazy, turbulent twenties brought an abrupt and radical change in viewpoint. Whether it was an emotional hangover from the war or merely the firing of imaginations by the most colorful and compelling stars any decade has seen is a moot question. Whatever the cause, America suddenly became sports-mad and its athletic heroes were canonized one cut below sainthood.

Babe Ruth, the most photographed personality in the world after Edward, Prince of Wales, received a salary greater than the President's. Red Grange, a football player from the University of Illinois, left college to turn professional and cleared a quarter of a million dollars in two months. More than two million dollars were paid to see Gene Tunney defend his heavyweight championship against Jack Dempsey. Bobby Jones won the golf titles of Britain and was given a ticker-tape reception down Broadway previously reserved only for visiting royalty, transatlantic aviators and Channel swimmers.

The honeymoon was wonderful while it lasted, but the depression and the 1930's threw up a granite wall of reality that smashed many illusions and concepts, and sport articles in the papers quickly reflected the trend of the times.

Flowery adjectives and high-powered superlatives were rationed with increasing severity as sportwriters commenced to analyze more critically performances and promoters' motives. The most obvious change in the sport pages was the drastic reduction in the length of stories.

During the 1920's the lead stories on major events—always represented solemnly as the spectacle of the century—ran interminably. It was not unusual for a metropolitan paper to carry a 4,000-word account of a World Series game or a heavyweight fight, accompanied by a crowd, or color, story of equal length. The crowd stories were written by "trained seals," prose poets from the city staff or celebrities such as Ring Lardner and Irvin S. Cobb, who had left newspaper work and returned to do a once-over-lightly. This, too, was the era in which ghosts tripped with muffled cadence across the sport pages, with the ink in their veins pumped by anonymous staff members who sometimes communicated with their spectral mouthpieces.

The trained seals and the ghosts vanished several years ago. Editors discovered that regular staff members of the sport department were capable of writing thoroughly acceptable crowd and feature yarns and compressing them into the body of news stories that consumed half the space formerly devoted to one aspect of the event. A growing appreciation for the esthetics of sport was apparent. Hendrik Van Loon admitted he never quite understood the real beauty of Greek sculpture until he saw Babe Ruth hit a home run. He also said a sliding demonstration by Ty Cobb and Knute Rockne in his living room was as uplifting a show as the best Russian ballet he ever saw.

Save for the correction of typographical errors and the cutting of material that was repetitious or no longer is pertinent to the action or result, every story appears here as it ran in the paper. Contemporary writers were asked to submit the stories liked best, and it is significant that the majority selected whimsical, reflective or philosophic pieces, and perhaps it's just as well. This book originally was conceived as a collection of news stories on famous events, but such copy, no matter how individual the treatment, would have followed a rather monotonous pattern. We trust the change of pace has made for wider scope and interest.

To repeat, this book is not offered as a series of essays in the classic literary tradition. It merely attempts to show why readers, when asked to name their favorite sections of the newspapers, consistently pick the sport pages for win, place or show.

STANLEY FRANK

May, 1944.

Coming of Age

CAVANAGH THE FIVES-PLAYER

BY

William Hazlitt

(LONDON EXAMINER) FEBRUARY 7, 1819

D IED AT HIS HOUSE in Burbage Street, St. Giles's, John
Cavanagh, the famous hand fives-player. When a person dies, who does any one thing better than any one else in
the world, which so many others are trying to do well, it
leaves a gap in society. It is not likely that any one will now
see the game of fives played in its perfection for many years
to come—for Cavanagh is dead, and has not left his peer behind him. It may be said that there are things of more importance than striking a ball against a wall—there are things
indeed that make more noise and do as little good, such as
making war and peace, making speeches and answering them,
making verses and blotting them, making money and throwing it away. But the game of fives is what no one despises who
has ever played at it. It is the finest exercise for the body, and
the best relaxation for the mind. The Roman poet said that
"Care mounted behind the horseman and stuck to his skirts."
But this remark would not have applied to the fives-player.
He who takes to playing at fives is twice young. He feels
neither the past nor future "in the instant." Debts, taxes,
"domestic treason, foreign levy, nothing can touch him further." He has no other wish, no other thought, from the moment the game begins, but that of striking the ball, of placing

3

it, of *making* it! This Cavanagh was sure to do. Whenever he touched the ball there was an end of the chase. His eye was certain, his hand fatal, his presence of mind complete. He could do what he pleased, and he always knew exactly what to do. He saw the whole game, and played it; took instant advantage of his adversary's weakness, and recovered balls, as if by a miracle and from sudden thought, that every one gave for lost. He had equal power and skill, quickness and judgment. He could either outwit his antagonist by finesse, or beat him by main strength. Sometimes, when he seemed preparing to send the ball with the full swing of his arm, he would by a slight turn of his wrist drop it within an inch of the line. In general, the ball came from his hand, as if from a racket, in a straight horizontal line; so that it was in vain to attempt to overtake or stop it. As it was said of a great orator that he never was at a loss for a word, and for the properest word, so Cavanagh always could tell the degree of force necessary to be given to a ball, and the precise direction in which it should be sent. He did his work with the greatest ease; never took more pains than was necessary; and while others were fagging themselves to death, was as cool and collected as if he had just entered the court. His style of play was as remarkable as his power of execution. He had no affectation, no trifling. He did not throw away the game to show off an attitude, or try an experiment. He was a fine, sensible, manly player, who did what he could, but that was more than any one else could even affect to do. His blows were not undecided and ineffectual—lumbering like Mr. Wordsworth's epic poetry, wavering like Mr. Coleridge's lyric prose, nor short of the mark like Mr. Brougham's speeches, nor wide of it like Mr. Canning's wit, nor foul like the Quarterly, nor *let* balls like the Edinburgh Review. Cobbett and Junius together would have made a Cavanagh. He was the best *up*-hill player in the world; even when his adversary was fourteen, he would play on the same or better, and as he never flung away the game through carelessness and conceit, he never gave it up through laziness or want of heart. The only peculiarity of his play was that he never *volleyed*, but let the balls hop; but if they rose an inch from the ground, he never missed having them. There was not only nobody equal, but nobody second to him. It is supposed that he could give any other player half the game, or beat them with his left hand. His service was tremendous. He once played Woodward and Meredith together (two of the best players in England) in the Fives-court, St. Martin's-street, and made seven-and-twenty aces following by services alone—a thing unheard of. He another time played Peru, who was considered a first-rate fives player, a match of the best out of five games, and in the first three games, which of course decided the match, Peru got only one ace.

Cavanagh was an Irishman by birth, and a house-painter by profession. He had once laid aside his working dress, and walked up, in his smartest clothes, to the Rosemary Branch to have an afternoon's pleasure. A person accosted him, and asked him if he would have a game. So they agreed to play for half a crown a game, and a bottle of cider. The first game began—it was seven, eight, thirteen, fourteen, all. Cavanagh won it. The next was the same. They played on, and each game was hardly contested. "There," said the unconscious fives-player, "there was a stroke that Cavanagh could not take: I never played better in my life, and yet I can't win a game. I don't know how it is!" However, they played on, Cavanagh winning every game and the bystanders drinking the cider and laughing all the time. In the twelfth game, when Cavanagh was only four, and the stranger thirteen, a person came in and said, "What! are you here, Cavanagh?"

The words were no sooner pronounced than the astonished player let the ball drop from his hand, and saying, "What! have I been breaking my heart all this time to beat Cavanagh?" and refused to make another effort. "And yet, I give you my word," said Cavanagh, telling the story with some triumph, "I played all the while with my clenched fist."

He used frequently to play matches at Copenhagen House for wagers and dinners. The wall against which they play is the same that supports the kitchen-chimney, and when the wall resounded louder than usual, the cooks exclaimed, "Those are the Irishman's balls," and the joints trembled on the spit!—Goldsmith consoled himself that there were places where he too was admired: and Cavanagh was the admiration of all the fives-courts where he ever played. Mr. Powell, when he played matches in the Court at St. Martin's-street, used to fill his gallery at half a crown a head, with amateurs and admirers of talent in whatever department it is shown. He could not have shown himself in any ground in England, but he would have been immediately surrounded with inquisitive gazers, trying to find out in what part of his frame his unrivalled skill lay, as politicians wonder to see the balance of Europe suspended in Lord Castlereagh's face, and admire the trophies of the British Navy lurking under Mr. Croker's hanging brow. Now Cavanagh was as good-looking a man as the Noble Lord, and much better looking than the Right Hon. Secretary. He had a clear, open countenance, and did not look sideways or down, like Mr. Murray the book-seller. He was a young fellow of sense, humour, and courage. He once had a quarrel with a waterman at Hungerford Stairs, and they say, served him out in great style. In a word, there are hundreds at this day who cannot mention his name without admiration, as the best fives-player that perhaps ever lived (the greatest excellence of which they have any notion)—and the noisy shout of the ring happily stood him in stead of the unheard voice of posterity!

The only person who seems to have excelled as much in another way as Cavanagh did in his was the late John Davies, the racket-player. It was remarked of him that he did not seem to follow the ball, but the ball seemed to follow him. Give him a foot of wall, and he was sure to make the ball. The four best racket-players of that day were Jack Spines, Jem Harding, Armitage, and Church. Davies could give any of these two hands a time, that is, half the game, and each of these, at their best, could give the best player now in London the same odds. Such are the gradations in all exertions of human skill and art. He once played four capital players together, and beat them. He was also a first-rate tennis-player, and an excellent fives-player. In the Fleet of King's Bench, he would have stood against Powell, who was reckoned the best open-ground player of his time. The last-mentioned player is at present the keeper of the Fives-court, and we might recommend to him for a motto over his door—"Who enters here, forgets himself, his country, and his friends." And the best of it is, that by the calculation of the odds, none of the three are worth remembering!

Cavanagh died from the bursting of a blood-vessel, which prevented him from playing for the last two or three years. This, he was often heard to say, he thought hard upon him. He was fast recovering, however, when he was suddenly carried off, to the regret of all who knew him. As Mr. Peel made it a qualification of the present Speaker, Mr. Manners Sutton, that he was an excellent moral character, so Jack Cavanagh was a zealous Catholic, and could not be persuaded to eat meat on a Friday, the day on which he died. We have paid this willing tribute to his memory:

"Let no rude hand deface it,
And his forlorn *Hic Facet*."

THE BOSTON STRONG BOY *

BY

John P. Marquand

A NEW BIOGRAPHY of the late John L. Sullivan cannot, even without national destiny at the crossroads, be placed completely in the category of escapist literature. For one thing, a thoughtful reader will encounter in this life of the Boston Strong Boy portents which are too ironic and prophetic to serve as sheer entertainment. For another, its subject is too starkly revealing as a mirror of his age, though now, from the point of view of manners and tastes, he is as extinct as the mustache cups that went with it.

He involuntarily provokes the most serious sort of social curiosity, for no one who reads this book can help but ponder on the peculiar and uneven aspects of the environment which produced him. Even those of us whose memories stretch back to the remnants of that era find it now as hard to grasp as, say, the pages of Scott's Ivanhoe or, better yet, a page of Bulwer-Lytton. It is difficult to reconcile its contradictions. There is John L. Sullivan's emergence from Boston, for example, in the quiet time which Van Wyck Brooks describes as New England's Indian summer—a strange fruit from Boston's tree of knowledge. There is an odder paradox. In the days when nice little boys wore long curls and velvet blouses and lace collars and cuffs and posed for their portraits with their

---

* Introduction to John The Great, by Donald Barr Chidsey, published in 1942 by Doubleday, Doran and Company.
8

hands on the heads of faithful Newfoundland dogs, Sir Galahad was not the hero of the youth of America, in spite of
Victorian effort to make this come to pass. The hero of this
age and the man who had the most influence on boyhood's
wish fulfillment was John L. Sullivan, the Champion of the
World. There has been no other pugilist in the history of
the prize ring, either in England or America, not excepting
the bookish Mr. Tunney or even the universally respected Joe
Louis, who has ever assumed such a role. It is difficult to explain the hold of John L. Sullivan upon his time; the present
biographer has not done so fully, and perhaps no one can.
He is bewildered by the man's non-exemplary qualities. Mr.
Sullivan never lectured on Shakespeare to the boys at Yale.
His education was rudimentary, though, be it said, his auto-
graph at one time was worth twice that of President Eliot's
of Harvard. He did not work hard and diligently, although
he amassed a million dollars in ephemeral and exhibitionist
ways, and very little of it by actual fighting. He did not save
a penny of it. The one discoverable way in which his private
life may have been a useful example was his dislike of cigarettes; he smoked only cigars, great quantities of large black
ones. He smoked these even as he trained for most of his
more arduous physical collisions. He underwent few of the
ascetic tortures which one associates with pugilism, until Mr.
Muldoon got hold of him. It was nearly always his opinion
that drinking and the prize ring went hand in hand.

From a study of his character, it does not seem that this
American boy's white knight was a very likable fellow, either.
His wit does not appear to have been scintillating, even when
he was sober. You will see him as a dull, quarrelsome, brag-
ging bully when he was drunk, and in his more active days
he was usually to be found in this unfortunate condition.
Yet he was the idol of his day: the press hung on his words;

he could pack the local theatres; young boys and old boys, too, followed him, much as we follow the circus now when it comes to town. You will see him conversing for two hours with the late King Edward, then the Prince of Wales. Everybody, including President Theodore Roosevelt, was glad to shake his hand. Even now his memory lingers somewhere in the past, not in the gallery of the statesmen or the scholars, but still on an unshaken pedestal in the gallery of American history.

He flourished at the time when you could make a meal from a free lunch in any self-respecting bar, in the days of "The public be damned," and of "God Almighty Baer," yet by some amazing alchemy his memory has outlived the Goulds and the Sages and the Harrimans and the Vanderbilts. His personality seems to offer only one valid reason for this. Mr. Sullivan said frequently and profanely, drunk or sober, that he could lick any so-and-so in the world. Others have made the same remark before and since, but Mr. Sullivan was different from most of the others: he was always ready to try it, and usually he could do it, and on those rare occasions when he couldn't he did not come to the reporters with an alibi. Even when he was an old man and his failing eyes encountered the hulk of the heavyweight, Jess Willard, John L. Sullivan wished that it were twenty years before. He did not know any fancy fighting, either; he could not dance or duck or roll with the punches. He was out there firmly on his feet to smash down his opponent's guard with clean, straight blows.

Furthermore, he was always ready to set up all the drinks for everyone in the house, all the wines and liquors that anybody wanted. Furthermore, he was a handsome physical monument. When he was not lightly clad in tights, with the jeweled belt of the Champion of the World around his middle, Mr. Sullivan was dressed in rich checkered raiment and fine cravats. His pockets were loaded with small change which he tossed freely to the urchins, and you could always touch John L. Sullivan for a bill if you were down and out. There was always more where it came from, and besides, he could lick any so-and-so in the world.

It makes up into a simple and not a wholly edifying prescription, but he offered the public then the same elements for hero worship that we now seek to find less successfully from Hollywood stars. The wishful thinking of their time fills in their vacuities and deficiencies. That is why you will find John L. Sullivan a useful guide in spite of his apparently useless wanderings. More than any other man in his period, John L. Sullivan can acquaint you with the spirit of his time, for you have shaken hands with it when you have shaken hands with John L. Sullivan. You meet in him quite shockingly the follies and deficiencies of our fathers and grandfathers. You will also learn the reasons for their strength and for much that is both right and wrong with the turbulent days of the present.

Arthur Brisbane

The following account of the Sullivan-Mitchell fight is a museum piece in American journalism for two reasons. It marked the first full-dress coverage of an international sporting event and it was the most important assignment up to that time given Arthur Brisbane, who was to become a power with few peers in his profession.

Tremendous interest attended the great John L. Sullivan's invasion of Europe in 1888. Newspapers in New York, Boston and other cities along the Atlantic seaboard disregarded the staggering cable tolls in their anxiety to give the sub-scribers an exclusive eye-witness description of the Strong Boy's meeting with the Englishman who had knocked the Great Man off his feet five years earlier.

Only forty spectators saw the fight and several wound up in the clutches of the law. The reporters who eluded the gendarmes rushed back to Paris and filed their stories in fe-verish haste to get their living, breathing, human documents on the street the following day ahead of the competition. It was a labor of love. The Great Blizzard of '88 struck New York and Boston on March 11, the day after the fight, and it was impossible to circulate the papers. The expense and the effort went for the indiscriminating Mr. Sweeney.

William Randolph Hearst's right bower and editorial pun-dit until his death at seventy-two in 1936, Brisbane was one of the most widely syndicated writers in America. His col-umn, "Today," famous for concise, simple, almost naive, expression on an astonishing variety of subjects, was enormously popular and generally is recognized as the cornerstone of Hearst's vast newspaper empire.

Brisbane was not a sport enthusiast and he was severely critical of professional pugilism ("A gorilla could lick them both"), but he did famously in spite of it all. He was the wealthiest ink-stained wretch ever to labor in the vineyard of the Fourth Estate.

THE EDITOR

DECLINE OF A HERO

BY

Arthur Brisbane

(NEW YORK DAILY TRIBUNE)

Paris, March 10, 1888.

THE SULLIVAN-MITCHELL fight at Chantilly to-day was an even gloomier and more depressing fiasco than the battle between Kilrain and Smith a few months ago on an island in the Seine. It took scarcely twenty minutes of sharp fighting to show that six years of a brutal, dissipated life had sapped the once astonishing power of the American champion. He could not close with his wiry English antagonist, and the effort to force the fighting cost him all the strength which his fatuous admirers counted on for the critical rounds at the finish.

Then the rain came, drenching the pugilists and turning the turf of the prize ring into a mass of slippery mud.

Mitchell held out doggedly in the wet, but Sullivan was seized with chills, and after thirty-nine rounds—most of them dragging and ineffectual—the contest ended in a draw. The American pugilist cried with mortification at his ignominious failure to make good the threats he had been hurling so lavishly at Mitchell. Mitchell's friends were equally chagrined at their champion's inability to fight out a decided victory. The credit, at any rate, remained with the London man and it was agreed on all hands—Sullivan's backers not excepted—that the Boston prize-fighter had met with a stinging reverse, as crushing to his hopes of international championship as an actual defeat.

The battle was fought on the country place of Baron Alphonse Rothschild, at Apremont, near the Chantilly station. The backers of both men had spent yesterday wrangling at Amiens over the details of the match, unable to agree on a place to pitch the ring. The lookout dispatched from London early in the week had arranged for a battle ground nearer at hand, but at the last moment the spot was found unsuitable. The Sullivan party thereupon charged Mitchell was trying to wriggle out of the fight, and much acrimonious discussion followed. Finally, Mitchell's backers agreed to leave the choice of a ring to the American contingent, and "Johnny" Gideon of "The London Sportsman," who had once hunted up a battle ground for Sayres, with two other of "The Sportsman's" representatives, started out late last night at Sullivan's request, to pitch a ring and make all ready for to-day's contest.

Gideon and his two assistants travelled as far toward Paris as Creil, and early this morning found a quiet spot on the Rothschild grounds, just behind the Baron's stable, the white villa showing through the trees in the distance. Forty people in all were in the secret and saw the fight, the scouting party sending word back at once, and the warring factions at Amiens arriving after a few hours' delay. The French police were on the alert all along the line, short files being drawn up at the different stations which the pugilists and their friends had to pass. Some officers were hanging around even at Creil, but they made no sign as the English and Americans got out of the railway carriages, and shortly afterward straggled by twos and threes over toward the woods at the back of the Baron's country seat.

The last man was on hand, finally, about 11 a.m. The ring was up and the seconds and backers were dividing into two hostile camps. The ropes were drawn about a little plat of turf under the trees. The ground was good and the weather fair enough, except for a threat of rain to the north.

Some well-known English sporting men were in the groups at each end of the ring. "Jake" Kilrain, the Baltimore pugilist, who fought the draw with "Jem" Smith, and Baldock, of the Pelican Club, were Mitchell's seconds. "Jack" Ashton and Macdonald were seconds for Sullivan. A London stockbroker, named Angle, was referee. "Jack" Bennett was Sullivan's umpire, and "Charlie" Rowell, the long-distance pedestrian, did a similar office for Mitchell. "Pony" Moore, Mitchell's father-in-law, and "Chippy" Norton, the well-known London bookmaker, and holder of the stakes in the coming match, stood in a group to one side with Carew Young, Sir Michael Sandys, Lord Wemyss and a few other aristocrats who figure as patrons of the London ring. On the American side were Dominick McCaffrey, "Charley" Dougherty and a few newspaper men.

Mitchell had been talking a good deal all the morning, and his face was flushed with excitement. He had trained hard, and his face was a trifle thin. Still, his spirits were good, and he said he was confident of holding his own. Sullivan had not pushed himself so hard in training, and his face and muscles showed it. He was as arrogant and contemptuous as ever, and boastfully pulled out a £500 note as he entered the ring and, flourishing it aloft, called for Mitchell to cover it. His manager, Phillips, also opened a roll of bills and offered odds of £1,000 to £300 on the Boston pugilist. No takers could be found, however. The English partisans had all their money up at long odds, and as the battle drew near they looked more and more despondently across at the big, self-confident bully who had never yet met his match in the prize-ring.

Sullivan, stripped to the waist, stepped out from his corner of the inclosure about half-past 12. He looked ruddy and burly enough, but as the crucial rounds soon showed, his staying powers had already vanished under the double bombardment of French champagne and American whiskey. Mitchell followed him into the ring four minutes later. The two men were old antagonists and personal enemies, and they glared at each other fiercely. Mitchell made the first movement toward shaking hands, the two men touched palms weakly, the referee called time, and the first round in the fight began. The time taken by the watchers was 12:30 p. m.

The first round opened savagely. Sullivan, as usual, forcing the fighting and making one or two powerful rushes. The American landed his first blow, a heavy left-handed, just to the left of Mitchell's jaw. The Londoner was dazed, but soon got in a light return on Sullivan's chest. Then he sparred cautiously about the ring, warding off successfully two or three of his pursuer's leads. Finally Sullivan got angry and rushed in close. His left hand fell in short, Mitchell dodging, but his big right fist crashed against the unlucky Englishman's head, and the wiry Londoner fell in a heap over toward the ropes in his corner.

The American contingent was jubilant, and odds ran up as

high as £1,000 to £100 on the big Bostonian. Sullivan was a trifle winded, but it looked as if the Briton could not stand up before many more rushes like that just ended.

After half a minute or so Mitchell was up again, sponged off and in the ring. Sullivan soon followed. This time Mitchell fought shy, retreating from one part of the ring to the other. Sullivan's fierce rush was too much for him, however, and the two were closed. The first blow caught the Londoner on the chest, and Mitchell staggered as if he had been hit by a pile-driver. He made a feeble effort to parry, and then to run away, but another blow on the head from Sullivan's deadly right hand laid him flat on the turf near the middle of the ring. His seconds lifted him over to the corner, where a little sponging brought him to in a minute.

The pace was too fast for the Englishman, but it was also beginning to tell on the greatest of short-distance "sluggers." Sullivan was red in the face, and the cool defensive strategy of his antagonist ruffled the big bully's temper. Still everything looked rose-hued to the little party at his back, which was now frantically waving the Stars and Stripes and the green flag of Ireland in anticipatory triumph. "Pony" Moore had a scowl on his face, and the Union Jack and the Royal ensign over Mitchell's quarters drooped disconsolately in the heavy air that threatened a coming storm.

THE ENGLISHMAN'S DILATORY TACTICS

Mitchell had profited by his experience so far, and from the beginning of the third round fought a waiting battle. He ran all over the ring, Sullivan bounding after him and getting in an occasional ineffective blow. The American champion at last made a desperate rush, broke down the Englishman's defences and sent him sprawling to the ground with a right-hand blow in the face. Sullivan seemed to have hurt his hand a little in this last rush, and Mitchell, though badly battered, was far from being "knocked out." Sullivan was pushing himself hard, and seemed to feel the strain.

In the fourth round Mitchell squirmed and dodged for several minutes before Sullivan could close with him. When he did reach the Englishman his blows fell lightly, and though Mitchell went down in the last rush, he fell more in the tussle than under any one blow. In the fifth and sixth rounds he took to the tactics that Smith had found so successful in his fight with Kilrain. Sullivan charged again and again, but every time the Londoner got away. Once when he was cornered he dropped to the ground on one hand and one knee—a foul by the London ring rules. Sullivan had come near striking him as he dropped, and the referee cautioned both men about making or causing a foul stroke.

In the next three rounds Sullivan kept up his ineffectual chase after the fleet-footed Englishman. Mitchell got off without any damage to speak of, and even planted his fist two or three times on Sullivan's face.

In the tenth round rain began to fall, and the shower soon turned into a steady pour. Sullivan was chilled to the bone and began to shake with ague. He kept pluckily on, however, pounding through the mud after his opponent, falling shorter and shorter on each rush. His backers kept up their courage, but looked for nothing better than a draw! Mitchell's backers hoped now that their man might outlast the American and win the championship and the £500.

The rounds from the tenth to the thirty-second dragged stupidly. Sullivan, who was beginning to shiver all over, could do nothing. Neither could Mitchell, though he tried with all his might. The terrible punishment of the first four rounds had nearly crippled him. The thirty-second round lasted twenty-seven minutes. The thirty-fifth round was fought through fifteen minutes. Both men were weak and could no longer hit out from the shoulder.

After half an hour's fighting in the last round, Baldock, Mitchell's second, broke into the ring and cried out that the men had enough. "Make it a draw," he urged. The fight had now lasted three hours and ten minutes. The principals readily agreed to stop, and shook hands, though the champion was soon after looking with rage and chagrin, and his backers folded up their flags, the most heart-sore set of sportsmen that has ever travelled 3,000 miles to see a great international fight.

Mitchell was badly trussed. There was a big lump on his jaw, his left eye was bunged up, and his body was a good deal battered. Sullivan was sick and worn out, but not much hurt. Both parties started for this city on the evening train.

The stakes, £500 a side, will be doubled, of course. But it looks as if Sullivan's fighting career was nearly over. His fight to-day will be a sad blow, at least, to his "hippodroming" box-office receipts.

Charles Dryden

The name of Charles Dryden rings no bells in the memories of newspaper readers whose experience has been confined to the last quarter-century. But to old subscribers and sport historians, Dryden strikes a clamorous gong awakening remembrance of baseball's first humorist and perhaps the greatest, with the possible exception of Ring Lardner, upon whom he exerted a profound influence.

Of all the pioneer chroniclers of sport, Dryden and his copy best survive the passage of time, which is the most rigorous test. His stuff today is as fresh and amusing and provocative as it was the day he wrote it forty years ago. It is no strenuous exercise of lily-gilding to say that this quiet, whimsical man was the prime mover in making baseball the best documented of all sports.

Although he was well grounded in technical baseball knowledge, Dryden preferred to stress the human-interest and humorous aspects of the game. While his colleagues were reporting in detail the scoring of runs, Dryden was telling of the foibles, fancies and foolishness of the ball players, of the brainstorms and brilliant plays they pulled on the field, and he dismissed the actual run-making in a few, casual sentences.

Dryden was an indefatigable phrase-maker and coiner of nicknames, although his copy was singularly free of the tedious slang and synonyms that marked most sport stories of his time. He portrayed Ed Walsh, the celebrated White Sox pitcher, as "the only man in the world who could strut standing still," a thumbnail description that has been lifted and paraphrased extensively. He waged a running feud with the copy desk in an effort to enliven his stories with bawdy references. He counted that day a triumph when the desk failed to catch something to the effect that "Joe Blow slid into the plate like Balaam rode into Jerusalem."

One of the first sport writers to be given a by-line, Dryden was such a circulation-puller that his stories ran on Page 1 in Philadelphia, New York, Chicago and San Francisco. The readers lapped up his racy, irreverent style, but the brass hats frequently were outraged by it. Andrew Freedman, irascible owner of the Giants, barred Dryden from the Polo Grounds in the early 1900's. Unperturbed, Dryden continued to write a story of the ball game for the New York Evening World every evening. He sat in City Hall Park, facing Newspaper Row, all afternoon observing nature and the queer customs of the natives, and after the game other reporters paused at his bench to give him all the facts and gossip he needed for his piece.

Born in 1860, Dryden embarked on his newspaper career comparatively late in life. He had been a hobo and he had been shanghaied off the docks of San Francisco for a trip around the world before he commenced to write. Working as an iron moulder in Monmouth, Ill., Dryden began to put down the amusing incidents that occurred around the foundry and a friend urged him to try writing for a living. Dryden thought it a good idea and went to San Francisco. He happened to be around a newspaper office the night a four-alarm fire erupted. Since no other reporter was available at the moment, Dryden was sent to cover the story. He neglected to mention that several firemen had been killed, but his story was so amusing that he immediately was put on the staff.

Although he flourished less than twenty years, Dryden left an indelible impression on the craft of sportswriting. He retired in 1915 and he died, at seventy-one, in 1931. A hopeless paralytic the last ten years of his life, Dryden played out his final innings living—and dying—by the monotonous tick of the clock.

THE EDITOR

ADDICTS' DELIGHT

BY

Charles Dryden

(PHILADELPHIA NORTH AMERICAN)

Washington, October 6, 1905.

ALL THE FRET and worry have been wiped from the schedule, and the fanatics may seek some needed repose. The Pennant is ours.

Mr. Mack's tired toilers lost today, 10 to 4, but they can do the shouting, since St. Louis cleaned up Chicago. The double-header here tomorrow carries no terrors. If necessary, we can drop both games while the White Sox pound away at the Browns until they are blue in the face. Nothing more doing until the post-mortem series to decide which is the dead one—Giants or Athletics. Let us all emit three cheers, anyhow, for luck.

The Rube broke into the busy whirl today, but he was too rusty to rescue like he once did. Coakley needed help, and

Rusty Rube gave the best he had, and which gives promise of the best there is later on.

The weary but willing Coakley again mounted the hill, only to be knocked off in the second round by a fusillade of five queer hits that scored four runs. One Falkenberg, the human whisper, went to the woods in one round. We reached him for three counts in the first, and tied in the third with Wolfe pitching.

At this time the Browns were pouring hot shot into the Sox far away, so Mr. Mack took a chance on Waddell. The giant won much applause and a few grunts and hisses as the old Stain of Guilt stride carried him to the slab.

He had the new snap ball, the whiffer and the smoke, but little control. Beyond spasms of wildness, Rusty Rube was as good as ever. The steam was there, the shoulder joint worked freely, and the Senators made but five hits. One of the five passes, a bunt hit and errors by Rube and Davis gave the enemy the game in the sixth round.

Plenty of work will put Rube in trim. He also pitched his head off to save the day for Andy and Mr. Mack. All the great flinger needs to put him right is a little dash of oil in his steering gear.

Wolfe was in excellent shape, holding the Athletics to four swats in eight rounds. But that made no difference while St. Louis was hitting the ball. The Pennant winners tore off enough yesterday to entitle them to one day of restful ease. Forget the weak poling of today.

A jubilee in honor of hard-earned and well-deserved victory broke out in the eighth inning. Sam Erwin, who is Uncle Ben's fishing pard at Phillie and elsewhere, had built here yesterday a number of flags and banners. One large pennant bore the inscription, "Champions of 1905." The smaller ones were labeled "Athletics," done in white on a blue ground.

Erwin smuggled these emblems into the boxes occupied by the wives of the Athletic players, back of the visitors' bench. The flags remained under cover until the eighth round, when the Browns had the Sox, 6 to 1. Then Erwin and the women turned on the jubilee, full blast. Mr. Schrenk's mother, who is an ardent fanatic, flapped the big flag and the little ones over the rail. Poor Rube was getting his bumps in that round. Four of the five hits came off in close order, and a wild pitch added to the tumult.

Another big crowd filled the stand, it being "Ladies Day." The good-natured howls of the home rooters, the bumps and the frantic flags had Reuben guessing some. He didn't know just what it all meant, being too busy to watch the score board while the Senators were scoring on him.

It certainly was an odd proposition to see a losing team win the pennant on alien soil, in the midst of rival demonstrations of joy on both sides. But that is the way the banner of 1905 came to Connie Mack.

Among the distinguished arrivals today was Mr. J. Schroeder, the talented groundkeeper for Columbia Park. He rode in a parlor car, and gave no thought to train sandwiches and sour mustard, for Joe was on pennant pleasures bent. In his face he carried a fine cigar, and under his arm a casket of little white metal elephants, attached to blue and white ribbons. These emblems of prowess were passed out to the players and Phillie rooters for breastplates.

Think of the contrast in groundkeepers, and how fate toys with them. Here was Joe, riding on the top wave of glory, while his rival, S. Payne, lingered at home alone with his dead and dying dandelions. Let us draw a veil over this harrowing picture. All hands are wearing lapel elephants tonight and floating the flag of the championship Athletics.

This historical old town, the home of more heroes, dead

and living, than any spot on earth, still sounds the tall praises of Mr. Bender. Even though he canned the Senators twice in one day, the fanatics are proud to grasp the hand of Charles Albert and shake his splendid hurling stem. By noon today he wore a moist and feverish palm, caused by too much adulation at short range.

Charles got his picture and large strings of words about himself in all the papers. He is the talk of the town, and deserves to be.

In the morning, Charles Albert took a steam lift to the top of the monument, which is more than five hundred feet high. He wanted to enjoy a calm and comprehensive view of the great city which he held under his brown thumb the day before. Mr. Bender said the general vista looked good to him, even at that altitude.

In the afternoon some tokens of esteem were lavished upon Charles Albert. A gentleman from Norfolk purchased a 25-cent cigar at the Riggs House and handed the same to Mr. Bender in the presence of a large throng. Then Gene Demont rushed in with a couple of pointer pups. Gene had more dogs than he needed and was just looking for a good place to unload a few.

Keeper Newhouse took charge of the live stock, which will be trained to hunt buffaloes at Devil's Lake, Dakota. Once a hero, and all sorts of rare and costly tokens roll in to the foot of the throne. The Indian is having a new card engraved "C. Albert Bender," for use in high society. He is a Pennant winner.

THE GOLDEN SMILE

BY

Jack London

(NEW YORK HERALD)

Reno, Nevada, July 5, 1910.

ONCE AGAIN has Johnson sent down to defeat the chosen representative of the white race and this time the greatest of them. And as of old, it was play for Johnson. From the opening round to the closing round he never ceased his witty sallies, his exchanges of repartee with his opponent's seconds and with the audience. And, for that matter, Johnson had a funny thing or two to say to Jeffries in every round.

The golden smile was as much in evidence as ever and neither did it freeze on his face nor did it vanish. It came and went throughout the fight, spontaneously, naturally.

It was not a great battle after all, save in its setting and significance. Little Tommy Burns, down in far off Australia, put up a faster, quicker, livelier battle than did Jeffries. The fight today was great only in its significance. In itself it wasn't great. The issue, after the fiddling of the opening rounds, was never in doubt. In the fiddling of those first rounds the honors lay with Johnson, and for the rounds after the seventh or eighth it was more Johnson, while for the closing rounds it was all Johnson.

Johnson played as usual. With his opponent not strong in attack, Johnson, blocking and defending in masterly fashion, could afford to play. And he played and fought a white man, in the white man's country, before a white man's audience. And the audience was a Jeffries audience.

When Jeffries sent in that awful rip of his the audience would madly applaud, believing it had gone home to Johnson's stomach, and Johnson, deftly interposing his elbow, would smile in irony at the audience, play acting, making believe he thought the applause was for him—and never believing it at all.

The greatest fight of the century was a monologue delivered to twenty thousand spectators by a smiling Negro who was never in doubt and who was never serious for more than a moment at a time.

As a fighter Johnson did not show himself a wonder. He did not have to. Never once was he extended. There was no need. Jeffries could not make him extend. Jeffries never had him in trouble once. No blow Jeffries ever landed hurt his dusky opponent. Johnson came out of the fight practically undamaged. The blood on his lip was from a recent cut received in the course of training and which Jeffries managed to reopen.

Jeffries failed to lead and land. The quickness he brought into the fight quickly evaporated, and while Jeffries was dead game to the end, he was not so badly punished. What he failed to bring into the ring with him was his stamina, which he lost somewhere in the last seven years. Jeffries failed to come back. That's the whole story. His old-time vim and endurance were not there. Something has happened to him. He lost in retirement outside of the ring the stamina that the ring itself never robbed him of. As I have said, Jeffries was not badly damaged. Every day boys take worse lacings in boxing bouts than Jeffries took today.

Jeffries today disposed of one question. He could not come

back. Johnson, in turn, answered another question. He has not the yellow streak. But he only answered that question for today. The ferocity of the hairy-chested caveman and grizzly giant did not intimidate the cool-headed Negro. Many thousands in the audience expected the intimidation, and were correspondingly disappointed. Johnson was not scared, let it be said here, and beyond the shadow of any doubt, not for an instant was Johnson scared. Not for a second did he show the flicker of fear that the Goliath against him might eat him up.

But the question of the yellow streak is not answered for all time. Just as Johnson has never been extended, so has he never shown the yellow streak. Just as any man may rise up, heaven alone knows where, who will extend Johnson, just so may that man bring out the yellow streak; and then again he may not. So far the burden of proof all rests on the conclusion that Johnson has no yellow streak.

And now to the battle and how it began! All praise to Tex Rickard, the gamest of sports, who pulled off the fight after countless difficulties and who, cool, calm and quick with nervous aliveness, handled the vast crowd splendidly in his arena and wound up by refereeing the fight.

Twenty thousand filled the great arena and waited patiently under the cloud-flecked, wide Nevada sky. Of the many women present some elected to sit in the screened boxes far back from the ring, for all the world like old-time Spanish ladies at the theatre. But more, many more women, sat close to the ringside beside their husbands or brothers. They were the wiser by far.

Merely to enumerate the celebrities at the ringside would be to write a sporting directory of America—at least a directory of the four-hundred sportsmen, and of many more hundreds of near four-hundreds. At four minutes to two Billy Jordan cleared the ring amid cheers and stood alone. the focal point of twenty thousand pairs of eyes, until the great William Muldoon climbed through the ropes to call ringing cheers from the twenty thousand throats for the State of Nevada, the people of Nevada and the governor of Nevada.

Beginning with Tex Rickard, ovation after ovation was given to all the great ones, not forgetting Bob Fitzsimmons, whom Billy Jordan introduced as "The greatest warrior of them all." And so they came, great one after great one, ceaselessly, endlessly. Until they were swept away before the greatest of them all, the two men who were about to do battle.

It was half past two when Johnson entered. He came first, happy and smiling, greeting friends and acquaintances here and there and everywhere in the audience, cool as ice, waving his hand in salute, smiling, smiling, ever smiling with eyes as well as with lips, never missing a name nor a face, placid, plastic, nerveless, with never a signal of hesitancy or timidity. Yet he was keyed up, keenly observant of all that was going on, ever hearing much of the confused babble of the tongues about him—hearing, aye, and understanding, too.

There is nothing beary or primitive about this man Johnson. He is alive and quivering, every nerve fibre in his body, and brain. Withal that it is hidden so artfully or naturally under the poise of facetious calm of his. He is a marvel of sensitiveness, sensibility and perceptibility. He has the perfect mechanism of mind and body. His mind works like chain lightning and his body obeys with equal swiftness.

But the great madness of applause went up when Jeffries entered the ring two minutes later. A quick, superficial comparison between him and the Negro would have led to a feeling of pity for the latter. For Jeff was all that has been said of him. When he stripped and his mighty body could be seen covered with mats of hair, all the primordial adjectives ever applied to him received their vindication. Nor did his face belie them. No facial emotion played on that face, no whims of the moment, no flutterings of a light-hearted temperament.

Dark and sombre and ominous was that face, solid and stolid and expressionless, with eyes that smouldered and looked savage. The man of iron, grim with determination, sat down in his corner. And the carefree Negro smiled and smiled. And that's the story of the fight. The man of iron, the grizzly giant, was grim and serious. The man of summer temperament smiled and smiled. That is the story of the whole fight. It is the story of the fight by rounds.

At the opening of the first round they did not shake hands. Knowing the two men for what they are, it can be safely postulated that this neglect was due to Jeffries or to the prompting of Jeffries' corner. But it is not good that two boxers should not shake hands before a bout. I would suggest to these protagonists of a perishing game, if they wish to preserve the game, that they make most of these little amenities that by custom grace their sport and give it the veneer of civilization.

Both men went to work in that first round very easily. Johnson smiling, of course; Jeffries grim and determined. Johnson landed the first blow, a light one, and Jeffries in the clinches gave a faint indication of his forthcoming tactics by roughing it, by crowding the Negro around and by slightly bearing his weight upon him. It was a very easy round, with nothing of moment. Each was merely feeling the other out and both were exceedingly careful. At the conclusion of the round, Johnson tapped Jeffries playfully on the shoulder, smiled good naturedly and went to his corner. Jeffries, in the first, showed flashes of catlike quickness.

Round two—Jeffries advanced with a momentary assump-

tion of his famous crouch, to meet the broadly smiling Johnson. Jeffries is really human and good-natured. He proved
it right here. So friendly was that smile of Johnson's, so irre-
sistibly catching, that Jeffries, despite himself, smiled back.
But Jeffries' smiles were doomed to be very few in this
fight.

And right here began a repetition of what took place down
in Australia when Burns fought Johnson. Each time Burns
said something harsh to Johnson in the hope of making him
lose his temper, Johnson responded by giving the white man
a lacing. And so today. Of course, Jeffries did not talk to
Johnson to amount to anything, but Corbett, in the corner,
did it for Jeffries. And each time Corbett cried something in
particular, Johnson promptly administered a lacing to Jeffries.

It began in the second round. Corbett, in line with his
plan of irritating the Negro, called out loudly:

"He wants to fight a little, Jim."

"You bet I do," Johnson retorted, and with that he landed
Jeffries a stinger with his right uppercut.

Both men were tensely careful, Jeffries trying to crowd and
put his weight on in the clinches, Johnson striving more and
more than the other to break out of the clinches. And at the
end of this round, in his corner Johnson was laughing glee-
fully. Certainly Jeffries showed no signs of boring in, as had
been promised by his enthusiastic supporters.

It was the same story in the third round, at the conclusion
of which the irrepressible Negro was guilty of waving his
hands to friends in the audience.

In this fourth round Jeffries showed up better, rushing
and crowding and striking with more vim than hitherto
shown. This seemed to have been caused by a sally of Johnson's, and Jeffries went at him in an angry sort of way.

Promptly Jeffries rushed, and even ere they came together Johnson cried out: "Don't rush me, Jim. You hear what I'm telling you?"

No sign there of being intimidated by Jeffries' first dynamic display of ferocity. All he managed to do was to reopen the training cut in Johnson's lip and to make Johnson playful. It was most anybody's round and it was certainly more Jeffries' than any preceding one.

Round five brought Jeffries advancing with his crouch. The blood from Johnson's lip had turned his smile to a gory one, but still he smiled, and to balance things off he opened Jeffries' lip until it bled more profusely than his own. From then until the end of the fight, Jeffries' face was never free from blood, a steady stream, later flowing from his right nostril, added to by an open cut on his left cheek. Corbett's running fire of irritation served but to make Johnson smile the merrier, and to wink at him across Jeffries' shoulder in the clinches.

So far, no problems have been solved, no questions answered. The yellow streak has not appeared. Neither had Jeffries bored in, ripping awfully, nor put it over Johnson in the clinches. Yet one thing had been shown. Jeffries was not as fast as he had been. There was a shade of diminution in his speed.

Johnson signalized the opening of the sixth round by landing stinging blows to the face in one, two, three order. Johnson's quickness was startling. In response to an irritating remark from Corbett, Johnson replied suavely, "Too much on hand right now," and at the same instant he tore into Jeffries. It was Johnson's first real aggressive rush. It lasted but a second or two, but it was fierce and dandy. And at its conclusion it was manifest that Jeff's right eye was closing fast. The round ended with Johnson fighting and smiling strong, and with Jeff's nose, lip and cheek bleeding and his eye closed. Johnson's round by a smile all the way through.

The seventh round was a mild one, opening with Jeff grim and silent and with Johnson leading and forcing. Both were careful and nothing happened, save that once they exchanged blows right niftily. So far Jeff's roughing and crowding and bearing in of weight had amounted to nothing; also he was doing less and less of it.

"It only takes one or two, Jeff," Corbett encouraged his principal in the eighth round. Promptly Johnson landed two stingers. After a pause he landed another. "See that?" he chirruped sweetly to Corbett in the corner. Jeff perceptibly showed signs of slowing down in this round, rushing and crowding less than ever. Jeff's slowing down was not due to the punishment he had received, but to poorness of condition. He was flying the first signals of fatigue. He was advertising, faintly, it is true, that he had not come back.

The ninth round was introduced by a suggestion from Corbett, heroically carrying out the policy that was bringing his principal to destruction. "Make the big stiff fight," was Corbett's suggestion.

"That's right. That's what they all say," was Johnson's answer, delivered with the true Chesterfield grace across his adversary's shoulder. In the previous rounds Johnson had not wreaked much damage with the forecasted cut, the right uppercut.

In this round he demonstrated indubitably that he could drive the left hand in a way that was surprising. Be it remembered that it had long been denied that he had any sort of punch in that left of his. Incidentally, in this round, it led all the others, and he landed a blow near to Jeffries' heart that must have been discouraging.

The tenth round showed Johnson with his unexpected left,

as quick as ever, and Jeffries going slower and slower. The conclusion of the first ten rounds may be summed up as follows:

The fight was all in favor of Johnson, who had shown no yellow, who had shown condition, who had shown undiminished speed, who had not used his right uppercut much, who had developed a savage left, who had held his own in the clinches, who had gotten the best of the in-fighting and all the out-fighting, who was unhurt, and who was smiling all the way.

Jeff was in bad shape: He was tired, slower than ever, his rushes had been futile, and the sports who had placed their money against him were jubilant.

There were men who proclaimed they saw the end. I refused to see this end, for I had picked Jeff to win, and I was hoping hugely for what I did not know, but for something to happen, for anything that would turn the tide of battle. And yet I could not hide from myself the truth, that Jeff slowed down.

The eleventh round looked better for Jeff. Stung by a remark of Corbett's, Johnson rushed and provoked one grand rally from Jeff. It was faster fighting and more continuous than at any time in the preceding ten rounds, culminating in a fierce rally in which Jeff landed hard.

Round twelve found Johnson, if anything, quicker and more aggressive than ever. "Thought you were going to have me wild?" Johnson queried sweetly of Corbett. As usual every remark of Corbett's brought more punishment to Jeffries. And by the end of this round the second of the two great questions was definitely answered. Jeff had not come back.

The thirteenth round was the beginning of the end. Beginning slowly enough, but stung by Corbett, Johnson put it all over him in the mouth fighting, and all over Jeff in the out-fighting and in-fighting. From defense to attack and back again and back and forth Johnson flashed like the amazing fight mechanism he is. Jeff was silent and sick, while as the round progressed Corbett was noticeably silent.

A few entertained the fond hope that Jeff could recuperate, but it was futile; there was no comeback in him. He was a fading, heart-sick, heart-broken man.

"Talk to him, Corbett," Jeff's friends appealed in the fourteenth round, but Corbett could not talk. He had long since seen the end. And yet through this round Johnson went in for one of his characteristic loafing spells. He took it easy and played with the big gladiator, cool as a cucumber, smiling broadly as ever, and yet, as careful as ever. "Right on the hip," he grinned out once as Jeff in a desperate dying flurry managed to land a wild punch in that vicinity.

Corbett likewise desperate ventured a last sally. "Why don't you do something?" he cried to the loafing, laughing Johnson. "Too clever, too clever, like you," was the reply.

Round fifteen and the end. It was pitiful. There happened to Jeff the bitterness that he had so often made others taste, but which for the first time, perforce, he was made to taste himself.

He who had never been knocked down was knocked down repeatedly. He who had never been knocked out was knocked out. Never mind the technical decision. Jeff was knocked out and through the ropes by the punch he never believed Johnson possessed—by the left and not by the right. As he lay across the lower rope while the seconds were tolled off, a cry that had in it tears and abject broken pride went up from many of the spectators.

"Don't let the Negro knock him out! Don't let the Negro knock him out!" was the oft repeated cry.

There is little more to be said. Jeff did not come back.

Johnson did not show the yellow streak. And it was Johnson's fight all the way through. Jeff was not the old Jeff at all.

Even so, it is to be doubted if this old Jeff could have put away this amazing Negro from Texas, this black man with the unfailing smile, this king of fighters and monologists.

Corbett and Berger and the others were right. They wanted Jeff to do more boxing and fighting in his training. Nevertheless, lacking the comeback, as he so patently did, this preliminary boxing and fighting would have profited him nothing. On the other hand, it would have saved his camp much of the money with which it backed him.

It was a slow fight. Faster, better fights may be seen every day of the year in any of the small clubs in the land. It is true these men were heavyweights, yet for heavyweights it was a slow fight. It must be granted that plucky Tommy Burns put up a faster fight with Johnson a year and a half ago. Yet the American fight followers had to see this fight of today in order to appreciate just what Burns did against this colored wonder.

Johnson is a wonder. No one understands him, this man who smiles. Well, the story of the fight is the story of a smile. If ever man won by nothing more fatiguing than a smile, Johnson won today.

And where now is the champion who will make Johnson extend himself, who will glaze those bright eyes, remove that smile and silence that golden repartee?

The Golden Age

It has been called the era of wonderful nonsense and no-where was the hysteria more boisterous or the screaming louder than in sports during the third decade of the twentieth century. Throwing off its bush-league trappings, sports suddenly erupted in the 1920's as big business and lavish entertainment. This was the decade that witnessed the first million-dollar fight and World Series; that made inadequate stadia accommodating 100,000 spectators for a football game; that spawned sprawling country clubs where golf and tennis were practised with a fervor verging on religious zeal; that spread a red carpet for men with swift and strong and skillful muscles.

This was the Golden Age of sport and the times produced more vital, vibrant performers than any other decade in the chronicles of athletics. Every sport had a dominant personality who attracted and held public attention, for this was the era of Babe Ruth, Jack Dempsey, Red Grange, the Four Horsemen, William Tatum Tilden III, Suzanne Lenglen, Bobby Jones, Man o' War, Paavo Nurmi, Charley Paddock, Nat Holman, Tommy Hitchcock and Johnny Weismuller.

Pioneer sportswriters had stimulated interest in sport and the men who followed put a glittering polish on the patina of tradition they inherited. The temper of the expansive times called for garish embellishment and the boys laid on the superlatives and breathless adjectives with a trowel.

Too many stories were overwritten, stridently and strenu-

ously. By present-day standards, the color is glaring, the straining for effect is self-conscious, the round-eyed wonder is juvenile and a competent copyreader could perform a major operation on the superfluity of words. Yet these were the stories that were considered very hot stuff and it is significant that every news story ran on Page 1 of the newspaper.

With the notable exceptions of a few men such as Lardner, McGeehan and Broun, sportwriters of the 1920's brought an attitude to their work that was not generally apparent in other sections of the papers. They sat down at their typewriters prepared to invest the event they were covering with the epic grandeur of the Creation.

That attitude was best expressed in an anecdote concerning Laurence Stallings, who was hired to do a trained seal act for Red Grange's first appearance in the East, at Franklin Field in 1925. Stallings had written the realistic, hardboiled "What Price Glory?", an enormously successful play, and had seen the mass murder of World War I. Grange had a large afternoon for himself against Pennsylvania and as soon as the game was ended, the newspapermen in the press box took the wraps off their typewriters and went to work to preserve the event for posterity.

Stallings, going through the agony pains of composition, paced up and down the press box for an hour. He tore at his hair, clutched at his brow and breast and uttered hoarse, hollow groans of despair. One of the colleagues who had completed his deathless document asked Stallings what in the world was the matter.

The blood-and-thunder historian threw out his arms in a gesture of bleak frustration.

"I can't write it!" Stallings cried. "The story's too big for me!"

THE EDITOR

H.R.H. SMITH

BY

Harry Cross

(NEW YORK TIMES)

Cleveland, October 10, 1920.

THE UNROMANTIC name of Smith is on everybody's lips in Cleveland tonight, for Elmer Smith, the right fielder of Speaker's Indians, accomplished something in the fifth world's series clash this afternoon that is the life ambition of every big league ball player. Elmer crashed a home run over the right field fence with the bases full in the first inning and sent the Indians on their merry way to a 8 to 1 victory over Brooklyn. Fate tried to conceal this lucky boy by naming him Smith, but with that tremendous slap Elmer shoved his commonplace identity up alongside the famous Smiths of history, which include Captain John, the Smith Brothers, and the Village Smithy.

This home-run punch which shoved over four runs in a cluster is the first of its kind that has ever been made in a world series game. Cleveland now has won three games to Brooklyn's two, and an overjoyed city this evening has about come to the conclusion that the championship streamer will float over the proud fifth city of the U. S. A.

While the delirious crowd of more than 25,000 was still rejoicing over Smith's sumptuous smash, Bill Wambsgans broke into the celebration to steal some of Smithy's thunder by accomplishing the first unassisted triple play that has ever whisked a world series populace up to the heights of happiness.

The crowd was already husky-voiced and nerve-wrecked with wild excitement when Wamby started to make baseball history. It seemed as if everything that could happen to make Cleveland's joy complete had happened.

Along in the fifth inning, when Bagby, with a commanding lead behind him, was taking it easy, Kilduff and Otto Miller both made singles and were perched on second and first. Clarence Mitchell, who had long since succeeded the badly wrecked Burleigh Grimes on the pitching mound, was at bat, and for the first time during the afternoon it looked as if the slipping Robins were going to accomplish something.

Uncle Robbie had evidently wigwagged a sign from the bench for a hit and run play, which means that the runners were expected to gallop just as soon as Mitchell swung his bat.

Mitchell connected solidly and jammed a tearing liner over second base. Wamby was quite a distance from second, but he leaped over toward the cushion and with a mighty jump speared the ball with one hand. Kilduff was on his way to third base and Miller was almost within reach of second.

Wamby's noodle began to operate faster than it ever did before. He hopped over to second touched the bag, retiring Kilduff, who was far down the alley toward third base. Then Wamby turned and saw Otto Miller standing there like a wooden Indian. Otto was evidently so surprised that he was glued to the ground, and Wamby just waltzed over and touched him for the third out.

The crowd forgot it was hoarse of voice and close to nervous exhaustion and gave Wamby just as great a reception as it had given Elmer Smith.

Those two-record-breaking feats were not all that happened in today's game to make Cleveland feel proud of its baseball club and itself. Not by a long shot! Along in the fourth inning when Grimes was still trying to pitch, Jim Bagby, the Indians' big, slow, lazy boxman, became suddenly inspired and with two fellow Indians on the bases he soaked a home run into the new bleachers which protrude far out into right centrefield.

No World's Series pitcher has ever received such a humiliating cudgeling as Grimes did this afternoon, for the simple reason that no other pitcher has ever been kept in the box so long after he had started to slip. Uncle Robbie kept him on the mound for three and two-third innings and in that time he was badly plastered for nine hits, including two home runs and a triple.

With half a dozen able-bodied pitchers basking in the warm sun, Grimes was kept in the game until he was so badly battered that the game became a joke. Instead of being enormously wealthy in pitchers as Robbie was supposed to be, he became a pauper as far as pitching talent is concerned. When the Indians had the score 7 to 0 Grimes limped out of the game and Clarence Mitchell, who had been faithfully warming up ever since he hit Cleveland, went out to the box and one more run was the best that the Indians could do off him.

That first inning is one which will ever linger in baseball memory. The Sunday crowd jammed every inch of the park and was even more enthusiastic than the throng at the opening game here. Strong-lunged young men went through the grandstands with megaphones and implored the fans to give the Indians their vocal and moral encouragement as they had at the opening game. "We want to make it four straight," they yelled, "and fly the world's championship silk from our flagpole."

The memory of Grimes's great pitching still lingered in the minds of the spectators, but the Cleveland Club on its own meadow is a far different kind of ball club from that which the residents of Flatbush saw last week. The Indians were on their toes and ran back and forth to their positions in the field like a college baseball nine.

The roar of the faithful followers was like a tonic and Speaker's men reveled in the wonderful reception they received. The thing that was uppermost in their minds was to show the home folks that they appreciated the loyalty. The best way they could show it was to win and they showed 'em. It didn't matter that it was a one-sided ball game and that the Brooklyn Club, minus good pitching, looked woefully weak and with the absence of the injured Jimmy Johnston at third base was inclined to be panicky. The only thing that mattered was that Cleveland was winning the ball game and the more runs the Indians could make the more fun there was in it for the Cleveland fans.

Jamieson was the first Indian to face Burleigh Grimes in the opening inning. He pounded a roller down through Koney which was too warm for the Dodger first baseman to handle. Wamby poked another single off Grimes and Jamieson went to second. The crowd chanted a flattering chorus of cheers to Speaker when he came to the bat. The wee bit of a tap which bounded off Tris's bat dropped in the infield and Grimes ran over to pick up the Indian manager's bunt and throw him out at first. Grimes slipped as he was about to pick up the ball and he was reclining on his back when he made a useless throw to first. It was a hit, and the bases were loaded with no one out.

The National Boiler Works laboring overtime never made

the racket that was now taking place in the ball park. The noise waves flowed up in gushes and echoed all over the city of Cleveland, finally rumbling far out on Lake Erie.

Elmer Smith is at the bat. You'll find Smiths here, there and everywhere, so there was nothing about the name to arouse enthusiasm. Elmer took a fond look at the high screen on top of the right field fence and Grimes began to pitch to him. The three Indians on the bases jumped up and down on their toes impatiently.

Elmer took two healthy swings at the ball and missed, and the next one was wide and he let it waft by.

Grimes looked around the bases and saw that he was entirely surrounded by Indians. He was ambushed by the Redskins. He felt that danger lurked in this Smith boy at the bat.

When Grimes hurled the next ball over, Smith took a mighty blow at the ball and it rose like a bird, went so far up in the air that it looked like a quinine pill.

Jamieson, Wamby and Speaker all took one good look at that rapidly rising ball, then they bent their heads, dug their spikes into the dirt and started to run. Grimes was knocked dizzy. As he looked about him he could see nothing but Indians chasing themselves around in a circle.

Smith, who just a few seconds before was just plain Elmer Smith, had become Home Run Smith before he had trotted as far as second base. When he had reached third, he was Hero Smith, and by the time he had crossed the plate he was a candidate for a bronze statue in City Square along with General Moses Cleveland, who founded this town, and Tom L. Johnson, who decorates the park just opposite old General Mose.

Manager Speaker, still a young man, yet gray and bald from baseball worries, was waiting at the plate when Smith touched the platter. Around Smith's neck went Tris's arm and he was the first to pat him on the back. Grimes stood out in the pitcher's box stupefied. The other Brooklyn players walked about in a daze and waited for the noise riot to subside.

Grimes was still pitching when the game was resumed. The Cleveland players wondered just what had to be done to a Brooklyn pitcher before he is taken out of the game. However, Grimes became a little better, and the side was retired after Burleigh had been aided by a double play.

The next citizen to be hailed as a hero is lazy James Bagby. No pitcher was ever before pounded for thirteen hits in a world's series and emerge a hero. Jim Bagby, big Sergeant Jim, did it. He pitched what was really a bad game of ball, but when it was over he was proud of it.

Doc Johnston opened the fourth inning when he bounded a hit off Grimes's leg. Yes, Grimes is still pitching for Brooklyn. Clarence Mitchell is warming up out in left field. He warmed up all day yesterday and started warming up early today.

Anyway, Doc got his hit off Grimes's leg. He went to second on a passed ball and to third as Sheehan was retiring Sewell at first. Grimes walked O'Neill purposely to get Bagby, and that is just where Jim, the barge, has the laugh on Grimes. Bagby slammed a long drive to right centre which dropped just inside the fence that is built around the new centre field bleachers. Johnston and O'Neill both romped home ahead of Jim amid scenes of wild, barbarous disorder.

When the riot was quelled, Grimes was still pitching for Brooklyn. Does this fellow Grimes stand so strongly with Uncle Robbie that he is never taken out of a game, no time, no place, no how?

Jamieson spanked a roller down to first base, and although three Brooklyn fielders, Grimes, Koney and Kilduff, tried to retire the runner at first, Jamieson was too swift and got a hit for himself out of the confusion.

It suddenly dawned upon Manager Robinson that the Indians were hitting Grimes, so he took him out and Mitchell went to the box.

Brooklyn's run came in the ninth inning when many of the jubilant Cleveland spectators were hurrying toward the gates. They were already shouting the Cleveland victory to the world and the scoring of the lone tally commanded absolutely no attention at all.

Bagby fanned Griffith as a starter, and then, as he listlessly chucked the ball over, Wheat singled to right. Jim was still listless when he threw the ball at Myers, who slapped a single to centre which sent Wheat to second. Konetchy hit a mean hopper down through Doc Johnston, the ball bounding out into the field as Wheat scampered home and saved the Dodgers from a shutout.

Brooklyn's stock has taken an awful drop.

ORCHID IN THE JUNGLE

BY

Irvin S. Cobb

(NEW YORK TIMES) JULY 3, 1921.

THROUGH A HUNDRED entrances the multitude flows in steadily, smoothly, without jamming or confusion. The trickling streams run down the aisles and are absorbed by capillary attraction in the seats. If it takes all sorts of people to make up the world then all the world must be here already. That modest hero of the cinema, Tom Mix, known among friends as the Shrinking Violet of Death Valley, starts a furore by his appearance at 12:15, just as the first of the preliminary bouts is getting under way. His dress proclaims that he recently has suffered a personal bereavement. He is in mourning. He wears a sea-green sport suit, a purple handkerchief, a pair of solid-gold filled glasses and a cowboy hat the size of a six-furlong track. Actress ladies in make-up and also some few in citizens' clothes jostle against society leaders and those who follow in their wake.

The arts, the sciences, the drama, commerce, politics, the bench, the bar, the great newly risen bootlegging industry—all these have sent their pink, their pick and their perfection to grace this great occasion. A calling over of the names of the occupants of the more highly priced reservations would sound like reading the first hundred pages of Who's Ballyhoo in America. Far away and high up behind them, their figures cutting the skyline of the mighty wooden bowl, are perched the pedestrian classes. They are on the outer edge of events if not actually in it.

Conspicuous at the front, where the lumber-made cliffs of the structure shoal off into broad flats, is that type which is commonest of all alongside a fight ring. He is here in numbers amounting to a host. There must be thousands of him present. He is the soft-fleshed, hard-faced person who keeps his own pelt safe from bruises, but whose eyes glisten and whose hackles lift at the prospect of seeing somebody else whipped to a soufflé. He is the one who, when his favorite pug is being hammered to a sanguinary Spanish omelet, calls out: "That's all right, kid, he can't hurt you." I see him countlessly repeated. For the anonymous youths who in the overtures are achieving a still greater namelessness by being put violently to sleep he has a listless eye. But wait until the big doings start. Then will his gills pant up and down as his vicarious lusting for blood and brute violence is satisfied.

Bout after bout is staged, is fought out, is finished. Few know who the fighters are and nobody particularly cares. Who is interested in flea-biting contests when he came to see a combat between young bull elephants? Joe Humphries, the human Cave of the Winds, bulks as a greater figure of interest as he vouches for the proper identities of these mute, inglorious preliminary scrappers than do the scrappers themselves.

It's one o'clock now. Where an hour ago there were wide vacant stretches of unoccupied seating space, now all is covered with piebald masses—the white of straw hats, the black of men's coats, with here and there bright patches of cola-like peonies blossoming in a hanging garden, to denote the presence of many women in gay summer garb. The inflowing tides of humanity have inundated and swallowed up the desert. Still there has been no congestion, no traffic jams. However the fight may turn out the handling of the crowd has been competent. Tex Rickard is the world's greatest showman.

The hour of one has arrived. Harry Stevens, the official caterer, can't figure within ten thousand of what the full attendance will be and so prepares to slice another ham. One thing is sure—today Boyle's Thirty Acres has given to Tex Rickard a richer harvest than any like area of this world's surface ever yielded.

At this moment—one-sixteen—atmospheric troubles impend. A drizzle has begun to fall. It is a trickle as yet but threatens to·develop into an authentic downpour. The air has grown sodden and soggy with moisture thickened to the saturation point. It is as though one breathed into a wet sponge. I figure this sort of thing, continuing or growing worse, will slow up the two chief clouters when their turn comes.

Governor Edwards of New Jersey comes at one-thirty: the first good solid knock-down in the ring at one-thirty-six. Both are heartily approved with loud thunders of applause. Not everyone can be the anti-dry sport-loving governor of a great commonwealth, but a veritable nobody can win popular approval on a day like this by shoving his jaw in front of a winged fist. There are short cuts to fame though painful.

The shower has suspended, but the atmosphere is still as soppy as a wet shirt. This certainly is a stylish affair. I have just taken note of the fact that the corps of referees all wear white silk blouses and white trousers like tennis players and that the little fat boy who holds up big printed cards with numerals on them to show the number of the next round is done up in spotless white linen like an antiseptically bandaged thumb. The humidity with which the air is freighted is beginning now to be oppressive. Even the exertion of shoving a pencil across paper brings out the perspiration and the two ambitious novices up in the ring are so wet and so slick with their own sweat that they make you think of a pair of fresh-caught fish flapping about in a new sort of square net.

It's three o'clock. Prompt on the appointed hour, for once in the history of championship goes, the men are brought forth on time. Carpentier comes first, slim, boyish, a trifle pale and drawn-looking, to my way of thinking. He looks more like a college athlete than a professional bruiser. A brass band plays the "Marseillaise," ninety-odd thousand men and women stand to greet him—or maybe the better to see him—and he gets a tremendous heartening ovation. Dempsey follows within two minutes. A mighty roar salutes him too, as he climbs into the ring and seats himself within the arc of a huge floral horseshoe; but so near as may be judged by the applause for him, an American born, it is not so sincere or spontaneous as the applause which has been visited upon the Frenchman.

He grins—but it is a scowling, forbidding grin—while photographers flock into the ring to focus their boxes first on one and then on the other. Dempsey sitting there makes me think of a smoke-stained Japanese war idol; Carpentier, by contrast, suggests an Olympian runner carved out of fine grained white ivory. Partisans howl their approval of the champion. He refuses to acknowledge these. One figures that he has suddenly grown sulky because his reception was no greater than it was.

A little crowd of ring officials surround Dempsey. There is some dispute seemingly over the tapes in which his knobby brown hands are wrapped. Carpentier, except for one solicitous fellow-countryman, is left quite alone in his corner.

Dempsey keeps his eyes fixed on his fists. Carpentier studies him closely across the eighteen feet which separates them. The

Gaul is losing his nervous air. He is living proof to give the lie to the old fable that all Frenchmen are excitable.

Overhead aeroplanes are breezing, and their droning notes come down to be smitten and flung up again on the crest of the vast upheaval of sound rising from the earth. A tiresome detail of utterly useless announcements is ended at last.

As the fighters are introduced, Dempsey makes a begrudged bow, but Carpentier, standing up, is given such an ovation as never before an alien fighter received on American soil. It is more plain by this test who is the sentimental favorite. The bettors may favor Jack; the populace likes Georges.

Without handshaking they spring together; Carpentier lands the first blow. Dempsey, plainly enraged, is fast; Carpentier is faster still. But his blows seem to be wild, misplaced, while Dempsey, in the clinches into which they promptly fall, plans punishing licks with swift, short-armed strokes. The first half minute tells me the story. The Frenchman is going to be licked, I think, and that without loss of time. A tremendous roar goes up as Dempsey brings the first blood with a glancing lick on the side of his opponent's nose; it increases as the Frenchman is shoved half through the ropes. The first round is Dempsey's all the way. He has flung Carpentier aside with thrusts of his shoulders. He has shoved him about almost at will.

But midway of the second round Carpentier shows a flash of the wonderful speed for which he is known. With the speed he couples an unsuspected power. He is not fighting the defensive run-away-and-come-again fight that was expected of him. He stands toe to toe with Dempsey and trades 'em. He shakes Dempsey with a volley of terrific right-handed clouts which fall with such speed you do not see them. You only see that they have landed and that Dempsey is bordering on the state technically known as groggy.

It is a wonderful recovery for the Frenchman. His admirers shriek to him to put Dempsey out. To my mind the second round is his by a good margin. Given more weight I am sure now that he would win. Yet I still feel sure Dempsey's superiority in gross tonnage and his greater aptitude at in-fighting will wear the lesser man down and make him lose.

The third round is Dempsey's from bell to bell. He makes pulp of one of Carpentier's smooth cheeks. He pounds him on the silken skin over his heart. He makes a xylophone of the challenger's short ribs. The Frenchman circles and swoops, but the drubbing he gets makes him uncertain in his swings. Most of his blows go astray. They fly over Dempsey's hunched shoulders—they spend themselves in the air.

In the fourth round, after one minute and sixteen seconds of hard fighting—fighting which on Carpentier's part is defensive—comes the foreordained and predestined finishment. I see a quick flashing of naked bodies writhing in and out, joining and separating. I hear the flop, flap, flop of leather bruising human flesh. Carpentier is almost spent—that much is plain to every one. A great spasmodic sound—part gasp of anticipation, part groan of dismay, part outcry of exultation—rises from a hundred thousand throats. Carpentier totters out of a clinch; his face is all spotted with small red clots. He lunges into the air, then slips away, retreating before Dempsey's onslaught, trying to recover by footwork. Dempsey walks into him almost deliberately, like a man aiming to finish a hard job of work in workmanlike shape. His right arm crooks up and is like a scimitar. His right fist falls on the Frenchman's exposed swollen jaw; falls again in the same place even as Carpentier is sliding down alongside the ropes. Now the Frenchman is lying on his side.

Dempsey knows the contract is finished—or as good as finished. Almost nonchalantly he waits with his legs spraddled and his elbows akimbo harkening to the referee's counting. At the toll of eight Carpentier is struggling to his knees, beaten, but with the instinct of a gallant fighting man, refusing to acknowledge it. At nine he is up on the legs which almost refuse to support him. On his twisted face is the look of a sleep-walker.

It is the rule of the ring that not even a somnambulist may be spared the finishing stroke. Thumbs down means the killing blow, and the thumbs are all down now for the stranger.

For the hundredth part of a second—one of those flashes of time in which an event is photographed upon the memory to stay there forever, as though printed in indelible colors—I see the Frenchman staggering, slipping, sliding forward to his fate. His face is toward me and I am aware at once his face is no vestige of conscious intent. Then the image of him is blotted out by the intervening bulk of the winner. Dempsey's right arm swings upward with the flailing emphasis of an oak cudgel and the muffled fist at the end of it lands again on its favorite target—the Frenchman's jaw.

The thud of its landing can be heard above the hysterical shrieking of the host. The Frenchman seems to shrink in for a good six inches. It is as though that crushing impact had telescoped him. He folds up into a pitiable meager compass and goes down heavily and again lies on the floor, upon his right side, his face half covered by his arms as though even in the stupor following that deadly collision between his face and Dempsey's fist, he would protect his vulnerable parts. From where I sit writing this I can see one of his eyes and his mouth. The eye is blinking weakly, the mouth is gaping, and the lips work as though he chewed a most bitter mouthful. I do not think he is entirely unconscious; he is only utterly helpless. His legs kick out like the legs of a cramped swimmer. Once he lifts himself half-way to his haunches. But the effort is his last. He has flattened down again and still the referee has only progressed in his fateful sum of simple addition as far as "six."

My gaze shifts to Dempsey. He has moved over into Carpentier's corner and stands there, his arms extended on the ropes in a posture of resting. He has no doubt of the outcome. He scarcely shifts his position while the count goes on. I have never seen a prizefighter in the moment of triumph behave so. But his expression proves that he is merely waiting. His lips lift in a snarl until all his teeth show. Whether this be a token of contempt for the hostile majority in the crowd, or merely his way of expressing to himself his satisfaction is not for me to say.

The picture lingers in my mind after the act itself is ended. Behind Dempsey is a dun background of gray clouds, swollen and gross with unspilt rain. The snowy white horizontals of the padded guard ropes cut across him at knee and hip and shoulder line; otherwise his figure stands out clear, a relaxed, knobby figure, with tons of unexpended energy still held in reserve within it. The referee is close at hand, tolling off the inexorable tally of the count—"seven, eight, nine"—but scarcely is one cognizant of the referee's presence, of his arithmetic either. I see only that gnarled form lolling against the ropes and, eight feet away, the slighter, crumpled shape of the beaten Frenchman, with its kicking legs and its sobbing mouth, from which a little stream of blood runs down upon the lolled chin.

In a hush which instantaneously descends and as instantaneously is ended, the referee swings his arm down like a semaphore and chants out "ten."

The rest is a muddle and mass of confusion—Dempsey

stooping over Carpentier as though wishful to lift him to his feet; then Dempsey encircled by a dozen policeman who for some reason feel called upon to surround him, two weeping French helpers dragging Carpentier to his corner and propping him upon a stool. Carpentier's long, slim legs dangling as they lift him and his feet slithering in futile fashion upon the resined canvas; Dempsey swinging his arms aloft in tardy token of appreciation for the whoops and cheers which flow toward him; all sorts of folks crowding into the ring; Dempsey marching out, convoyed by an entourage of his admirers; Carpentier, deadly pale, and most bewildered-looking with a forlorn, mechanical smile plastered on his face, shaking hands with somebody or other, and then the ring is empty of all save Humphries the orator, who announces a concluding bout between Billy Miske and Jack Renault.

As I settle back now to watch with languid interest this anti-climax, three things stand out in my memory as the high points of the big fight, so far as I personally am concerned.

The first is that Carpentier never had a chance. In the one round which properly belonged to him he fought himself out. He trusted to his strength when his refuge should have been in his speed.

The second is that vision of him, doubled up on his side, like a frightened, hurt boy, and yet striving to heave himself up and take added punishment from a foe against whom he had no shadow of hope.

The third—and most outstanding—will be my recollection of that look on Dempsey's towering front when realization came to him that a majority of the tremendous audience were partisans of the foreigner.

FIASCO AT SHELBY

BY

Warren Brown

(CHICAGO HERALD-EXAMINER)

Shelby, Mont., July 5, 1923.

JACK DEMPSEY WAS GIVEN the Shelby stand-off here yesterday when after 15 rounds of good, bad and indifferent fighting on his part, the champion saved his title, but lost his reputation as a superman, one who could batter through any sort of defense his smaller opponent might offer, one who could call the round in which he would knock over the challenger. Dempsey did none of these things, and some explanation is therefore in order. At this time we can offer nothing better than a few items of comment heard as the fight went on.

At the end of the fifth round Dan McKettrick, a member of the Dempsey-Kearns combine, leaned over into the press box and announced: "The champ ain't fightin."

At the end of the tenth, a skeptic in the nearby seats piped up: "This makes the fight pictures worth some dough."

At the end of the twelfth a newspaper man chirped: "It's a good thing Dempsey has his own referee with him."

At the end of the fourteenth round, when it became evident that Gibbons was going to pull the unexpected and stay the limit with the champion, a fan away in the background proposed "three cheers for Tommy Gibbons."

They were given, and with plenty of enthusiasm.

Three minutes later a weary face-puffed challenger returned to his corner, and Referee Jimmy Daugherty raised the water-soaked gloved hand of the champion of the world in token of the fact that Dempsey had won the decision after fifteen rounds of fighting, good, bad, and indifferent.

Gibbons stayed the limit because he is a super-hanger-on and game as a pebble.

As a fight the Dempsey-Gibbons thing left much to be desired. Most of the solid punches that were landed—and there were not a great many of them, were landed by Dempsey. Gibbons occasionally slid a solid left hook against Dempsey's chin and body, but few of the punches carried great force, or if they did they failed to have much effect on the champion.

Gibbons resorted to clinching from the start to finish, and in the last round caught Dempsey's right arm in both hands and hung on so tight that the referee was unable to pry him loose. He was then a thoroughly well-beaten fighter, but through gameness kept on his feet.

Neither fighter was marked to any great extent, though Gibbons opened that old cut over Dempsey's eye with a left hook in the second round. Dempsey bruised Gibbons' lips with a steady battering in the first round and Tommy put a red mark under Jack's right eye in the fourth. Outside of this both men ended the fight as they had begun it, with the exception that Dempsey was upwards of $250,000 richer, while Gibbons had the satisfaction of knowing he was the only man able to keep from being knocked out by Dempsey since the latter became world's champion. Gibbons will probably capitalize on this later, as will Dempsey when the inevitable return match is staged as far away from Shelby as possible. This may, or may not, account for the result of yesterday's encounter.

The crowd showed up for the fight all right, but not until a last minute cut in prices was authorized, and $25,000 worth of customers came in at the reduced rates. Later in the afternoon the gates were thrown open and the entire town of Shelby and visitors from outlying districts swarmed in to take advantage of the first chance ever given the American public to see a world's championship prize fight without laying down the old dough in one bunch or another.

For a time it looked as if the champion and the challenger would have to step their fifteen rounds to empty seats, less than 8,000 being present in the arena built for 47,000 when the last preliminary started. The reduction of prices and the decision to have a free list ran the crowd up in an amazingly short time to well over 20,000, and even those who paid to get in had the satisfaction of seeing something worth while.

Before the main bout started there was more difficulty over the money question, as if this show had not had enough of this during the past few weeks. There was only $8,000 ready to pay Referee Daugherty and the preliminary fighters, and when that was not forthcoming at once Daugherty and the fighters refused to go on. Of the $8,000 Kearns put up $5,000 and it was said that he put up an additional $500 to square a Government tax difficulty before they would permit the gates to be opened at all. So all in all, Kearns had something more on his mind than getting Dempsey into the ring to meet the challenger.

Kearns argued it out with Daugherty and the referee finally agreed to go on. The preliminaries were cut down to two bouts, however, neither of them much good; and the long waits between them, and before the first one started, did not serve to put the crowd in good humor.

Towards the close of the fight when it looked certain that Gibbons was going to stay the limit, the crowd near the ringside started in to razz Dempsey and the newspaper men who had picked the champion to win by a knockout. As the rounds wore on the boys became a bit more noisy in their compliments to gentlemen of the press, and after the fight was over those scribes who sat in Dempsey's corner were treated to a shower of straw cushions. Most of the news gathering mob, having become used to pop bottle showering in the St. Louis ball park, didn't mind a little thing like soft cushions any more than they did the stings of half-starved Shelby mosquitos.

As a matter of fact most of the mosquitos whose presence was one more of the delights of this little boom town a few days ago had either died or disappeared when the time came for the fight to be called. Perhaps the insects, like most of the folks who had been asked to pay from twenty to fifty dollars for seats, could not quite decide whether it was worth it. The mosquitos, off stinging in another part of the State, did not hear about the free list until it was too late.

The most remarkable thing about the battle was the fact that Gibbons was able to absorb the punishment meted out to him by Dempsey. Only a man game to the core could have withstood the mauling he received and then come back for more. He proved that he is a gamester of the first water and that a "good little man" shouldn't be expected to beat a "good big man."

Gibbons was sentimentally the favorite for the reason that he was regarded as the underdog. Furthermore, he fought for nothing. Dempsey got $210,000 cash and a little more than that came into the gate to-day, but Gibbons was not to share in the proceeds until the receipts reached $300,000.

He does not get a dime. However, his pugilistic fortune is

made by the great fight he put up. He can claim the right
to meet the champion of the world again.

Gibbons is one of the master boxers of the game. He had
been often cited, too, as an example of clean living, a rare
attribute among prize fighters. The years he spent in taking
care of himself, in eschewing wine and song, were fully re-
paid to Tom Gibbons yesterday.

His body stood up under a merciless hammering in a long
fight that was under rules which made it a rough house
affair. The men were to protect themselves at all times and
could hit on the breakaways.

These are technical expressions which may be best explained to the readers by saying that the fighters could do to
each other things that are generally looked for only in a street
fight. Dempsey benefited by the rules because of his superior
strength.

He would catch Gibbons in the clinches, and maul him
around as if Tom were nothing more than a rag doll, smashing him with body punches, hammering the back of his neck
with the murderous "rabbit punch," a form of blow com-
monly used by hunters to kill a wounded rabbit.

Either Dempsey cannot hit as he used to hit, or Gibbons
has a body made of rubber. Once or twice Gibbons looked a
bit sick, once or twice it looked as if the coyote had been
finally run to earth, then Tom would make a quick twist and
turn and come bobbing up in a new quarter, apparently as
fresh as ever.

His elbows were breaking the force of a lot of Dempsey's
inside punches. He was letting Dempsey spend a lot of the
energy behind his drives in the air. Gibbons was nearly always going away from the smashes, and at times he made the
champion of the world miss so badly that Dempsey looked
annoyed.

For the first time in his ring career, Dempsey made a remark to an opponent in the ring. That was when Gibbons speared him with a good hard blow. The champion's lips drew back in a snarl and he muttered something.

Dempsey looked in perfect condition, but he couldn't "step" as he used to step. He could not move around. The two years he has spent in idleness have rusted the springs in his legs. He had all his old-time "form"—that is to say, he had all his old appearance, but he wasn't the fighter yesterday that beat down the giant Willard at Toledo.

It was the old story of the unexpected that makes sport. Not one man in the crowd, that was so small in the early stages of the show that it looked pathetic in the huge arena, thought Gibbons could go the full distance with Dempsey. Only one man, Bill Brennan, has gone beyond ten rounds with the champion since the earliest days of his fighting career. Practically every pugilistic prophet in the country found himself wrong at the finish.

Dempsey looked quite chagrined as he shook hands with Gibbons at the close of the fight. He said something, perhaps congratulating Gibbons on his showing, which is the code of the ring, but there was no smile on his face.

MOONLIGHT SONATA

BY

Walter Davenport

(NEW YORK HERALD) SEPTEMBER 15, 1923.

———————

IN LESS THAN FOUR minutes of slugging Jack Dempsey battered Luis Firpo into a twilight state.

More than 85,000 persons paid nearly a million and a quarter of dollars to be present in the Polo Grounds for those few terrific moments. For those wild minutes the throng became a mob. In that round and a third the 85,000 went back to the mentality of their hairy ancestors. Dempsey smashed Firpo at the outset and then until the end, a brutal end. That mob screamed. A shrill, wild scream such as the jungle explorers talk of.

All that had gone before was forgot. All the orders of the police to remain seated went for nothing. Eighty-five thousand men and women, for a few minutes gone mad as the beast goes mad at the smell of blood, forgot their fine civilization, their boast of superiority over the animal, and screamed for what they were seeing.

All sorts and conditions of mankind saw the sulking man from Argentina do his savage best and fail. They saw him lash out with his beamlike right arm and knock the American through the ropes.

And then, having got what they paid to see, they sank back to tell each other that they had told each other so.

A million and a quarter for a four-minute thrill, a thrill that had your temples pounding and your heart bursting. But ask any person who sat in that wild crowd. It was worth it!

It was a magnificent night for it. The luck of Tex Rickard continues. There have been other such dramas as this, and the experience of this reporter has been too brief to warrant fair comparisons. The old-timers, however, say that they've never felt the spirit of prize fight as they did last night.

And probably there never was a crowd so perfectly attuned to the occasion. A thousand newspaper stories have been written about the man from Argentina. In his training he had scoffed at convention. Trainers of athletes groaned when they read his carnivorous menus. He would defeat himself with his teeth, they said.

Here was a man who had stubbornly refused to listen to men supposed to know all about pugilism. In the newspapers this giant from South America has been set forth as something a little less than human and so far back in the ruck of civilization as to be just emerging from the dawn of things. The inference was that were he to be badly wounded, so badly as to cause him to admit defeat, he would slink away to whatever it is he uses as his lair and lick his wounds, after the manner of the beast.

It made no difference that Luis Firpo is a man of average intelligence; propaganda has made him a creature of instinct rather than reason. Eighty thousand persons, vaguely recalling that back in their early geography lessons they had been taught that away down there in the lower Argentine and Patagonia crude giants went about in savage isolation, living by strength of muscle rather than might of government, came forth to see a monster stand up against one of us. To be sure, all these analyses of the man Firpo were colored with absurdity, but the fact remained that such was the feeling that filled this wonderful crowd.

There was zest to the occasion. There was sharpness to the weather. Of those who came early, the wisest were those who fetched heavier overcoats and thermos bottles. Just what those thermos bottles contained is for you to guess.

It was a fine night for fighting. It was almost football weather. The preliminary boxers shivered in their corners while waiting the call to amuse the throng that had come to see champions. The throng itself hugged its overcoats closer as the night wore on.

There was no call for ice cream or cold drinks. Hot dogs went well, not because they really were hot, but because the name was suggestive.

It was a New York crowd. That is to say, a well-disciplined crowd. Turn back to the pages that record the scenes attending the Jeffries-Johnson spat, the Corbett-Fitzsimmons battle, or even the Heenan-Sayres or Sullivan-Mitchell engagements, and it occurs to you that either prize fighting has come up several leagues socially, or business methods have robbed it of its oldtime glamour. If the historians tell the truth the crowds attending one of these gone-by affairs were as eager to do battle as they were to see it.

Before attending one of those fights the spectator went into training just as the pugilist did. He went prepared to defend his ticket, his seat, his honor, his life and his country. One counted the fight a failure if one did not become embroiled in a little side encounter.

Not that there were not occasional passages at arms to enliven last night's crowds. Now and then, out among the gentlemen occupying the far away centerfield bleacher's seats, some one would attempt to occupy another gent's seat or to speak out of his turn. Sometimes he was dared to step

forth to defend his stand. Again he was walloped before being challenged. But always a merry battle, brief and inde-
cisive, ensued. And usually the cops joined in. The cops
always won. Moreover, the side battles were not limited to
the boys in the bleachers. There was a tall, well set up man
occupying a seat where second base is wont to be when
needed. In a loud tone of voice, he let it be understood that
Dempsey was, in his opinion, a bum. He denounced the
champion in a manner indicating that he and Dempsey were
on the outs.

A neighboring seat holder ventured to ask the enemy of
the champion whether he was willing to risk a few dollars
upon the outcome of the impending battle.

"I'll bet you a thousand bucks," said the big fellow, "that
this Firpo knocks him loose from his family."

"Very well," was the reply. "I presume you have the thousand with you."

"Well, what if I have. I'm looking for odds."

"What's your price?"

"One to six. What are you looking for: a sucker or something?"

"I'll tell you," said the second man. "You oughtn't to be
taking any chances. What you need is somebody who will bet
you that this ain't Friday night."

"Who said it ain't?" demanded the enemy of the king.

"Well, my friend, you wouldn't know whether it was or
not if somebody didn't tip you off."

With that the two men had words. Others joined in. Pretty
soon it became a general argument. Some one in the rear of
Dempsey's hater decided to snuff out one side by jamming
the latter's hat down upon his nose. In one terrific swipe,
aimed at nobody in particular, but scythe-like in its sweep,
the originator of the racket swung his fist into the face of

an innocent bystander, who instantly retaliated with his foot, the same taking the big boy in the ribs or thereabouts. The cops arrived, selected five of the noisiest and dragged them out. As luck would have it, the man responsible for the whole ruction was included among those hurled out of the park. It doesn't often happen that way.

The arrival of Luis Angel Firpo was attended by pain and disappointment. A large number of men struggled to get a closeup of the man from Argentina who looks enough like the Neanderthal man to be none other. It would seem that Luis's friends, before he set forth for the scene of dueling, had been told to be most careful lest harm befall him, rendering him incapable of slugging at Mr. Dempsey.

Luis arrived in a motor car. With him were his seconds, trainers, interpreters and a few elegantly dressed gentlemen who eloquently waved their hands at the walls of the Polo Grounds. Taking this to mean that Luis was about to leap the said walls or, as a last piece of training, butt his way through the masonry, the crowd stood back a bit. That gave the seconds, &c., an opportunity to form a hollow square in the center of which was Luis.

With their hands on their watches and scarfpins, the South Americans dashed through the gates. They went so fast that Luis was forced to shift one hand to his hat, which, having been bought by an enemy and being therefore too small, was in constant danger of flying off. In the Argentinian dash through the gate several too-eager men had their feet trod upon by Luis's entourage. Another received a vigorous poke in the neck for getting in the way. A third was tripped up and, losing his balance, was precipitated into a collection of refuse cans.

On the other hand, Jack Dempsey's arrival was minus casualties. Dempsey, too, arrived in a motor car, a magnificent car of British make. Time was when the gladiator arrived on foot and thanked the man at the gate if he was allowed to get in without a ticket. They called John L. a dude once (only once) because he rode from Boston to Revere and back in a carriage on the night he tucked away a celebrity known as Ruffles Brogan.

Jack leaped out of the car in advance of Kearns, his public accountant, and an assortment of combative looking gentlemen who looked very important. He wore a very old sweater and a cap that would cause the arrest of anybody wearing it south of Chambers Street after dark. He hotfooted it into the tradesmen's entrance and a cheer greeted him. He snatched the cap from his head and waved it. Several ticketless members of the crowd saw a possible chance of squeezing in in Dempsey's wake, thinking they might be mistaken for a second or a trainer or a private secretary. They failed. Stout guardians of the gate grabbed them as they appeared.

"Hey, watcha doin'?" demanded one of these gate crashers. "Can't ye see I'm wit Jack?"

"No," was the disheartening reply, "I couldn't see you with anybody, you big cheese."

Ordinarily such insult would have been resented. A battle should have followed. But the cops were on the job once more.

Never was an occasion so thoroughly copped. The gate crasher was hurled across the pavement and into the arms of a patrolman who hadn't much exercise.

It was one time that Jack Dempsey has crawled into a prize ring the sentimental favorite. The applause that greeted him at Toledo was tinged with scepticism. Willard, not overpopular himself (and for a reason not dissimilar to that which has removed Luis Firpo far from the mob heart), was considered impregnable. He couldn't be hurt. He was too big. Quite a number of the gentlemen present at Toledo rather hoped that both of the gladiators would fail to survive.

When Jack slaughtered the impotent Mr. Miske he fought with hoots ringing in his ears. He did for the valiant Brennan, and the crowd was half hoping that Bill would swing over a lucky one and end the career of the champion, who escaped the joys and tribulations of France.

Carpentier was a howling favorite because he had been drafted into the French army whereas Jack avoided such induction into the A. E. F., and great was the joy at Shelby when Tom Gibbons hung on for fifteen rounds. But last night the order of things had changed. Dempsey received quite an ovation. He was urged to "kill the spiggoty" by sportsmanlike patrons of the manly art.

He was bidden to decimate, annihilate and otherwise do away with Luis Angel Firpo, who, for no reason worth listening to, had come into great unpopularity. Sterling patriots begged Jack to keep his sacred title in the United States. Such was the feeling they put into their prayers that one shuddered to think what was going to happen were the Argentine to land one of his rights on the ear of the champion. A financial panic and the capture of Chicago by the I. W. W. would be the very least to expect.

Luis received comforting applause too. Shrill vivas greeted him as he lumbered into the ring. There were enough South Americans present to carry on a spirited revolution anywhere south of El Paso. There were other celebrities present. Restless John Reilly of Palestine, Ohio, and upper West Side occupied a $10 seat and was celebrating his place in society by wearing a necktie. He admitted, after some heckling, that he found both the ticket and the necktie. The amazing part of it is that John should have been anywhere where either a ticket or a necktie would be lying about unattached.

With Mr. Reilly was Joe Knickerbocker, the Yonkers ice man. Mr. Knickerbocker has become an ardent admirer of Mr. Louis Fall, otherwise Battling Siki, who is training for something or other at the old armory in Yonkers. In turn, Mr. Fall, who was among those present at the festivities last night, has developed a strong attachment for Luis Firpo, who, he says, bears a startling resemblance to Pete, a water buffalo presented to him by admiring citizens of British East Africa.

The truth of the matter is that Siki's admiration for Luis is founded upon envy. Mr. Knickerbocker informed Siki that once upon a time Luis knocked a full fledged horse cold with a punch on the submaxillary, using nothing but his uncovered right fist. For the moment Siki was not impressed. He inquired whether Luis had ever bitten a lion. Joe told him that Luis had not only bitten but eaten lions, whereat Siki asked Joe whether he had a good strong horse that could be punched without getting too sore about it.

Joe says that he offered two horses, one an ice wagon servant and the other a puller of coal wagons. All this happened last Monday on Chick Island, Yonkers.

Mr. Fall walloped the first animal and stepped back. He didn't want the brute to fall on him. The horse all but giggled and swished his tail.

"He can swat flies too, battler," was Knickerbocker's biting comment.

Mr. Fall pegged the second horse. Absolutely no result. This one didn't even whisk his tail. Mr. Fall rubbed his knuckles. He was silent for a moment and then said to Joe Knickerbocker:

"Oh, well, there must be some knack about it. Have you got a good lion about you?"

Battling Siki held quite a reception after he reappeared on the field.

Harry Wills, John Lester Johnson, the Jamaica Kid, Kid Norfolk, Clem Johnson, Panama Joe Gans, Jack Johnson, Kid Buller, Bill Tate, George Godfrey, Jeff Clark, and other knuckle dusters of the same pigmentation as the Senegalese bruiser, shook his right hand. Repartee was absent at first. The English-speaking Negroes grinned at Siki and Siki grinned back at them. He cocked his alpine hat forward and to the left giving the impression of a small peanut shell precariously balanced upon a large chestnut burr. He bowed and stood on one foot.

Kid Norfolk executed a rapid double shuffle and cocked his hat forward and to the left. Siki allowed that he was gratified and wished all hands much luck. Norfolk slid his hand along the Siki arm and gave his hat another shove.

"He ain't awful big or nothin' like that," said Norfolk, "but boy, he do look like he can make a mess if he's let."

Big Bill Tate was inspecting Siki from the rear. He appealed to Jack Johnson.

"Jack," said Bill, "you all make talk with this boy. You know all them words he talks. Ask him is he lookin' fo' a good all around fightin' evenin' some night."

Jack Johnson, one time heavyweight champion, bowed to Battling Siki. Siki pitched at his cuffs and declared himself charmed. Likewise, and with vast pride, he delivered himself of some lately acquired English.

"How do, meestair, yes," said Battling Siki.

But Jack was not to be put off. Had he not spent much time in Paris? But yes.

He unloosed a flock of wicked French. Bill, Jeff, Norfolk, John Lester, Panama Joe, George and Clem cried their admiration.

"Talk at him, Jack," cried Norfolk. "Talk at him whar he live."

Siki listened attentively. When Jack had finished Siki looked a bit baffled but came back with:

"Merci bien. Much oblige, meestair, yes."

The Siki reply didn't fit. Jack tried once again, adding gestures this time.

"Stick to him, Jack," crowed the encouraging Norfolk. "Tell him, him and me can pack Madison Square Garden with customers."

But when Jack was through talking French Siki, still mystified, replied:

"Yes, meestair. Much oblige. Yes."

"Trouble is," explained Jack retiring from the rostrum, "I speak just French and not this skinigelese language Mr. Siki speaks."

And then with a magnificent gesture Jack Johnson made his departure of Battling Siki.

"Mr. Siki, I am happy to meet up with you. You and me may never meet in the ring. Every time a promoter sees me he says there ain't goin' to be no fightin' with me. I bids you good evening."

Mr. Siki bowed to the ebony gathering, purchased four hot dogs painted with mustard and was ushered toward his seat.

"There," said Norfolk, "is a boy who I kin go some with. To-morrow I calls on Mr. Rickard and talks."

That part of the crowd that saw Battling Siki proceed to his seat was rent with emotion. So was Siki. Had he just emerged from a double victory over Jack Dempsey and Luis Firpo he could have been no more proud. Not the least of Siki's charm is his naïveté. Laugh at him and he laughs back at you. Bow and he bows. Indulge in a hearty cheer and Siki echoes the salutation. Tip your hat and Siki flourishes his.

He bowed himself through crowds. Once, blocked by a traffic jam, he executed a kind of elephant dance, a flatfooted treading that called for tom-tom beating. Only Siki knows what keeps that hat on his head. Near his chair a black Ichabod with an enormous diamond in his shirt arose to shout a welcome. And with the loose Negro arose an equally dark woman with a yellow aigrette in her hat.

"Git up there in that ring, Siki boy, and do yo' stuff," yelled the tall sport.

"Hi," squealed Siki. "Yes, meestair."

And then the police saw to it that Siki got his seat and order was restored.

Heywood Broun

Whenever the familiar observation is made that the sport pages have been used by famous writers as springboards to loftier heights, admiring lip service is paid the memory of Heywood Broun. Technically, the great liberal was a sport writer only a few years. He progressed rapidly to book reviewer, dramatic critic and then to enduring renown in journalism as one of the first—and still the greatest—political and social columnists. But Heywood Broun never forgot he had been a sport writer, nor would he let his readers forget it.

Although Broun was off the daily sport beat during the last quarter-century of his career, he constantly drew upon his first experiences as a newspaperman. When he needed an apt simile, analogy or a sharp, pithy phrase, he invariably went back to baseball, football or boxing for the figure of speech he wanted.

Broun liked nothing better than to descend from his ivory tower and inhale the old smells of the clubhouse and listen to the familiar roar of a sport mob. Long after his column, "It Seems To Me," had gained international acceptance as prescribed intellectual reading, Broun wrote the lead stories on World Series and an occasional championship heavyweight fight.

He mourned the passing of John J. McGraw, whose Giants he had covered on his first newspaper assignment in 1912, and he crowed as extravagantly as any bleacher fan when Babe Ruth caught hold of one and drove it out of sight and

*mind. His touch never was lighter or more amusing than
when he wrote on baseball—and he wrote about it constantly
with affection and enthusiasm.*

*Among the countless tributes paid Broun when he died
in 1939 at the age of fifty-one was a telegram from President
Roosevelt: " . . . He will be missed and mourned, particularly by the underprivileged, whose staunch champion he
always was."*

THE EDITOR

RUTH WILL OUT

BY

Heywood Broun

(NEW YORK WORLD) OCTOBER 12, 1923.

THE RUTH IS MIGHTY and shall prevail. He did yesterday.
Babe made two home runs and the Yankees won from
the Giants at the Polo Grounds by a score of 4 to 2. This
evens up the World's Series with one game for each con-
tender.

It was the first game the Yankees won from the Giants
since Oct. 10, 1921, and it ended a string of eight successive
victories for the latter, with one tie thrown in.

Victory came to the American League champions through
a change of tactics. Miller Huggins could hardly fail to have
observed Wednesday that terrible things were almost certain

to happen to his men if they paused any place along the line from first to home.

In order to prevent blunders in base running he wisely decided to eliminate it. The batter who hits a ball into the stands cannot possibly be caught napping off any base.

The Yankees prevented Kelly, Frisch and the rest from performing tricks in black magic by consistently hammering the ball out of the park or into sections of the stand where only amateurs were seated.

Though simplicity itself, the system worked like a charm. Three of the Yankees' four runs were the product of homers, and this was enough for the winning total. Aaron Ward was Ruth's assistant, Irish Meusel of the Giants also made a home run, but yesterday's show belonged to Ruth.

For the first time since coming to New York, Babe achieved his full brilliance in a World's Series game. Before this he has varied between pretty good and simply awful, but yesterday he was magnificent.

Just before the game John McGraw remarked:

"Why shouldn't we pitch to Ruth? I've said before and I'll say again, we pitch to better hitters than Ruth in the National League."

Ere the sun had set on McGraw's rash and presumptuous words, the Babe had flashed across the sky fiery portents which should have been sufficient to strike terror and conviction into the hearts of all infidels. But John McGraw clung to his heresy with a courage worthy of a better cause.

In the fourth inning Ruth drove the ball completely out of the premises. McQuillan was pitching at the time, and the count was two balls and one strike. The strike was a fast ball shoulder high, at which Ruth had lunged with almost comic ferocity and ineptitude.

Snyder peeked at the bench to get a signal from McGraw.

Catching for the Giants must be a terrific strain on the neck muscles, for apparently it is etiquette to take the signals from the bench manager furtively. The catcher is supposed to pretend he is merely glancing around to see if the girl in the red hat is anywhere in the grandstand, although all the time his eyes are intent on McGraw.

Of course the nature of the code is secret, but this time McGraw scratched his nose to indicate: "Try another of those shoulder high fast ones on the Big Bum and let's see if we can't make him break his back again."

But Babe didn't break his back, for he had something solid to check his terrific swing. The ball started climbing from the moment it left the plate. It was a pop fly with a brand new gland and, although it flew high, it also flew far.

When last seen the ball was crossing the roof of the stand in deep right field at an altitude of 315 feet. We wonder whether new baseballs conversing in the original package ever remark: "Join Ruth and see the world."

In the fifth Ruth was up again and by this time McQuillan had left the park utterly and Jack Bentley was pitching. The count crept up to two strikes and two balls. Snyder sneaked a look at the little logician deep in the dugout. McGraw blinked twice, pulled up his trousers and thrust the forefinger of his right hand into his left eye. Snyder knew that he meant: "Try the Big Bozo on a slow curve around his knees and don't forget to throw to first if you happen to drop the third strike."

Snyder called for the delivery as directed and Ruth half topped a line drive over the wall of the lower stand in right field. With that drive the Babe tied a record. Benny Kauff and Duffy Lewis are the only other players who ever made two home runs in a single World's Series game.

But was McGraw convinced and did he rush out of the dugout and kneel before Ruth with a cry of "Maestro" as the Babe crossed the plate? He did not. He nibbled at not a single word he has ever uttered in disparagement of the prowess of the Yankee slugger. In the ninth Ruth came to bat with two out and a runner on second base. By every consideration of prudent tactics an intentional pass seemed indicated.

Snyder jerked his head around and observed that Mc-Graw was blowing his nose. The Giant catcher was puzzled, for that was a signal he had never learned. By a process of pure reasoning he attempted to figure out just what it was that his chief was trying to convey to him.

"Maybe he means if we pitch to Ruth we'll blow the game," thought Snyder, but he looked toward the bench again just to make sure.

Now McGraw intended no signal at all when he blew his nose. That was not tactics, but only a head cold. On the second glance, Snyder observed that the little Napoleon gritted his teeth. Then he proceeded to spell out with the first three fingers of his right hand: "The Old Guard dies, but never surrenders." That was a signal Snyder recognized, although it never had passed between him and his manager before.

McGraw was saying: "Pitch to the Big Bum if he hammers every ball in the park into the North River."

And so, at Snyder's request, Bentley did pitch to Ruth and the Babe drove the ball deep into right centre; so deep that Casey Stengel could feel the hot breath of the bleacherites on his back as the ball came down and he caught it. If that drive had been just a shade to the right it would have been a third home run for Ruth. As it was, the Babe had a great day, with two home runs, a terrific long fly and two bases on balls.

Neither pass was intentional. For that McGraw should receive due credit. His game deserves to be recorded along with the man who said, "Lay on, MacDuff," "Sink the ship, Master Gunner, split her in twain," and "I'll fight it out on this line if it takes all summer." For John McGraw also went down eyes front and his thumb on his nose.

Some of the sportsmanship of the afternoon was not so admirable. In the sixth inning Pep Young prevented a Yankee double play by diving at the legs of Ward, who was just about to throw to first after a force-out. Tack Hardwick never took out an opposing back more neatly. Half the spectators booed Young and the other half applauded him.

It did not seem to us that there was any very good reason for booing Young, since the tradition of professional baseball always has been agreeably free of chivalry. The rule is, "Do anything you can get away with."

But Young never should have been permitted to get away with interference. The runner on first ought to have been declared out. In coming down to second Young had complete rights to the baseline and the bag, but those rights should not have permitted him the privilege of diving all the way across the bag to tackle Ward around the ankles.

It was a most palpably incompetent decision by Hart, the National League umpire on second base. Fortunately the blunder had no effect on the game, since the next Giant batter hit into a double play in which the Giant rushline was unable to reach Ward in time to do anything about it.

Ruth crushed to earth shall rise again. Herb Pennock, the assistant hero of the afternoon, did the same thing. In the fourth inning, Jack Bentley topped the slim Yankee left-hander into a crumpled heap by hitting him in the back with a fast ball. Pennock went down with a groan which could be heard even in the $1 seats. All the players gathered around him as he writhed, and what with sympathy and some judicious massage, he was up again within three or four minutes, and his pitching efficiency seemed to be in nowise impaired. It was, of course, wholly an accident, as the kidney punch is barred in baseball.

Entirely aside from his injury, Pennock looked none too stalwart. He is a meager athlete who winds up with great deliberation, as if fearful about what the opposing batter will do with the ball. And it was mostly slow curves that he fed to the Giants, but they did nothing much in crucial moments. Every now and then Pennock switched to a fast one, and the change of pace had McGraw's men baffled throughout.

Just once Pennock was in grave danger. It looked as if his three-run lead might be swept away in the sixth inning. Groh, Frisch and Young, the three Giants to face him at that point, all singled solidly. It seemed the part of wisdom to remove Pennock immediately after Young's single had scored Groh. Here Huggins was shrewd. He guessed wisely and stuck to Pennock.

Irish Meusel forced Young, and it would have been a double play but for Young's interference with Ward's throw. Cunningham, who followed, did hit into a double play, Scott to Ward to Pipp. The Giants' rally thus was limited to one run.

Their other score came in the second inning, when Irish Meusel drove a home run into the upper tier of the left field stands. It was a long wallop and served to tie the score at that stage of the game, as Erin Ward had made a home run for the Yankees in the first half of the inning. Ward's homer was less lusty, but went in the same general direction.

Ruth Will Out

In the fourth the Yankees broke the tie. Ruth began it with his over-the-fence smash, and another run came across on a single by Pipp, Schang's hit to right—which Young fumbled long enough to let Pipp reach third—and Scott's clean line hit to centre. This is said to be Scott's last year as a regular and he seems intent on making a good exit, for, in addition to fielding spryly, he made two singles.

The defensive star of the afternoon was Joe Dugan, third baseman of the Yankees. He specialized on bunts. McQuillan caught him flat-footed with an unexpected tap, but he threw it on the dead run in time to get his man at first.

Again he made a great play against Kelly, first batter up in the last half of the ninth. Kelly just nicked the ball with a vicious swing and the result was a treacherous spinning grounder that rolled only half way down to third. Dugan had to run and throw in conjunction this time, too, but he got his man.

For the Giants, Frisch, Young and Meusel batted hard, and Jack Bentley pitched well after relieving McQuillan in the fourth. He was hit fairly hard and he was a trifle wild, but the only run scored against him was Ruth's homer in the fifth.

As for the local color, the only bit we saw was around the neck of a spectator in a large white hat. The big handkerchief, which was spread completely over the gentleman's chest, was green and yellow, with purple spots. The rooter said his name was Tom Mix, but offered no other explanation.

THE BIG TRAIN

Frank "Buck" O'Neill

Washington, October 10, 1924.

A KING RETURNED to his throne today in this land of the free heart's hope and home. An emperor came back from Elba to find his worshiping following rallying in serried ranks to his standard.

The king was Walter Johnson, and his diadem of victory was placed upon his brow amid scenes without parallel in the history of baseball. For Walter Johnson, idol of American fandom, stepped into the breach and guided the staggering Senators out of the vale of defeat and perched them upon the pinnacle of the baseball world.

He guided them to the championship of the world in a terrific battle that raged through 12 innings. The score was 4 to 3.

The prayer of fandom was answered. Johnson, twice defeated by the Giants, his life's dream shattered, entered the game in the ninth inning with the score tied. Then, until Earl McNeely's double down the left field line scored Muddy Ruel with the winning run of the game, Johnson fought back the Giants with the courage that years ago won him the *nom de guerre* "Walter, the Lion-Hearted."

And Johnson had to pitch. There were moments when the

least mistake would have plunged Johnson into the yawning abyss that engulfed him here in the first game of this hectic series, and again on the Polo Grounds. The slightest error of the men behind him would have been ruinous, but Johnson, the true-hearted, made no mistake, nor did the men behind him err. They fought behind their idol as gamely as he fought for them. Their catches and pegs were as true and as swift as the baffling curves he projected to the plate. And Walter Johnson won.

Walter Johnson won because of his courage as much as his cunning, and that makes the victory the sweeter. Twice in the waning innings of the contest he struck out George Kelly, the man who started him along the rocky highway to defeat in the first contest. In the ninth inning he passed Young with Frisch on third and then blazed his fast one through the middle for Kelly. Kelly could hardly see the ball, let alone hit it. In the eleventh with Southworth on second, Johnson passed Young, the left-hander, and then turned his speed on Kelly once more. The long Californian went down. Great was Walter Johnson.

Johnson strode boldly to the gateway of Valhalla and bade the door be opened. And this time the doorkeeper obeyed the challenge. Johnson at last, after 18 years, has won his place with the heroes of other years.

What tho' he pitched only four innings? His hurling was as great as any pitcher ever offered. His trials were many, but his mastery was complete.

Washington fans realized their long dream as Johnson was crowned king of the diamond. For 40 years they have waited and dreamed with a faith that would not down, and when at last the game was done, perfectly normal men and women suddenly became bereft of reason. They cheered hysterically as they rushed in disorganized masses toward the Washington bench. They wept as they threw away their score cards, their newspapers, their hats and overcoats.

President Calvin Coolidge was transported to the heights with the crowd. When Earl McNeely caught the ball on the end of his bat and sent it whistling down the left field foul line, Coolidge leaped to his feet and swung his hat in the air. As Ruel dug his cleats viciously into the turf across the plate, the chief executive of our country became just a normal fan reacting to the common urge that turned all men mad. He cheered with the fervor of Jimmy Smithers of the left field bleachers. He cheered with the wild excitement of Sambo Jones, who perched on a roof of a neighboring house. The president was just a fan, and no president ever had greater cause for exulting.

Ruel scored amidst cheers that rolled along the Potomac to the sea. And when he scored the winning run the stands erupted, hurling fans on the field. A headlong rush to the Washington bench followed, and there, led by cheer leaders in true college style, the crowd thundered their applause for the team.

Each man kills the thing he loves, Oscar Wilde said many years ago, and the fans this afternoon almost killed Walter Johnson. They slapped their hero on the back, wrung his hand, hugged him and almost knocked him under the feet of the throng that rushed for him. Swift work by a police battalion saved Johnson from his friends.

For half an hour then they remained in front of the stands and cheered the several members of the team, cheered Coolidge, cheered themselves and tore the roof off the stands. Rome never howled as the capital is howling tonight. And Rome never had a greater reason. The searchlight battery illuminating the dome of the Capitol blazes more brilliantly than ever. The city pulses with a new life, a life conceived in enthusiasm and dedicated to the exaltation of the Senators.

Victory snatched from the jaws of defeat is sweet, and never was victory sweeter than this today. The Senators took the lead in the fourth inning when Bucky Harris smashed a ball into the left field seats for a home run, the first hit made by the Senators off the baffling delivery of Virgil Barnes, up to that moment.

But the lead was short-lived. In that sixth inning the defense of the Senators cracked wide open and the Giants scored three runs on two clean hits and two errors.

The Senators then tied the count in the eighth inning, making three hits and getting a base on balls off Barnes. In the ninth they had a chance to win the game with Judge on third, Bluege on first and one out, but Miller hit into a double play, and the chance failed.

In the eleventh, with Bentley in the box, the Senators might have ended the contest with Goslin on second, Judge on first and two out, but Bluege forced Judge at second base. It was maddening to the crowd, this profligate waste of opportunities. Hope fled before the rush of fear only to rush back once more into the breasts of the 40,000 or more who prayed with fervor for a triumph long delayed.

There is poetic justice in sport and poetic justice scored in this classic of the field. Muddy Ruel, who scored his first hit of the series in the eighth inning, a weak rap down the first base line, started the Senators on their way to final victory. Little Muddy raised a weak and puny foul which Gowdy muffed, and then strode into the box, gritting his teeth, registering high resolve, on the next ball. Bentley got the curve over the middle of the plate and Ruel swung.

The ball whistled down the left field foul line like a white meteor, a flashing beacon of hope to the crowd.

Walter Johnson then came to the plate and the crowd rose en masse to cheer him, pleading for a hit that would end the game. Walter laced the ball down to Travis Jackson, who fumbled for a fraction of a second and Walter, legging it with might and main, was safe at first base. The din was almost deafening. Here was victory, here was the chance of success.

Then came McNeely to the plate. He took a cut at the first ball pitched and raised a foul into the netting for a strike. Groans arose, but Bentley put the next ball over, waist high and slightly inside. The swing of a yellow bat, a crash and the ball started for left field. It rolled along the ground for 30 feet and then took a wild hop for liberty. Ruel rushed for the plate, and Irish Meusel raced in to retrieve the ball.

Meusel picked the ball up, but seeing Ruel just a few feet from the plate, he did not throw. Instead, he looked ruefully at the ball, put it in his pocket and walked slowly in. The game was over, the championship was won by Washington. Walter Johnson was crowned emperor of a realm long denied him by the connivance of fate and the vicissitudes of baseball.

Loud and long rolled the cheers of Washington fans in honor of Walter Johnson and Earl McNeely and little Muddy Ruel. But there were cheers due for the black-haired, fighting Bucky Harris, leader of the new world champions, crowned champion at the age of 28, his first year as a major-league manager.

Harris put the Senators in the running, and kept them in the ball game. His batting in the pinch in the lucky eighth tied the score and made ultimate victory possible.

In the fourth inning Harris smashed a wallop high over the head of Hack Wilson and into the left field stands for a home run. In the eighth inning, with Nemo Liebold on third and Ruel on second, there by virtue of base-hits, Harris slapped a ball into left field just beyond the clutch of Travis Jackson. The two runs scored, and the game was knotted tight.

Harris had no spectacular plays to make in the field but he accepted with alacrity every chance that came his way. The defensive fireworks were supplied by Ossie Bluege. Bluege, who was in turn the Jekyll-Hyde of the infield. Bluege, replacing the sorely wounded Roger Peckinpaugh at shortstop, turned in two marvelous stops, one on Hack Wilson, in the second inning, and another on the same player in the fourth. In the second Bluege went over to the right side of second base and snatched a single off the turf, tossing it to Judge in the nick of time. Wilson's wallop in the fourth was well placed and well meant, but Bluege headed it off and got his man.

Yet it was Bluege's doleful error on Gowdy that sent a runner over the plate and allowed the final New York run to count. Taylor, playing with a broken hand, made a fine stop of Kelly's rifle shot down the left field line and took a base hit right out of the average of the Giant's first sacker.

Both managers were hard pressed for pitchers. The Giants were right down to the ragged edge and, for that matter, so were the Senators. But Harris had an ace in the hole.

He had not used Curley Ogden for the good reason that Ogden has been troubled with a sore arm. But Ogden went out on the line and McGraw switched his lineup for a right-hander. He had Terry on first base and Kelly in the outfield.

Ogden struck out Lindström, passed Frisch and then out from the bullpen came George Mogridge. It was a pre-arranged plan.

McGraw sent Barnes into the game and until the eighth the Kansas boy pitched great ball. He met his match in Mogridge. The left-hander, however, retired in favor of

Marberry in the seventh, while Barnes remained around until the eighth, when Harris blasted him off the mound with a wallop to left. Nehf replaced Barnes and retired in favor of McQuillan. Bentley came into the game in the eleventh and lost the game in the twelfth.

Desperate indeed was the battle of managers. McGraw made one of his famous strategic moves in the eleventh inning. The Senators had Goslin on second and Judge on base with Bluege, a left-handed hitter, coming to the plate. At once McGraw called time and sent Irish Meusel over to right and placed Ross Young in left because of the latter's superior throwing ability. The move was not necessary, for Bluege spilled a weak grounder into a force play and the frame was over.

It may well be said by National League rooters that Barnes deserved a kinder fate. For three innings the Senators were toy soldiers in his hands. Then in the fourth Harris hit his homer, the first hit. Rice was robbed of a single by Wilson's great diving, sliding capture of his low liner. In the fifth and sixth frames the drab order of one, two, three was preserved. In the seventh inning the Senators got two runners on bases, but could not break through.

But in the eighth the break came. Nemo Liebold hit in place of Taylor and sliced a double to left. Ruel beat out a roller to Kelly, the first hit of the series for him. Tate hit for Mogridge and walked, filling the bases. McNeely failed to take cognizance of the fact that Barnes was slipping and he hit the first good ball. He was out. But Harris also hit the first good ball and scored two runs. That ended Barnes.

When Walter Johnson went down to the bullpen in the sixth inning, the crowd roared a welcome. They sensed in Johnson the presence of victory. Johnson stepped into the lists in the ninth inning. He got Lindstrom, but Frisch hit a triple to center, and it looked bad. Young received a free pass and Johnson then struck out Kelly amidst scenes that beggar description.

In the eleventh Groh was rushed into the game and started with a pinch single in place of McQuillan. Southworth ran for Heinie and got to second on Lindstrom's bunt. Frisch struck out this time and again Young was passed. Kelly struck out for the second time in the pinch, and the crowd went stark, raving mad.

Johnson held his rivals down under the speed of his fast ball. Old Lion Heart was himself again, and all men looked alike to him.

Grantland Rice

The dean of American sport writers, Grantland Rice has written more words—good words—on major events than any other man in the business. In this, his sixty-fourth year, Rice still retains his enthusiasm and the ability to outwrite the opposition on a spot news story when he gets his teeth into an assignment.

The gentleman from Tennessee, an eminent versifier, sentimentalist, golf nut and an indefatigable jouster of the daily double, has an unchallenged distinction in a highly competitive—and sometimes acrimonious—field. Everyone loves the guy. There is hardly a sport writer alive who has not been the beneficiary of Rice's experience and friendship.

There is only one black mark in the Rice dossier. It has been said, somewhat facetiously and inelegantly, that he inadvertently loused up sportswriting more than any man of his time. His dramatic style—the most famous example of which is the following article, where the Notre Dame backfield was called the Four Horsemen for the first time—was copied extensively and all the imitations were pretty terrible, of course. In time, the bright young men despaired of snatching Rice's royal mantle and applied themselves to the task of putting one little word after another. Rice remained supreme in the technique of lush leads and giving rich elaboration to a story while, by no means incidentally, weaving all the essential facts into his colorful pattern.

The best-known contemporary sport writer in the country, Rice still flourishes in the New York Sun.

THE EDITOR

THE FOUR HORSEMEN

Grantland Rice

(NEW YORK HERALD TRIBUNE)
OCTOBER 19, 1924.

———

OUTLINED AGAINST a blue-gray October sky, the Four Horsemen rode again. In dramatic lore they are known as Famine, Pestilence, Destruction and Death. These are only aliases. Their real names are Stuhldreher, Miller, Crowley and Layden. They formed the crest of the South Bend cyclone before which another fighting Army football team was swept over the precipice at the Polo Grounds yesterday afternoon as 55,000 spectators peered down on the bewildering panorama spread on the green plain below.

A cyclone can't be snared. It may be surrounded, but somewhere it breaks through to keep on going. When the cyclone starts from South Bend, where the candle lights still gleam through the Indiana sycamores, those in the way must take to storm cellars at top speed. Yesterday the cyclone struck again as Notre Dame beat the Army, 13 to 7, with a set of backfield stars that ripped and crashed through a strong Army defense with more speed and power than the warring cadets could meet.

Notre Dame won its ninth game in twelve Army starts through the driving power of one of the greatest backfields that ever churned up the turf of any gridiron in any football

age. Brilliant backfields may come and go, but in Stuhldreher, Miller, Crowley and Layden, covered by a fast and
charging line, Notre Dame can take its place in front of the
field.

Coach McEwan sent one of his finest teams into action, an
aggressive organization that fought to the last play around
the first rim of darkness, but when Rockne rushed his Four
Horsemen to the track they rode down everything in sight.
It was in vain that 1400 gray-clad cadets pleaded for the
Army line to hold. The Army line was giving all it had, but
when a tank tears in with the speed of a motorcycle, what
chance has flesh and blood to hold? The Army had its share
of stars in action, such stars as Garbisch, Farwick, Wilson,
Wood, Ellinger and many others, but they were up against
four whirlwind backs who picked up at top speed from the
first step as they swept through scant openings to slip on by
the secondary defense. The Army had great backs in Wilson
and Wood, but the Army had no such quartet, who seemed
to carry the mixed blood of the tiger and the antelope.

Rockne's light and tottering line was just about as tottering as the Rock of Gibraltar. It was something more than
a match for the Army's great set of forwards, who had earned
their fame before. Yet it was not until the second period that
the first big thrill of the afternoon set the great crowd into
a cheering whirl and brought about the wild flutter of flags
that are thrown to the wind in exciting moments. At the
game's start Rockne sent in almost entirely a second string
cast. The Army got the jump and began to play most of the
football. It was the Army attack that made three first downs
before Notre Dame had caught its stride. The South Bend
cyclone opened like a zephyr.

And then, in the wake of a sudden cheer, out rushed Stuhldreher, Miller, Crowley and Layden, the four star backs

who helped to beat Army a year ago. Things were to be a trifle different now. After a short opening flurry in the second period, Wood, of the Army, kicked out of bounds on Notre Dame's 20-yard line. There was no sign of a tornado starting. But it happened to be at just this spot that Stuhldreher decided to put on his attack and begin the long and dusty hike.

On the first play the fleet Crowley peeled off fifteen yards and the cloud from the west was now beginning to show signs of lightning and thunder. The fleet, powerful Layden got six yards more and then Don Miller added ten. A forward pass from Stuhldreher to Crowley added twelve yards, and a moment later Don Miller ran twenty yards around Army's right wing. He was on his way to glory when Wilson, hurtling across the right of way, nailed him on the 10-yard line and threw him out of bounds. Crowley, Miller and Layden—Miller, Layden and Crowley—one or another, ripping and crashing through, as the Army defense threw everything it had in the way to stop this wild charge that had now come seventy yards. Crowley and Layden added five yards more and then, on a split play, Layden went ten yards across the line as if he had just been fired from the black mouth of a howitzer.

In that second period Notre Dame made eight first downs to the Army's none, which shows the unwavering power of the Western attack that hammered relentlessly and remorselessly without easing up for a second's breath. The Western line was going its full share, led by the crippled Walsh with a broken hand.

But there always was Miller or Crowley or Layden, directed through the right spot by the cool and crafty judgment of Stuhldreher, who picked his plays with the finest possible generalship. The South Bend cyclone had now roared eighty-five yards to a touchdown through one of the strongest defensive teams in the game. The cyclone had struck with too much speed and power to be stopped. It was the preponderance of Western speed that swept the Army back.

The next period was much like the second. The trouble began when the alert Layden intercepted an Army pass on the 48-yard line. Stuhldreher was ready for another march.

Once again the cheering cadets began to call for a rallying stand. They are never overwhelmed by any shadow of defeat as long as there is a minute of fighting left. But silence fell over the cadet sector for just a second as Crowley ran around the Army's right wing for 15 yards, where Wilson hauled him down on the 33-yard line. Walsh, the Western captain, was hurt in the play but soon resumed. Miller got 7 and Layden got 8 and then, with the ball on the Army's 20-yard line, the cadet defense rallied and threw Miller in his tracks. But the halt was only for the moment. On the next play Crowley swung out and around the Army's left wing, cut in and then crashed over the line for Notre Dame's second touchdown.

On two other occasions the Notre Dame attack almost scored. Yeomans saved one touchdown by intercepting a pass on his 5-yard line as he ran back 35 yards before he was nailed by two tacklers. It was a great play in the nick of time. On the next drive Miller and Layden in two hurricane dashes took the ball 42 yards to the Army's 14-yard line, where the still game Army defense stopped four plunges on the 9-yard line and took the ball.

Up to this point the Army had been outplayed by a crushing margin. Notre Dame had put under way four long marches and two of these had yielded touchdowns. Even the stout and experienced Army line was meeting more than it could hold. Notre Dame's brilliant backs had been provided

with the finest possible interference, usually led by Stuhldreher, who cut down tackler after tackler by diving at some
rival's flying knees. Against this each Army attack had been
smothered almost before it got under way. Even the great
Wilson, the star from Penn State, one of the great backfield
runners of his day and time, rarely had a chance to make any
headway through a massed wall of tacklers who were blocking
every open route.

The sudden change came late in the third quarter, when
Wilson, raging like a wild man, suddenly shot through a
tackle opening to run 34 yards before he was finally collared
and thrown with a jolt. A few minutes later Wood, one of
the best of all the punters, kicked out of bounds on Notre
Dame's 5-yard line. Here was the chance. Layden was forced
to kick from behind his own goal. The punt soared up the
field as Yeomans called for a free kick on the 35-yard line.
As he caught the ball he was nailed and spilled by a Western
tackler, and the penalty gave the Army 15 yards, with the ball
on Notre Dame's 20-yard line.

At this point Harding was rushed to quarter in place of
Yeomans, who had been one of the leading Army stars. On
the first three plays the Army reached the 12-yard line, but it
was no fourth down, with two yards to go. Harding's next
play was the feature of the game.

As the ball was passed, he faked a play to Wood, diving
through the line, held the oval for just a half breath, then,
tucking the same under his arm, swung out around Notre
Dame's right end. The brilliant fake worked to perfection.
The entire Notre Dame defense had charged forward in a
surging mass to check the line attack and Harding, with open
territory, sailed on for a touchdown. He traveled those last 12
yards after the manner of food shot from guns. He was over
the line before the Westerners knew what had taken place. It

was a fine bit of strategy, brilliantly carried out by every member of the cast.

The cadet sector had a chance to rip open the chilly atmosphere at last, and most of the 55,000 present joined in the tribute to football art. But that was Army's last chance to score. From that point on it was seesaw, up and down, back and forth, with the rivals fighting bitterly for every inch of ground. It was harder now to make a foot than it had been to make ten yards. Even the all-star South Bend cast could not longer continue to romp for any set distances, as Army tacklers, inspired by the touchdown, charged harder and faster than they had charged before.

The Army brought a fine football team into action, but it was beaten by a faster and smoother team. Rockne's supposedly light, green line was about as heavy as Army's, and every whit as aggressive. What is even more important, it was faster on its feet, faster in getting around.

It was Western speed and perfect interference that once more brought about Army doom. The Army line couldn't get through fast enough to break up the attacking plays; and once started the bewildering speed and power of the Western backs slashed along for 8, 10 and 15 yards on play after play. And always in front of these offensive drives could be found the whirling form of Stuhldreher, taking the first man out of the play as cleanly as though he had used a hand grenade at close range. This Notre Dame interference was a marvelous thing to look upon.

It formed quickly and came along in unbroken order, always at terrific speed, carried by backs who were as hard to drag down as African buffaloes. On receiving the kick-off, Notre Dame's interference formed something after the manner of the ancient flying wedge, and they drove back up the field with the runner covered from 25 and 30 yards at almost every chance. And when a back such as Harry Wilson finds few chances to get started, you can figure upon the defensive strength that is barricading the road. Wilson is one of the hardest backs in the game to suppress, but he found few chances yesterday to show his broken field ability. You can't run through a broken field until you get there.

One strong feature of the Army play was its headlong battle against heavy odds. Even when Notre Dame had scored two touchdowns and was well on its way to a third, the Army fought on with fine spirit until the touchdown chance came at last. And when the chance came Coach McEwan had the play ready for the final march across the line. The Army has a better team than it had last year. So has Notre Dame. We doubt that any team in the country could have beaten Rockne's array yesterday afternoon, East or West. It was a great football team brilliantly directed, a team of speed, power and team play. The Army has no cause for gloom over its showing. It played first-class football against more speed than it could match.

Those who have tackled a cyclone can understand.

W. O. McGeehan

A coincidence in chronology joins W. O. McGeehan and Grantland Rice in this book, just as they were teamed for many years in adjoining columns of the New York Herald Tribune. McGeehan did not enjoy the national reputation held by some of his contemporaries, and it is a great pity. There are many who insist he was the ablest reporter and commentator sportswriting has produced.

The juxtaposition of McGeehan and Rice offers an interesting study in contrasting attitudes. Rice, with his enthusiasm and kind word for every event, is an outstanding exponent of the "Gee whiz" style of writing. McGeehan, on the cynical, critical side, was the founder of the "Aw nuts" school, although he was not a professional aginner. He properly belongs between those extremes, a little to the left of center.

McGeehan at his best was a satirist; he had an ironic touch but he never descended to the slang caricature fancied during his period. His language was formal and precise and it was singularly free of the weary clichés and telltale turns of expression that date today so much of the copy written twenty years ago.

A strict realist and a stern debunker of phony piety, McGeehan was rough on rats and professional promoters. He referred to spectators as cash customers, not fans; he regarded prize-fighting as a business rather than a sport and he invariably called it "the cauliflower industry" or "the manly art of modified murder." The appellation he hung on *the New York Boxing Commission, "The Three Dumb Dukes," still is in use.*

Yet McGeehan was capable of the tender, tremulous touch when the occasion called for such treatment. His column on Lindbergh's solo flight across the Atlantic in 1927 and his story on the funeral of Christy Mathewson are models of controlled, restrained sentiment.

Bill McGeehan was born in San Francisco in 1879 and gave luster to that city's renown as an incubator of great newspapermen. He left Stanford University in 1898 to enlist in the First California Volunteers and served with the outfit for two years in the Philippine insurrection. Returning to his home grounds in 1900, McGeehan went into newspaper work on the San Francisco Call and never left the field.

A talented, all-around craftsman, McGeehan was city editor and managing editor of the San Francisco Post after leaving the Call and he also worked on the Bulletin and Examiner before migrating to New York in 1914. There he quickly became one of the top men in the toughest of all newspaper leagues. He was appointed sport editor of the Tribune in 1916 and five years later was promoted to the managing editor's throne.

Executive work palled on McGeehan, though, and in 1922 he abdicated to devote all his time to his column, "Down the Line." Ostensibly a sport writer, McGeehan liked to make side excursions on other beats. His color stories on the Scopes "monkey trial" were considered the best feature stuff to come out of Dayton, Tenn., and in later years the readers looked for his light travelogues throughout the world, accompanied by "the lady who is driving me," his wife, Sophie Treadwell, a famous reporter and dramatist in her own right.

Like Ring Lardner, McGeehan died in 1933 of a heart ailment at the age of fifty-four while he was visiting his old friend, Uncle Wilbert Robinson, in Georgia. Hospital attendants reported that up to the end he demanded a typewriter in bed so that he could turn out his daily piece for the paper.

THE EDITOR

A POX ON PERFECTION

BY

W. O. McGeehan

(NEW YORK HERALD TRIBUNE)

———————

Washington, October 9, 1925.

AFTER MATURE DELIBERATION I have come to the conclusion that only those who know little or nothing about the national pastime really enjoy a World Series. The experts are interested only in the games that put the non-experts into a state of somnolence, while they suffer great mental anguish at the games that produce thrills for those who know little or nothing about the intricacies of inside baseball.

For instance, after the opening game of the current Series Mr. Wilbert Robinson, president of the Brooklyn Baseball Club, approached me beaming with enthusiasm. "Now there," said Mr. Robinson, "was a great game of baseball." "Why?" I demanded. Mr. Robinson withered me with a look of scorn. "And they send saps like you to report baseball games," he said, bitterly.

Following the second game Mr. Robinson held me with his glittering eye. "You saw it?" he asked. "Surely," I replied evasively and tried to hurry on. "You got the big story of the game?" he demanded. "Oh, yes," I replied airily. "Peck fumbled one and then Cuyler drove out a home run, and it was all over."

The World Series guest here beat his breast and emitted loud raspberry. "Do you mean to tell me," demanded Mr. Robinson, "that you did not notice the big feature of the game? Didn't you see the Pittsburgh infield come in during the ninth inning? Anybody who knows anything about base-ball would have noticed that. I asked Fred Clarke about it after the game and all he said was, 'You go to hell!' and here you are going to write a piece about the baseball game and you didn't even see that."

"If the infield did come in, what of it?" I demanded, a trifle nettled. "If the infield wanted to play in why shouldn't it? This is a free country, including Pittsburgh, even if every hotelkeeper in the place is named Jesse James."

"Everybody noticed it," continued Mr. Robinson, ignoring the flippancy of your correspondent. "John McGraw nearly tore out of the ball park. Even Colonel Huston, who has been sleeping through the Series, woke up and said, 'Somebody tell that Pittsburgh infield to deploy as skirmishers, double time.' Of course he went right back to sleep again, but he noticed it.

"Then there was Jim Tierney, of the Giants. Why even he noticed it, and Judge McQuade was hollering for some-body to get injunction or an alibi or a habeas corpus or something to get that Pittsburgh infield where it belonged! I heard Barney Dreyfuss yelling, 'Tell that infield to play looser! Tell Bill McKechnie to tie the infield loose!' "

"But," I insisted, "nobody hit where the infield wasn't.

Also Pittsburgh won the game. So once more I ask, what of it?"

"What of it?" demanded the indignant Mr. Robinson. "It wasn't right, that's all! It wasn't baseball!"

"But Pittsburgh won the game!" I persisted.

"Oh, what is the use of talking to a sap?" said Mr. Robinson. As a parting shot he added, "When you talk to Ma Robinson about the ball game do not admit that you did not notice that Pittsburgh infield. She thinks that you are intelligent. So, for heaven's sake, do not tip your mitt and your secret will be safe with me. I never will tell anybody that you did not notice the Pittsburgh infield."

Mr. Robinson merely strengthened a conviction which I have held concerning the national pastime for these many years. This conviction is that the great majority of the cash customers never get a thrill out of inside baseball, and that the perfect baseball game, if it could be ballyhooed in advance, would not draw a corporal's guard.

In support of this conviction I would offer in evidence the almost perfect Athletics owned by Mr. Cornelius McGillicuddy. They won ball games with such monotonous regularity that the customers became so wearied of seeing them win baseball games that they did not come to the ball park. When the customers do not come to baseball parks the enthusiasm of the owner for a perfect ball club and perfect baseball begins to die a very painful death. Mr. McGillicuddy scattered his perfect ball club all over the open ivory market and started fresh.

In the first game of the current World Series they staged some perfect baseball and set all of the cash customers to yawning. Mr. McGraw, Mr. Jennings, Mr. Cobb and Mr. Babe Ruth were thrilled by it, but the non-experts were not. As the experts do not contribute to the support of the national pastime to any marked extent, it looks as though the magnates should strive for imperfection by all legal and reasonable means.

Baseball is a circus, and as is the case with many a circus, the clowns and the side shows frequently are more interesting than the big stuff in the main tent.

Mr. Pie Traynor, who broke out into a rash of boils, base hits and fancy fielding at the start of the current Series, once posed in the role of opportunity knocking at the gates of Fenway Park, the home grounds of the Boston Red Sox.

Young Mr. Traynor is from the rock-ribbed, rock-headed coast of Massachusetts. He wanted to play baseball; consequently he used to haunt Fenway Park at practice time. He would worm himself into the practice infield and work himself into large gobs of perspiration.

The Red Sox manager (it may or may not have been Cousin Egbert Barrow, who is now filling the post of secretary to the Yankees with ease, grace and abandon) noticed him one day. Said the manager of the Red Sox to Mr. Pie Traynor, "I wish you would get to hell out of here and stay out! I am tired of watching you cut our nice infield to pieces with your spikes."

Stung to the quick, young Pie Traynor left the park abruptly and in a fit of despondency moved south, where he obtained employment, as they say, with a minor league club. It was not long before Mr. Traynor was annexed by a Pirate scout.

The Red Sox could use a young man of Traynor's size, weight and general make-up at the current writing. It is very unwise to discourage earnest young men. They return later bearing wreaths of raspberries.

The downpour that stopped the game today caused some of the veteran World Series followers to reminisce in a spirit of brooding melancholy about the Series of 1911, when the inmates of the traveling madhouse were held seven days in Philadelphia by the rain.

There is something to be merry about in the thought that if the rain had come it came in Washington instead of Pittsburgh. A week in Pittsburgh at World Series rates would bankrupt organized baseball.

The conversation with a Pittsburgh hotel clerk during this Series runs to this effect:

"How much for a room?"

"How much have you got with you? That's what it costs and it has to be paid in advance."

TENNIS À LA MODE

BY

John R. Tunis

(BOSTON GLOBE)

———————

Cannes, France, February 17, 1926.

NEVER WAS ANY amateur sporting event the world over staged under such atrocious conditions."

Those were the words of the man who sat next to me—I was going to say in the press stand, but there was no press stand—at the great match here yesterday between Miss Helen Wills, champion of the United States, and Mademoiselle Suzanne Lenglen, champion of France, at the Carlton Tennis Club of Cannes. This man is no beginner at the business of watching bit sporting events, either. He follows them from Alaska to Albania. He has seen Wills and Firpo battle in a ring; six-day bicycle races in London, in Paris and Berlin; football games in the Yale Bowl and the vast Stadium at Stanford; the Cup Tie at Wembley, World Series in New York and Washington and the Olympic Games in Europe and the United States.

I looked around as he uttered these words; at the boys and girls climbing the high wire fence beside us, at the crowd of Frenchmen in the huge eucalyptus tree behind the court, at the workmen hammering and pounding on the stands, although the players were due to appear in less than five minutes, at the yelling mob in the alleyway parallel to the club, at the newspaper men around me, men whose names are known from Maine to Montana, sitting with their typewriters on their laps, pushed, shoved and crowded on every side. I looked at these things and I was forced to agree with his remarks. Atrocious conditions is an understatement of the case.

Let me give you an idea of the Carlton Tennis Club of Cannes. When you think of the Riviera, of Cannes, you doubtless picture a deep blue sea, an azure sky, a soft and languorous sun seeping down upon gardens and flowers of all sorts—upon palm trees and orange trees and mimosa and roses and carnations, and bougainvillea climbing up the walls along the roadside. Forget it. Put that out of your mind. Here is the Carlton Tennis Club as it actually is.

A small space between four mean back streets. Above towers the mass of the Carlton Hotel, one of those Grand Palace hotels where it is bad form to appear before noon, and anyone who earns a living is liable to be ejected directly his crime is discovered. Opposite, a saw mill rises beyond the central court—or, as the French so euphemistically put it, *le court d'honneur*—its raucous buzzing anything but soothing to the nerves in the middle of an important match. Behind the stands rises the blank wall of a garage. Opposite, the back doors of the couple of villas peep through the scrawny hedge. The six courts composing the club property are so ranged that three are always placed wrongly into the sun. The "clubhouse" is a little hut enclosing one room seventeen by eleven feet inside. It has a couple of dozen lockers, a shower bath which does not shower, several washstands discharging cold water, and that is all. No towels. No electric light. In short, nothing.

What a place to stage a match of this kind, the greatest match of tennis between two women that the world has seen for many years, may ever see for years to come! One thinks with regret of the vast arenas at Wimbledon, at Forest Hills, at Saint Cloud, with their spacious seating accommodations— and one wonders why a meeting like this was played under such circumstances. The answer to that is easy.

Meet Mr. F. M. B. Fisher.

"F.M.B." his friends call him. He is a heavy man with a large frame and a big paw which he extends cheerily when he meets you. Formerly a cabinet minister in his own country (New Zealand), he served with distinction in the war. He is a tennis player who has represented his country in international competition, a sportsman of renown, a facile and mellifluous conversationalist, and at the present moment in the employ of an English tennis ball company. Now perhaps you begin to see the light. Obviously if a match of this importance could be played with a certain kind of ball it would be worth many millions of dollars to the corporation in question.

Now the Carlton Tennis Club is run by three young sportsmen: the brothers Burke, sons of old Tom Burke, one of the first and the most famous of all tennis professionals. They are openly and avowedly professionals. Albert is the present holder of the French professional title, and as professionals they have the sympathy and respect of everyone who is engaged in the dubious entertainment of earning a living. Regarding this match, however, they appear to have been figureheads. The man who apparently ran the show is, so far as can be discovered, none other than our friend F. M. B., the Tex Rickard of Riviera tennis.

Mr. Fisher, and he alone, seemed to know what was coming. At any rate, weeks beforehand when correspondents from the biggest dailies of New York and London were running around saying that the two would never meet, Mr. Fisher was saying nothing. But his company was placing advertisements with magazines to appear some time later showing that at least he had a pretty good guess when the two women would meet and where it would be.

Although the match was not to take place until 11:15, I had a fear that there might be a struggle to get in, and therefore rolled up about 9:30. At that time, an hour and a half before the players were to come on court, a line four deep stretched from the gates of the club to the Croisette, five hundred yards away. And it was growing rapidly. I was told the first arrivals had been there at the entrance shortly after daybreak.

Just outside us in the little alley—it was hardly more than that—which ran beside the court, a mob seethed and yelled and rushed up and down in an effort to get in, to get a glance at the match somehow, anyhow. Many of the more nimble Canois and Canoises grabbed branches of a big eucalyptus tree and climbed up into its boughs. As the members of the club committee saw this vast number of non-payees so comfortably installed they brought pressure to bear in the shape of a Cannes traffic cop. As a tree climber he was a good traffic cop. French model. As he went up, the invaders went higher still. Finally he decided he had gone high enough. Down he came, amid the cheers and jeers of the multitude. In a small house facing the court an enterprising Frenchman with a long beard was renting places at his second story windows for twenty francs a place. When his wife came downstairs, shouting that the windows were all filled six or seven times over, he began to rent places in the roof. I say "in the roof" advisedly. The roofs of the Riviera are so constructed that the tiles laid on beams can be removed from within. You took a chair to the attic, mounted it, removed the tile, and poked your head out. Pretty soon every house in the vicinity looked half undressed. A hundred faces stuck out of the attics as though the villas were made of cardboard. On the wide, gently sloping roof of the garage more people began to appear. The large painted sign announcing that this particular garage moved itself to the Hotel Majestic at Cobourg in the summer was soon covered. That was how the French saw the match. For have you any idea what seats for this super-spectacle cost?

They cost—if you wished to sit down and were lucky enough, through your influence with F.M.B., to obtain a chance to buy one—three hundred francs apiece, Now three hundred francs even to an American is about eleven dollars. For the finals of the singles at Forest Hills, or for the Davis Cup matches, where you can see Tilden and Johnston, those giants of the court in mortal combat, you pay two or three dollars. Or at the present rate of exchange about 50 to 75 francs. One-sixth of what was taken away from you to see this battle for feminine supremacy. To a Frenchman three hundred francs is exactly sixty dollars. It will buy, among other things, an overcoat, a pair of custom-made shoes, a first class railroad ticket from Paris to Cannes, or room and board at a moderate hotel in Cannes or Nice. Do you wonder that the compatriots of Suzanne Lenglen gasped when they heard the prices? That they preferred to stand on ladders, sit on the top of garages, poke their heads through the roofs or mount motor buses drawn up behind the court?

As the excitement and confusion at the gate in front increases, a cheer arises in the alley behind the court. It is Suzanne, Suzanne the Queen, triumphant, arriving in a Voisin car from her villa at Nice. She throws a kiss to the crowd through the windows and is greeted by another roar. Inside the stands are filling. And they are still being rushed to completion by the workmen, while down in front the distinguished guests take their places—Manuel, the ex-king of Portugal, the Baron de Graffenried, the Count de Bourbel, the Rajah of Pudakota, lords and ladies without number, writers and authors from all over the world, capitalists and financiers and notables from every big city in Europe. At a little after eleven the air becomes positively electric. It is— no—yes—it is the players at last.

An army corps of camera men assault them. Suzanne, ever the actress, smiles and poses for them with her usual grace. Beside her stands the American, as emotional as a Methodist minister at a funeral. The umpire, Commander G. W. Hill-yard, R.N., of the All England Club at Wimbledon, takes his chair, and the linesmen, among whom are Lord Charles Hope, Cyril Tolley, Najouch, the professional player of the Cannes Tennis Club, Cazalet, Sir Francis Towle, R. Dunkerley and others seat themselves. *There is no foot fault judge apparent.*

The match starts. With great difficulty the workmen pounding on the unfinished stands are persuaded to refrain. When the American unexpectedly takes the second game Suzanne registers some surprise. But her supporters, perched on roofs and balconies, yell when she moves ahead in the fifth. The umpire at this point tries vainly to control the crowd. His control is somewhat less effective than W. Johnson's. At last Charlie Aeschliman, who is sitting with Promoter Fisher on a bench just below the chair, rises and addresses the crowd in English and French. With true British phlegm the Commander does not or will not speak anything but English, although fully sixty per cent of the spectators are French and the match is taking place in France.

The sun is hotter overhead as Suzanne finally takes the first set amid great cheering. But she is tired. The stubborn fight of the girl from the Golden West has upset her, try as she will to contain herself. No love sets today.

In the second game of the second set the American passes her cleanly at the net. See, Suzanne is attempting to smile as she returns to serve. But it is rather a wan smile, and when her opponent goes to 3-1 in games the French champion stops beside the court and sips a brandy. The fact is that Miss Wills is standing up to her so well that Mademoiselle Lenglen is getting tired, mentally as well as physically.

The excitement is intense as the score reaches 5-all. A number of compatriots of the great Suzanne, standing on top of motor buses backed up behind the court, make a demonstration as their champion evens the score. This seems to bother her; she turns around and requests them to be quiet, in a tired voice. Observe again that this demand was not made by the umpire but by one of the players. Surely never a championship match was ever played under such conditions!

At last the French player gets to match point. A shot crashes into her forehand corner. She thinks it is out, tosses the balls to the court and rushes to the net to shake hands with a rueful young American girl. But the ball was not out. A courageous linesman informs the umpire who, for some reason, was descending from his chair. The players at once resume their positions, the spectators reseat themselves, while Charlie Aeschliman waves back the horde of camera men, already assuming possession of the court. They retreat reluctantly to behind the baseline where they have been standing, turning cranks and taking pictures all through the match.

In a minute the score is evened. The match is not over yet. Ah, that is where Suzanne showed herself the true champion. Without a word, without a murmur, without any protest visible or otherwise, she returned to her task. Faced by a superhuman game, meeting unexpected and stern resistance, she had, as she thought, won the match. Her title of the greatest woman player in the world was safe. But no. She was not through. The match was not, as she imagined, over. So back to that court she went with a quick, nervous gesture. There was the real champion of champions.

In five minutes the real end came. The players were only saved from being swallowed alive by a half a hundred camera men by the long arms of—no, not Commander Hillyard. Nor yet Promoter Fisher. Neither of these gentlemen were on the job. It was the long arms of Charlie Aeschliman who kept back the photographers like tugs after a liner entering port.

Surely never was any sporting event played under such conditions. Never such a lack of preparation, of arrangements, of any attempt at caring for and handling the press, the crowds, for the thousand and one incidental things that arise at times like these. Tickets were to be had—at a price—only if you were in with the gang. One of the crowd. If not you might just as well attempt to buy a Pullman reservation to heaven. It simply couldn't be done, that's all. Under the circumstances need I say there was speculation which would have caused Mr. Tyson to grow green with envy?

What the actual receipts are or were seems to be a mystery. Neither the Burkes nor Promoter Fisher will tell, and there is no honorable way of finding out. However, there were by their admission some three thousand seats sold, at an average of two hundred francs apiece. This, by the way, is a low estimate, as most of the seats were sold at three hundred francs, and furthermore it does not take into account the daily admissions nor extra places added the last day which could not have reached any inconsiderable sum. Now deducting a hundred thousand francs for the taxes due the French government, and one hundred thousand for the expenses of the tournament—advertising, erecting the stands, hiring chairs, and so forth (and this again is a liberal estimate)—

and you have left a total of four hundred thousand francs as any college graduate will tell you.

At one of those highly entertaining meetings between Mr. Fisher, representing the Burkes, and the members of the press and movie firms, which took place before the match, Mr. Fisher fixed me with his beady eye and remarked:

"Have you any idea what the Burkes are going to clear on this match, Mr. Tunis?"

I replied that I hadn't the foggiest idea, but that if the Burkes did not clear a half a million francs they were exceedingly poor business men.

Mr. Fisher sniffed. That is the only word describing his attitude at the moment.

"For your information," he said, "allow me to tell you that the Burkes will not clear more than one hundred thousand francs."

Now, personally I believe Mr. Fisher implicitly. In fact, there can be not the slightest shadow of a doubt whatsoever, although of course I have not had the pleasure of seeing the actual figures, of the truth of this statement. Let us, then, as an example in arithmetic, subtract the one hundred thousand francs which the Burke brothers as owners of the Carlton Tennis Club cleared on the Wills-Lenglen match, from the four hundred thousand remaining.

If I am correct that leaves a total of three hundred thousand francs. Where has this sum gone to? The answer is easy. I don't know. But one of two things are sure. Either the Burkes have failed to put down certain sums which they have spent or which have been spent for them, or else they have been shockingly negligent in their accounting. In what direction has the leakage occurred? To find this out might prove of much interest to the governing bodies of tennis in England, in the United States and in France.

ALEX THE GREAT

BY

James Harrison

(NEW YORK TIMES) OCTOBER 11, 1926.

———————

THE CARDINALS WON.

The baseball drama had a happy ending after all, for as the last reel faded out the sentimental favorites were holding the championship. They beat the Yankees and the Yankees beat themselves, and between the two the greatest game of the series went to St. Louis, 3—2.

The old story can be written again. The breaks of the game decided it. To baseball history can be added one more chapter where the seventh game of the big series was decided, not by skill or courage, but by fate.

After millions of words had been scribbled and tons of white paper covered with expert calculations, the world's series worked itself down to four short words: Koenig's fumble, Meusel's muff.

If Mark Koenig, the Yankee shortstop, had gripped his fingers around a grounder in the fourth inning; if the veteran Bob Meusel had caught an easy fly that bobbed out of his hands in the same round, the Yanks would have won and would be world's champions this morning.

If the Cardinals had not scored three unearned runs on those two devastating errors, Waite Hoyt would not have been robbed for the second time in his career of the glory

of a shut-out in the final game of the world's series. Babe
Ruth would not today be mourning the fact that his home
run in the third did not bring the championship to New
York single-handedly and unaided.

And St. Louis last night and through the early hours of the
morning would not have been celebrating the happy ending
to its wait of thirty-eight years.

Everything was incidental to those two errors. It was incidental that Herb Pennock came back to pitch in a hopeless
cause. It was incidental, even though highly dramatic, that
in the seventh inning, with the bases full and two out,
Alexander the Great came out of the shadows of the bullpen
to strike out Tony Lazzeri and throttle the Yankees' last great
rally. It was incidental, too, that Tommy Thevenow, Cardinal shortstop, drove in the winning runs with a single in the
fourth.

Alexander wrote finis to the hopes of the surging Yanks
with an old hand but a steady one. To his already superb
work in the series he added this one climax. His pitching in
the series was probably the greatest since the days of Matty
and Babe Adams, but if Meusel and Koenig had held on to
the ball, Alex would have been merely a gallant old pitcher
on a losing ball team.

Fate made a hero of Alexander and a victim of Hoyt. Fate
was the scene shifter who set the stage in the seventh, out
upon which Alexander shuffled. His cap was perched on one
side of his head and he was slowly chewing a quid of tobacco.
He was a quaint, almost humorous, figure with his jaunty
cap, his old man's gait and his quizzical face, but when he
wound up his arm and threw, the Yanks had reached the
end of the trail.

There was nothing more left for them. They had battled
through six games and now had the championship at the

ends of their fingers when suddenly they came face to face with Alex. While 40,000 went wild with delight, he stood across the path and the Yanks took a detour to second-place money in the greatest money series of all time.

In the third, Babe Ruth hit his fourth homer, setting a new record for a single series. With Hoyt pitching the game of a lifetime, this run looked enough to win. But in the fourth Koenig fumbled and Meusel muffed, and the Yanks found themselves two runs behind.

Miller Huggins reorganized his scattered battalion and the Yanks charged on. They swirled at Jess Haines in the sixth and luck was with them this time, for Chick Hafey played a line drive rashly and when the ball rushed past him Dugan scored with the second run.

Only one to go now, and Haines, his pitching hand bearing the bruise of a batted ball, was weakening. In the seventh, Combs opened with a single over Thevenow's head. The Yanks were coming again. There was confidence in their mien and menace in their bats. Koenig sacrificed Combs to second and Ruth was walked intentionally.

Meusel, the unfortunate lad with the feeble fingers of an earlier inning, had his chance to wipe the slate clean, but his grounder to Bell was turned into a forceout of Ruth at second while Combs dashed on to third.

Gehrig now at bat, whose single had won one game and his double helped to win another. Haines faltered after he had thrown two strikes on the native-born New Yorker. Something suddenly went wrong with the Haines right arm. He floated three bad balls up to the plate, and another high one, around the neck of the Yankee, sent Gehrig to first and filled the bases.

Rogers Hornsby called his men into a huddle and they grouped themselves around the pitcher's box like the Yale backfield. Hornsby, O'Farrell, Haines, Bottomley, Bell, Thevenow—they were all there. When the conference broke up, Haines took off his glove and walked to the bench.

The Cardinals were going to try a new pitcher. Forty thousand pair of eyes peered anxiously through the gray mist toward the bullpen out in deep left. There was a breathless pause, and then around the corner of the stand came a tall figure in a Cardinal sweater. His cap rode rakishly on the corner of his head. He walked like a man who was going nowhere in particular and was in no hurry to get there. He was a trifle knock-kneed and his gait was not a model of grace and rhythm.

Any baseball fan would have known him a mile away. It was Grover Cleveland Alexander. Alexander the Great was coming in to pull the Cardinal machine out of the mudhole. The ancient twirler, who had gone nine full innings the day before, was shuffling in where younger men feared to tread.

On any other day he would have been sitting contentedly on the bench, chewing his quid and ruminating on life in general and the ball game in particular. This time he was plucked out from the bullpen and thrust into the limelight as the last hope of the Cardinals.

He warmed up in that leisurely, methodical way of his, and as he faced Lazzeri, fresh young slugger from the Coast, he was outwardly as unconcerned as if it were a Spring exhibition game. Throughout the park there came a silence. The fans slid forward to the edge of their seats. Hardly a mother's son of them seemed to be moving a muscle, but, although the crowd was rigid with the thrill of the moment, old Alex was undisturbed.

He had been through all that before. Apparently there wasn't a nerve in his body. Ball one to Lazzeri was low and the crowd stirred, but Alex calmly carved the outside corner with a strike, like a butcher slicing ham.

Another one outside and Lazzeri fouled it into the stand. The Yankee was now in the hole. "This lad is in a tighter fix than I am," thought Alex, and so he essayed a low curve that one of the Singer midgets couldn't have hit. Lazzeri swung and missed. The deed was done. Alex took off his glove and shuffled again to the bench. The Cardinals, young and impetuous, pounded his back and hugged him madly, but old Alex took it with placid good humor—not the shadow of a smile on his face.

Only once did he turn his head and send a half-smile toward the stand, and we suspect that that was his only gesture of triumph.

In the eighth the Yanks went out one-two-three. The old arm of Alexander was now rising and falling with a steady beat, tolling off the last minutes of the world's series. Against him was Pennock, but Alex had a one-run lead and there was nothing in his mellow past which made any one believe that Alexander would lose a one-run lead in the ninth inning of the last world's series game.

Combs and Koenig were child's play for him, as the Yankees' final onslaught began. With two strikes against him Combs grounded to Bell and was out. Koenig, with two strikes also showing on the scoreboard, gave the same fielder an easy roller.

And now the drama was almost done. There was only one more scene. Ruth was at bat—the Yankee's last hope. Would Alexander pitch to him as he had to lesser men?

It would have been the last great story of the series if Alex had fanned him. But Alex was not concerned with great stories, drama, climaxes, headlines or anything else of the sort. He pitched carefully and deliberately to Ruth. He brought the count to three and two, one being a called strike and another a foul, but Alex just missed the corner of the plate on the next one and the Babe walked.

The old-timer was taking no chances on Ruth hitting another into the far-flung bleachers. Meusel rather than Ruth was the program, but before Meusel could settle the issue Ruth did it for him by breaking for second base. O'Farrell whipped a fast throw to Hornsby and the series was over.

Now Rogers Hornsby can go back to Texas, where his mother lies dead, and Alexander the Great can go back to his easy chair, his slippers and a Winter fireplace and dwell pleasantly on the October afternoon when Tony Lazzeri swung at a low ball which a Singer midget could not have hit. If Alex wants to chuckle, he is clearly entitled to it.

He can look back to a series which saw him winning two masterful victories and helping to win a third. The man who was fired by Joe McCarthy, manager of the Cubs, in mid-summer came back in October to turn out one of the greatest world's series pitching achievements.

Matty, Babe Adams, Combs and Coveleskie twirled three victories in other baseball classics, but they were all young men and full of strength. Alex was not only old; he was a baseball discard, tossed onto the scrapheap as an antique without worth.

Rogers Hornsby can go back to Texas with the comforting thought that he "stayed with the team" and won. The young man who caught the imagination and sympathy of the country as only Walter Johnson before him had done is undoubtedly glad the series is over. Not for him any triumphant celebrations; he has discharged one duty only to take on another.

Hoyt pitched fine ball all the way through. For a short

spell he was again the Hoyt of 1921, when his work against the Giants earned him the brief sobriquet, a "second Matty." His fast ball was a work of art and his curve the best he has shown in five years—both wonderfully controlled and hopping through like the wind.

Hoyt, the staff on which the Yanks leaned in the big test, came through in magnificent style, but it was again his misfortune to be beaten by the breaks of the game. His mind must have wandered back to 1921. In the last ill-fated game of that series Roger Peckinpaugh booted a ball away and Hoyt lost, 1 to 0. Once again fate came along to kick him on the shins.

The series is over. The Yanks were outbatted and outfielded, but their superior experience and balance carried them along. Even those assets were failing them until Ruth completely turned the tide with his St. Louis homers. Those three pitched balls almost cost the Cardinals the title.

Ruth is still the Yankee team. The Cards made great talk about pitching to him, but in the deciding game they walked him four out of five times.

It was a series of great crowds and busy turnstiles, but not much action compared to many another series. Not a well-played series and not a thrilling one, except in spots. The breaks were evenly divided. The new champions earned what they got, and old Alex earned a quiet Winter in his rocking chair.

IN DEFENSE OF CRITICISM

BY

Paul Gallico

(NEW YORK DAILY NEWS)
SEPTEMBER 28, 1927.

———————

GENTLEMEN, GENTLEMEN, such names, such hard ones! Cannot we get together on this? A guy tries to be fair-minded and impartial, and what happens? Each side thinks I am against its own particular beloved bum, and all the letters are unpleasant. If this is to be the case, I am going back to a bias and stick to it. Then one side, at least, will think that I am all right. As it stands now the Tunney sympathizers feel that I am doing their idol an injustice, and those who think Dempsey "the greatest fighter that ever drew on a glove" maintain that I did not give Dempsey a fair break when I said that he fought a dirty fight and that, therefore, I am a this-and-that, not to mention a so-and-so.

In other words, what was wanted was a complete whitewash of both pugs. If I had prettied them both up I would have been a great guy. Well, live and learn. Next time I'll scent up both parties.

But in the meantime mebbe we can get straight on the way I look at this fight. Let us examine, for instance, the opening paragraph of a communication from one Tom Burns, who begins: "Where do you come off to pan Jack Dempsey when you picked him to win?"

I fail to see the connection. Cannot the gentleman disassociate the two ideas, picking a winner and reporting a fight? Because I happen to name Dempsey as my choice, do you want me to shut my eyes to his foul tactics or fail to report them? Everybody hold on while I break all high dudgeon records. That ain't honest, Nell, and I gotta be honest if it bores everybody to death. If this were to be the case I should have to stop making selections, and if I stopped making selections what would a lot of people do for laughs? I am willing to make prophecies so that the 98% Wrong club can continue to flourish, but I won't defend them. If my fighters cannot fight clean, that isn't my fault.

However, for the records, may I be permitted to restate my case, or rather clear up my impressions of the late unpleasantness in Chicago.

Gene Tunney, the champion, fought a clean, courageous, winning fight. As long as he was on his feet he won the argument unquestionably by proving himself the better boxer and the more punishing hitter.

Unfortunately, he was off his feet for fourteen seconds, which is four seconds more than Marquis of Queensberry rules allow. Those extra four seconds he got constitute a break, and as I wrote before, I am not inclined to quarrel with the fate that gave it to him. The champion is entitled to the breaks. Dempsey got plenty of them while he was champion. If you could get close to the real Dempsey and get him to open his heart you would find him unenvious of the magnificent break that Tunney got. Dempsey understands things like that. He's been around.

I say that Tunney is game because he took hard punches way below the belt line without a squawk. He made a thrilling picture of manhood when he and Dempsey were over in my corner and Dempsey drove three left hooks deep into his groin and Tunney looked him squarely in the eyes and never flinched. He kept punching.

Too, I maintain that Tunney's seventh round retreat was a piece of brilliant defensive thinking and strategy, but that, to the eye, it looked both undignified and ungallant. He looked a little like a preliminary boy who has had his first good crack on the lug and is skating around in the hopes that the ropes will miraculously open and let him out.

And a moment later, when Dempsey finally caught up with Gene, Tunney looked every inch a fighter as he lashed out at Dempsey with his right and shook the challenger up with it.

I saw Jack Dempsey foul Tunney repeatedly during their fight with punches to the groin. I saw Dempsey butt with his head and strike low blows that appeared to me in two instances to be deliberate, because Dempsey appeared to be looking where he was hitting. I do not consider any of the punches back of the head as being rabbit punches or in any way foul.

At the same time I saw Dempsey make a gallant stand in the final rounds when he was cut and bleeding and groggy. He came flailing in, semi-conscious, but punching, and he was punching FAIR.

I am afraid that I enjoyed those fourteen seconds in which Genie was on the deck.

Ring Lardner

Ring Lardner, poet laureate of the ball player and the most famous literary figure the craft of sportswriting yet has produced, once confided that he cherished three ambitions as a youth. The first, and most compelling, was a desire to see his fill of ball games. Then he hoped to write for national magazines and to have a play produced on Broadway. Lardner had the good fortune, and the great talent, to realize his three ambitions.

Baseball was good to Lardner—almost as good as he was to—and for—baseball. The game that impelled him to abandon engineering in favor of writing brought him national prominence as a reporter and columnist. His uncanny ear for dialogue, which enabled him to capture the humor, pathos, vanity and distortion in ball players' speech, gave him the memorable "You Know Me, Al" stories and international renown as a vital and peculiarly American writer. And baseball was his springboard to his ultimate success as a playwright.

In the preface to his authoritative work, "The American Language," H. L. Mencken wrote: "Its discovery (the speech of the masses as it is spoken) had to wait until Ring Lardner, a Chicago newspaper reporter. In his grotesque tales of baseball players, so immediately and so deservedly successfull, Lardner reports the common speech not only with humor but with the utmost accuracy. His writings are a mine of authentic Americana: his service to etymology incomparable."

Such extravagant praise was the fruit of Lardner's love of baseball and the fascination ball players held for him. The dour man, who was to become known as America's leading humorist, really got into sportswriting on a pass. He was a bookkeeper at twenty for a gas company at Niles, Mich., when an emissary from the South Bend Times stopped at the plant to inquire where Ring's older brother might be found. The paper wanted the elder Lardner for its sports staff. Ring gravely explained that his brother was bound by a contract he couldn't possibly break and wound up getting the job himself.

South Bend couldn't keep a man of Lardner's gifts for long and two years later, in 1907, he went to the Chicago Inter-Ocean. During the next six years he worked in Chicago, Boston and St. Louis, where he was editor of The Sporting News, the trade paper of baseball. In 1913, the second phase of Lardner's career was launched. He was hired by the Chicago Tribune to write its sport column.

The tedious job of turning out seven columns a week forced Lardner to hit upon the technique that was to make him famous. He had been listening to ball players talk on and off the field and one day, to fill out his column, he wrote a short, imaginary conversation between two White Sox heroes playing poker in a Pullman car. The innovation was popular immediately and Lardner, at the urging of Charley Van Loan, a well-known writer of sport fiction, sent a sample of his diamond dialogue to the Saturday Evening Post. A check and a demand for more of the same followed promptly and Al, the brash rookie, was born.

The enormous success of these classics in slang, with sharp, revealing flashes of characterization, encouraged Lardner to do more fiction. In the decade that followed he wrote such imperishable stories as "Champion," "Haircut,"

"Alibi Ike" and "The Love Nest"—stories that prompted critics to compare him with European and American masters, and the one-time baseball writer did not suffer by the comparison. More than one recognized authority has called Lardner the finest short-story writer America has produced.

In 1919 Lardner left the Chicago Tribune and went to New York to do a weekly piece for a newspaper syndicate. The theatre bug had bitten him violently and he confessed he wanted to be near Broadway, the nerve center of show business. He drew upon baseball for his first effort, a baseball sketch in the Ziegfeld Follies of 1922 with Will Rogers portraying a veteran pitcher. After that tentative nibble, Lardner got his teeth into Broadway with a full-length play, and again he turned to baseball for "Elmer the Great," which enjoyed a successful run in 1928 with Walter Huston in the leading role. A year later Lardner and George S. Kaufman collaborated on "June Moon," a smash hit featured by Lardner's songs.

The man who gave literary stature to sportswriting died in 1933 at the age of forty-eight. No one has usurped the unique position he holds in American letters and it is unlikely that anyone will. Ring Lardner compressed enough distinction and genius in an all-too-brief quarter-century for three careers.

THE EDITOR

YOU KNOW HIM, PAL

Ring Lardner

(NEW YORK WORLD)

———————————

Pittsburgh, October 6, 1927.

IN DIRECT VIOLATION of all the rules of the Baseball Writers'
Association of America, your boy friend got up at 7
o'clock this morning and was in the Schenley dining room
enjoying a shore dinner at 7:45. During the steamed clam
course in came Jack Fournier and Mrs. Jack Fournier, and
I asked them to join me.

I did this for two reasons: In the first place, it helps a man
relish his breakfast to have a lady share same with him and
especially when the lady in question is a whole lot easier to
look at than a World's Series ball game. In the second place,
there was only room for three people at the table, and if the
other two places were occupied it would remove the danger
of my being infested with Miss Helma Thoke, the Oklahoma
woman I told you about yesterday. (Miss Thoke, nicknamed
Ducky because her husband was a quack doctor in Enid,
Okla., had been given a free trip to the Series as a reward
for winning a popularity contest, much to Mr. Lardner's
bafflement.)

Mr. Fournier declined the invitation on the ground that
he wished to eat in a hurry and get right over to the ball
park. I thought this was kind of a queer ambition for a fella

that had his box seats bought and paid for, but then I figured that maybe Jack wanted to make a study of Forbes Field on the chance that he would play with the Pittsburgh club next season. It being the only club in the big leagues which has escaped him so far.

It turned out, however, that the Fournier family had got up by Mrs. Fournier's watch, which is one of these here costly little Swiss watches that if you look at it close you can tell what month it is, provided you carry a pocket calendar.

The Fourniers thought it was half past twelve, and if they didn't bolt their food they would miss the lady singing "The Star Spangled Banner."

Incidentally, this lady is the same one that sang it here two years ago and evidently don't know that there has been a lot of new songs written since then.

Well, anyway, I was left defenseless and sure enough it wasn't long before Miss Thoke burst into the room and plunked herself down beside me to whom she has evidently taken quite a fancy.

"You know," she said, "I am betting on Pittsburgh to win and I think they are throwing me down. In the first game they let Mr. Kremer play quarterback or whatever you call it till Columbia was way ahead and then they put in Mr. Miljus, who could of scored many more touchdowns if he had been there at the beginning."

I explained to her carefully that there are some pitchers, not quarterbacks, whose specialty is relief work. I spoke of men like Marberry and Wilcy Moore and old Charlie Hall that used to be with the Boston Red Sox, men that ain't so good for nine innings maybe, but can make a sucker out of their opponents late in the game.

"Well, then," said Miss Thoke, "why don't Mr. Bush and Mr. Huggins insist on starting the games in the seventh innings? This would permit them to release all their pitchers except Mr. Miljus and Mr. Moore and the money which they now waste paying these here other pitchers salary, why they could spent it in some worthy cause, the only question would be what worthy cause to spend it in."

"My suggestion," I replied, "is for them to buy you a one-way ticket from Pittsburgh to Manila and a life membership in the home for female fools."

She laughed heartily, and, in obedience to George Cohan's injunction to always leave them laughing when you say goodby, I hurried over to Forbes Field to tell the Fourniers what time it was. Accompanying me was Dan Howley, manager of the St. Louis Browns. He read me a piece in the paper to the effect that policemen had seized hundreds of tickets from the scalpers.

"I can't see," said Dan, "that this helps the situation. What is the difference whether you have to buy your ticket from a scalper or a cop?"

"Oh," I answered, "a policeman would not dast sell the tickets. If he did they would take his star."

"That is something that could never happen to me," said Mr. Howley.

There was nearly 42,000 people in the park, and 36,000 of them was helping Donie Bush manage his ball club. What I can't understand is how the Pirates ever won any games on the road where Donie had to do the managing all by himself. In the eighth inning, when it was time to put in a pinch-hitter, the usual cry for Cuyler went up. But Donie chose Earl Smith and the 36,000 booed him, showing that in spite of the inroad of visiting firemen there is still plenty of boos left in Pittsburgh.

The things that happened to Vic Aldridge in the third inning was not entirely his fault. The rally started with a

base hit by Combs that could of been fielded by a first baseman that ain't quite so much of a recluse as Joe Harris. The
next five guys participating in this rally were Koenig, Ruth,
Gehrig, Meusel and Lazzeri, and yet they call them Yankees.

The incidents of the eighth inning, however, was Vic's
own business and not even Donie's 36,000 assistants squawked
when he was taken out.

Miss Thoke's mouth was so full of candy all afternoon
that she couldn't say much. On one occasion, when Pipgras
and Bengough stopped the game for a conference, she wanted
to know what they was talking about and I told her they
were trying to find out how to pronounce each other's name
as this was the first time either of them had ever been in a
World's Series.

"Can you pronounce them yourself?" she asked me.

"No," I said. "But you certainly ought to be able to with
all that candy in your mouth."

Well, she tried, and the less said about the result the
better. Luckily I am going where I have got a clean suit of
clothes.

REQUIEM TO RICKARD

BY

Gene Fowler

(NEW YORK MORNING TELEGRAPH)
JANUARY 9, 1929.

NOT BEFORE the altar and the choir of the Cathedral,
   With surpliced boys intoning,
And dirges of holy bells beating down on the congregation;
Nor with cross bearers and robed clergymen marching;
Candles burning and sunlight groping feebly through
   stained glass while swaying censers are uplifted—

But beneath the high and bare girders of the hippodrome
   hall—
With twice ten thousand seats strangely empty,
And the chill of a January day stalking through the bleak
   corridors—
There, in a bronze coffin, lies the tall and silent Texan.

In the high hall he built, he lies in state.
Along the torn-up avenue, the laborers peer at the silk-
   hatted men leaving their motor cars and at the throngs
   passing into the black-draped foyer—
And near the ring-space is a floral platform and a bronze
   box.

And here is his Peace, where only yesterday—and again tomorrow—the bodies of boxers were wet with straining
and their flanks were cramped and tired from the blows,
While gutturals of the gallery men, sadistic, growled like
the surf of the Rockaways.

Not the Gothic sanctity of the Cathedral with its somber
ecclesiastics and the rituals—
But the stolid policemen in the hippodrome hall.
The crepe-festooned lobby, where the mourners pass the
picture gallery of the champions—
Portraits of muscular celebrities: Muldoon, his arms folded
and his loins draped bravely in a lion's hide and posing
in a studio setting simulating the arena of the Caesars;

Hairy-chested Jeffries in his ponderous crouch, poised for a
left-hand rip to the liver.
Huge, phlegmatic Willard, his unwieldy biceps flexed and
his steam-shovel fists framing a vacant face;
Dempsey, when his tapering legs were yet alert with youth
and when his body was a symbol of power;
Jack Johnson, the incorrigible black genius of defense;
Corbett in white tights, his pompadour suggesting a cocka-
too's crest and his darting left extended.
Skinny-legged Bob Fitzsimmons with his grotesque bald pate
and his abnormal shoulders—
The Maulers' Hall of Fame—and beyond it, in the high
hall, the sleeping Texan.

Upstairs, in the locked drawer of the bronze desk, are the
dry and shriveled gloves Battling Nelson wore when
bludgeoning the consumptive Gans;

And a trophy head of an African buck given by the younger
  Roosevelt, and a rhinoceros hide cane presented by
  T. R.
And an empty chair made from the horns of steers;
And a brass cuspidor the Texan seldom hit with his tobacco
  thrusts.
And drawn blinds on the wide windows fronting Forty-ninth
  street, where he often listened to the voices of playing
  children.

His friends—the millionaire and the beggar, too, come in to
  see the Texan.
The gate is shut forever between him and them and there
  is only Memory.
Lament and January Day—tomorrow the Spring, and flowers
  newly-blooming on a grave.
Not beneath the vaulted roof of the Cathedral,
But under the high and bare girders of the hippodrome hall,
There, in a bronze coffin, lies the tall and silent Texan.

RIVER RUMPUS

BY

Robert F. Kelley

(NEW YORK TIMES)

———————

Poughkeepsie, N. Y., June 25, 1929.

COLUMBIA'S VARSITY EIGHT brought back the rule of the Hudson to New York tonight and fought the river as well as eight other crews to do it. In the thirty-two years that this event has been held under the towering cliffs of Highland, there has never been a race like this one. Started after a long series of delays that finally saw the crews sent away from the marks in almost complete darkness, the biggest fleet in the history of eight-oared rowing started, but the river took its toll before they had finished.

Of the nine starting boats, only five rode through the rollers to the finish line. And in the four that went down were two that had been expected to provide some of the fighting.

California and Cornell, soon after the towering steel framework of the railroad bridge at the third mile had been passed, sank and Syracuse joined them in swimming. Early in the race, before the third mile had been completed, the Massachusetts Institute of Technology oarsmen, on their first visit to this greatest of regattas, stopped rowing with water around their waists and swam for it.

Columbia, rowing a great and gallant race, came from

behind in the last two miles and raced an amazing Washington crew into the river to win by two and a half lengths. These two, when the other eights filled up and dropped back, had the race entirely to themselves.

Washington was more than eight lengths ahead of Pennsylvania in third place and Penn had four and a quarter lengths over a Navy eight that had made a good deal of the racing through the opening stretches and hung on pretty well until a mile and a half from the finish. The last survivor was Mike Murphy's Wisconsin crew, sticking at a low beat all the way and just rowing to stay above water. Even so, the Middle Westerners closed in on Navy and were a bit more than three lengths behind it at the close.

There have not been such scenes of wild confusion in a big boat race in the modern history of rowing. At the end the scene beggared description, with coaching boats, their riding lamps lit, darting about the river rescuing men who had rowed for three miles and then found themselves called upon to swim about in the half light of early night.

The river, almost completely in the grip of night, was ablaze with the lights of the biggest fleet of yachts and river boats ever to see this race. Observers on the bank, in the observation train and on most of the boats, were unable to tell what crews were sinking in the wild, darkened scene of confusion. But one thing stood out vividly. There was no mistaking the Columbia crew.

There went Columbia, moved over in the outside lane left open by the sinking Syracuse boat, swinging along beautifully, rhythmically and powerfully, triumphant over the other crews in the race and over the river itself. Columbia's victory is among the greatest sporting achievements ever put down on record.

Out in the middle of the river, right bang into the worst

water in the lane between those of Tech, the first shell to swamp, and California, the New Yorkers rowed an intelligent and vividly courageous race to come through to the second championship scored by them in the last three years. Captain Horace Davenport's Columbia varsity has gone through its season undefeated and it deserves all of its laurels.

The varsity race came at the end of a day which broke all records for this event. Never before has this course seen the crowd that came here, promised one of the best boat races ever rowed. There must have been more than 125,000 persons watching in the eery murk of a cloudy twilight as the regatta progressed toward its weird final chapter.

When the varsity crews began coming to the start night had almost won a complete victory over the day. A haze hung over the river and added to the darkness, but along the hills behind Poughkeepsie a long, lighter line of clouds threatened a storm. Against them, on the hill just opposite the start, the lonely buildings of the monastery stood out in bold relief.

A few drops of rain fell, and the crowd, sitting in shirt-sleeves and light dresses in the oppressive, humid heat, started to move uneasily. But the rain held off. It might have been better if it had come, for then the waters would have flat-tened down. Instead, the wind rose a bit.

Several crews got up to the line early and lay there behind the starting stake boats, marshaled by their coaches' launches, a huge, strange armada of frail-looking craft. For quite a while they stayed there, waiting for Tech, and finally Cornell, which had apparently started late from its boathouse away down the river.

In the last, dying light of day, they paddled to the stake boats and stretched forth across the water, an unforgettable sight as eighty-one men moved into position for what was confidently expected to prove the greatest drama of history.

The tide, by this time running strong, gave them a terrific amount of trouble in lining up. It swung the crews around and kept the men frantically backing water to straighten out again.

Two or three times the booming, dramatic voice of Referee Curtiss roared out, "Are you ready, all?" as the train sat in silence, waiting. Each time two or three coxswains' hands rose high in the air to signal distress. Finally he called again, and then came the flash and bark of his starting gun. But he had overlooked Cornell's raised hand, and back came the crews again for another start. More delays, and finally another gun flashed, with this time Bob Berman, signaling from the stern of Columbia.

By this time it was impossible to distinguish the little flags set in the bows of the craft and the colors of oar blades. It was only at the start, while they held to their lanes, that the watchers on the train could find their eights. Finally, on the third try, they went away and immediately old Dick Glendon's Navy crew began the game fight it made to redeem a season disappointing and unsuccessful.

The Navy crew, swinging in well back in the Glendon stroke, was off in front, with Columbia behind and Cornell third. California was fourth, but people in the train had not yet begun to realize the terrific fight to live that faced the oarsmen out on the river. Behind them were Washington, Penn, Wisconsin, Syracuse and Tech in that order.

At the end of the first mile Navy was holding its lead by the slim margin of a few feet against the whitetipped blades of a Washington crew that was closing in like mad and had moved ahead of Columbia. The Californians, filling early, were steadily dropping back out of it. They had first rigged their shell high for rough water, changed their minds and rigged low again when it looked like smooth going and then were lost when it turned rough again.

Around the two-mile mark Tech, making heavy weather of it, began to sink at the stern, and immediately their coaches beat close in on them and took the men from the water as they sank. Then, for the first time, those on the train realized the state of the water. Leaving that accident behind, the race went along with Columbia, splashing but fighting hard out in the middle, staying gamely with Navy and Washington and the other crews dropping slowly behind.

Syracuse stayed up for a while, but dropped back in the middle distances. Wisconsin was never up far and California never a factor. Inside in the inner lane Penn plugged along, rowing well and gamely to finish up much higher than it had expected at the start of the race. In the meantime interest centered on the duel among the other three crews.

For the second mile and part of the third it looked as though Columbia was not going to be able to do it. The two other crews were staying at their work and holding out in front. They had a lead of almost a length at one period, but in the third mile Columbia, still rowing steadily and evenly, began closing in on them. Navy here began to fade and Columbia caught it at the two-and-a-half-mile point. Then Columbia moved up to within a half length of Washington, and as they rowed up under the pilings of the railroad bridge Columbia had caught the Huskies.

From there on Columbia added to its lead and went steadily away in the closing stretches to a great and completely earned victory. Nothing can be taken from Columbia's achievement today. The eight men—Walters, Murphy, Walker, Sanford, Douglas, Blesse, Davenport and MacBain—

steered by Berman, wrote their names indelibly into the history of this regatta.

For California, the end of the trail, that came here by way of Holland and a world's championship, ended neck-deep in the turbid waters of the Hudson. It was a terrific disappointment to the men from the Pacific Coast, but they have risen to the top of the heap in the past.

To Cornell, with the highest hopes in years, the result was also heart-breaking, but the luck of the game was against it today, as well as a superbly rowing and coached crew that would have been close to winning under any conditions as it rowed tonight.

In the past history of Poughkeepsie, only three crews have swamped in races, never all in one race. Today's conditions were the worst college rowing ever has seen.

Damon Runyon

A conservative statistician recently estimated that Damon Runyon has written 75 million words since 1900 and, to paraphrase the master himself, every word has been received with more than somewhat blatting of delight by the citizens. Runyon is the only sport writer who matches the versatility and facility possessed by Ring Lardner. In the last decade he has enhanced his prestige, first founded on newspaper work, with his enormously popular movies and light fiction.

In spite of his exciting adventures in Hollywood and the realms of higher finance, Runyon still considers himself a working newspaperman and turns out daily "The Brighter Side," a column distributed nationally by the King Features Syndicate. Arthur Brisbane said he was the best reporter in the world, a reputation gained largely on the sport beat, which he patrolled with debonair diligence until 1936, when he succeeded Brisbane in the big brains department of Mr. Hearst's congregation.

Flowing simplicity, flavored with humor and human interest, is the touchstone of Runyon's style, developed during the twelve years he travelled with the New York ball clubs. His deft talents were recognized early by Hearst, who found him a sure-fire circulation-puller on murder trials, political conventions, the Mexican revolution of 1912 and as one of four accredited correspondents sent with Pershing's punitive expedition against Pancho Villa in 1916.

Runyon showed a predilection for action and following his nose for news early in life. Born at Manhattan, Kansas, in 1884, the son of an itinerant printer, his formal education was spotty but his knowledge of the facts of life was extensive. He tried to enlist in the Spanish-American War with a Colorado regiment when he was fourteen. Rebuffed because of his age, he went to Minnesota, passed himself off as eighteen, and was accepted by the 13th Volunteers, with whom he fought the Philippine guerillas for two years.

Always a sport nut, the young warrior returned to Colorado and made the enchanting discovery that people actually were paid for going to ball games and fights and writing pieces in the paper about them. On the side, he was president of the Colorado State League, promoted boxing and rode horses on the leaky-roof circuit. Hired by the New York American in 1911, Runyon quickly established himself as a topflight sport and feature writer, a ranking that gave him all the pleasure, prestige and profit he wanted.

In 1931, Runyon finally obeyed an impulse that had been agitating him for years. He wrote his first fiction story. Again, like Lardner, he found sports a fertile field for plot and dialogue, but whereas Lardner used ball players for his source material, Runyon exploited the horse-players, hustlers, hangers-on and hoodlums of Broadway. His characterizations of guys and dolls and his unusual turns of expression, a shrewd blend of underworld and sport slang seasoned with precise five-dollar words that made for an effect at once pithy and incongruous, stamped him as the most refreshing stylist in the magazine field.

Overnight, he became the most sought-after writer in America. He was the oracle and unofficial mayor of Broadway. In 1933, the shining temples of Hollywood beckoned him and one of the first pictures adapted from a Runyon original resulted in the emergence of two exciting personali-

ties. The picture was "Little Miss Marker," starring Shirley Temple.

Runyon exerted an influence on sportswriting that was both good and bad. Novices studied his simple, straightforward style with profit, but those who attempted to copy his subtle tricks fell flat on their foolish faces. Fortunately, for one and all, the second phase soon was given a decent burial. The imitators wearied of knocking their brains out trying to throw fast balls and curves with the Old Master.

THE EDITOR

HANDY SANDE

BY

Damon Runyon

(NEW YORK AMERICAN)

Louisville, Ky., May 17, 1930.

I

Say, have they turned the pages
   Back to the past once more?
Back to the racin' ages
   An' a Derby out of the yore?
Say, don't tell me I'm daffy,
   Ain't that the same ol' grin?
   Why it's that handy
   Guy named Sande,
   Bootin' a winner in!

II

Say, don't tell me I'm batty!
  Say, don't tell me I'm blind!
Look at that seat so natty!
  Look how he drives from behind!
Gone is the white of the Ranco,
    An' the white band under his chin—
  Still he's that handy
  Guy named Sande,
  Bootin' a winner in!

III

Maybe he ain't no chicken,
  Maybe he's gettin' along,
But the ol' heart's still a-tickin',
  An' the ol' bean's goin' strong.
Roll back the years! Yea, roll 'em!
    Say, but I'm young agin',
  Watchin' that handy
  Guy named Sande,
  Bootin' a winner in!

WHY, IT WASN'T even close!
Gallant Fox, pride of the East, with the old master
mind of the horsemen sitting in his saddle as easily as if he
were in a rocking chair on a shady veranda, galloped off with
the $50,000 Kentucky Derby this afternoon. He won by two
lengths, going away.

Gallant Knight, owned by B. B. Jones, of Virginia, who
races under the name of the Audley Farm, was second, and
Ned O., belonging to G. W. Foreman, of Maryland, was
third. Gone Away, another Easterner, was fourth. He belongs

to William Ziegler, Jr., the baking powder king. The time was 2:07 3-5, which is a bit slow for the mile and a quarter of the Derby.

To William Woodward, owner of Gallant Fox, and President of the Harriman banks, of New York, who breeds horses in Maryland as a personal hobby, was presented the gold trophy that goes with the stake, by none other than Lord Derby of England, for whose family the English Derby, the Kentucky Derby and all other turf derbies are named.

When Gallant Fox came trotting back to the judges' stand with Sande bobbing on his back, the crowd of 60,000 let go a terrific roar. The demonstration was more for Sande than for the horse. The racing public loves the great jockey, whose victory today made his third Kentucky Derby. He won on Zev and again on Flying Ebony.

The field of fifteen horses was at the barrier not over two minutes when Starter Bill Hamilton yelled "Come on," and they shot out of the starting stalls like a big bundle of bright color.

Tannery, the hope of Kentucky, was first to break, but going past the stand the first time Hal Price Headley's filly Alcibiades was in front. High Foot, the Chicagoan, was second and Buckeye Poet, one of the Bradleys, was third. Sande lay about fifth with "The Fox." He began moving up as they rounded the first turn, the red hood on Gallant Fox's head slowly but surely shoving forward, with the red cap on Sande's head so far up on the withers of "The Fox" that it seemed almost a part of the blazing hood.

Not until he reached the back side, however, did Sande really set out for Alcibiades, the only filly in the race. About midway down the back stretch, Gallant Fox took the lead, and suddenly out of nowhere came his celebrated rival, Crack Brigade. The boys are commencing to call Crack

Brigade "The Fox's" sparring partner. He finished second to the Woodward horse in the Wood Memorial, and also the Preakness and the Kentucky Derby.

Crack Brigade's challenge was brief. Gallant Fox just naturally raced the ears off "Doc" Cassidy's steed going down the back stretch, and going into the far turn to the stretch, "The Fox" commenced to move away. He was galloping along easily, and the race was in little doubt. As they turned into the stretch, Sande urged "The Fox" gently and daylight showed between him and the next horse.

During the run down the stretch, Gallant Knight showed clear of the bunch back of Gallant Fox, and began making something of a bid, enough to encourage the crowd to cheer for him. But Sande just let out a link, and Gallant Fox moved off and on under the wire two lengths in front. Gallant Knight was an easy second. Ned O. had a scramble for third.

A great horse and a great rider was the combination that was too much for the best the West and the South could offer against the East today. Gallant Fox, whose daddy is Sir Galahad III, old rival of Epinard, the French horse across the pond, may be one of the best horses the American turf has had in years.

Sande's face was wrinkled with smiles as he trotted his mount back to the stand. The great jockey came back this season to some of his greatest triumphs, after a year in retirement. He was getting too heavy to ride, he thought, so he bought some horses and began racing his own stable, riding only occasionally. He lost $75,000 before he realized it was no game for him, and during the winter he sold his horses, and went back into training. He was on Gallant Fox when the Woodward horse, which is trained by Jim Fitzsimmons, won the Wood Memorial and the Preakness.

The smiles on Sande's face came and went in waves as he listened to the cheers of the crowd. They hung a floral horseshoe on Gallant Fox, and handed a bunch of roses to Sande. The horse has a curious trick of nodding his red-hooded head at a crowd after a race, as if taking bows. He nodded quite briskly in the gathering dusk of a late Kentucky afternoon day, apparently accepting the plaudits of the mob as the right of his new kingship of the horses of his time.

As the horses, blanketed from head to hocks, were led across the infield, a big crowd rushed for the paddock to watch the saddling. This is a ceremony that seems to intrigue strangely many racegoers. Also, they figure they may pick up a tip there. The Three D's declared to win with Broadway Limited, if possible, and put P. Walls, their crack jockey, on the steed that went for a price as a yearling that made it famous.

There was plenty of delay between the fourth and fifth races to permit the public to sock it into the windows, but, even so, many were shut out when the long line of silky-skinned steeds came stringing out of the paddock, and went teetering along the soft earthen path in what is called the post parade.

In his glass-enclosed cage in front of the grandstand, Lord Derby was seen to manifest considerable interest in the different horses. He inspected Gallant Fox closely. This is one of the finest-looking horses that ever peeked through a bridle, though some horse experts think he has too much leg, or something to that effect.

Crack Brigade is also a magnificent-looking colt. From the network of amplifiers on the lawn came the voices of the radio announcers quite distinct above the hum of the crowd.

The grandstand spectators sought their seats in some confusion. The air was very moist, and you couldn't call the track fast. Nor was it so very slow. It was what the experts pronounced dull. The Churchill Downs track is peculiar in that it is never fast in moist atmosphere, even if it isn't actually raining.

In many respects, the Derby is the classiest sports event of all, in personnel of the crowd. It draws heavily on what we are pleased to call society, and on the business and political spheres, not to mention the turf. However, it doesn't pull much from Broadway, which deems it too far away. Only a few of the real hot sports from the big white line were detected in the mob, and they looked lonesome.

Wall Street was well represented, however. The bankers and the brokers go for the Derby in a large way. They like to load up special cars with their pals, and bring their own licker. The local licker isn't so forte. Kentucky is still strong in its traditions as the home of fine horses and beautiful women, but the good whiskey that it used to brag about is a distant memory.

From the blue grass region of Kentucky came big delega-tions today, most of them talking of Tannery, though a lot of them wagered on Colonel E. R. Bradley's entry just from force of habit. The white, green hoops-and-cap of the Idle Hour farm is far away the most popular set of colors in this part of the world. Colonel Bradley is the home boy of Ol' Kaintuck. Of course when you come right down to it, most horses trace back to Kentucky in breeding, but once a nag falls into Eastern ownership, it is no longer regarded as a Kentucky horse.

The Kentuckians were more subdued today than usual about the Derby, for the reason that they didn't have a stand-out entry as in other years. When Kentucky has some-thing like Bubbling Over going in the big heat, the citizens make plenty of noise about it. Today they listened to the

Easterners rave about Gallant Fox, they heard the Chicagoans gabble of High Foot and said nothing. They slipped quietly to the mutuel windows and bet on the Bradleys just the same. The Kentuckian is a sentimental soul when it comes to horses.

I have often read windy dissertations as to the general significance of the Kentucky Derby. Loyal Southerners like to see it as a survival of the sporting spirit of the old, old South, and always give it a background of rebel yells. They love to picture Churchill Downs as the meeting place and the reunion premises of the scions of the Confederacy.

The only trouble with that etching now is that the sidewalks of New York, and the Chicago loop have commenced to move into Kentucky of late years, and when you go looking for a Kentucky Kunnel you are apt to bump into John Curry, Tammany Leader, or Palmer House Ryan, from Chi.

I mean to say the atmosphere of the sweet magnolia bloom, and the aroma of the mint julep that may have clung to Derby Day in other times, have gotten mixed up with cosmopolitan odors. The Derby hat of the effete East has largely supplanted the wide-brimmed black dicer that tradition tells us is typical of the old "Sooth."

I fear that unless the Southerners make a more determined stand, the New Yorkers and the Chicagoans will be claiming the Derby as their very own in a few years. Incidentally, Pittsburgh, Cleveland and Philadelphia are joining in the invasion. I saw special trains from these cities parked in the railroad yards, and passengers were walking around the streets of Louisville with a proprietorial air.

EMPEROR JONES

BY

O. B. Keeler

(THE ATLANTA JOURNAL)

Merion Cricket Club, Ardmore, Pa., Sept. 27, 1930.

ON THE FAMOUS East course at Merion, where as a shock-haired youthful phenomenon of 14 he first appeared in national championship competition, Robert Tyre Jones, Jr., today completed the greatest march of conquest in golf history.

By the one-sided margin of 8 up and 7 to go, Jones brushed aside Eugene Vanderpool Homans, of Englewood, N. J., to win the United States amateur championship and score his fourth straight national victory for the year—the "grand slam" of golf.

There are no more golfing worlds left to conquer for this 28-year-old citizen-lawyer of Atlanta, Ga., who made his final triumph look so ridiculously easy that the wonder is he hasn't been doing this sort of thing every year since he first began to scale the heights.

Bobby's triumph today after a solid week of competition was by far the easiest of any of the quartet he scored to sweep everything in sight for the campaign of 1930. It was just a breeze in comparison with the battles he waged earlier to capture the British open, the British amateur and the American open.

147

There was drama and a surging, rushing, and at the finish, an uncontrollable crowd of perhaps 15,000 spectators, running wild as they sought to see golfing history made such as may never be recorded again, but there were few, if any, competitive thrills to a final match that was just another big parade for the all-conquering son of the south.

The end was in sight when Jones ended the morning eighteen holes of the thirty-six-hole final, 7 up. Good and game a young golfer as Homans is, he was no match whatever for the stocky king of the links. It was just a question of how long it would go in the afternoon and Bobby kept the galloping gallery in suspense longer than it was anticipated, largely because Calamity Jane, the Jones putter, was not her usually consistent self.

Jones became 9 up at the twenty-second, with only 14 to go, and the crowd became frenziedly anxious to be in on the "kill," but it went seven more holes. At the twenty-seventh, Homans cut away a hole with a fine birdie 2. At the twenty-eighth it looked to be all over until Bobby took two shots to get out of a trap and barely saved a half in "buzzard" 6s. It was now dormie 8 and the throng broke all bounds in its wild gallop to the eleventh hole, down into the woods and along the creek—the twenty-ninth hole of the match.

Gallery marshals were ruthlessly brushed aside or knocked down in the wild charge to catch a glimpse of the last putt. Jones and Homans were nearly engulfed after they played their second shots well on to the green. Surrounded by Marines, the contestants and officials pushed their way to the green.

Jones was 25 feet away from the cup and putted dead for his 4. A hush fell over the tremendous crowd, covering the hills and knolls, the woods and fairway. Homans putted from 20 feet, the ball rolled close but missed and a wild shout went up from the crowd. Almost instantly there was a wild rush for the green and Jones.

For a few seconds it looked as though the quadruple monarch of all the golfing kingdoms would be overwhelmed, but as if by magic command, the Marines rose from nowhere, a score of them under Lieutenant Whitey Lloyd, former Annapolis fullback, to form a solid phalanx around the Georgian. The vanguard hit Lloyd and bounded back, shaken off like he used to block would-be tacklers. Others slowed up as they saw the protective cordon and the danger of a mob scene was avoided.

In flying wedge fashion, the Marines escorted Jones, Homans and officials of the United States Golf Association through the throngs, and up to the clubhouse lawn where the massive championship trophy, on a spotless table cloth, sparkled in the sun for the ceremony of presentation again to this Georgia marvel.

Twenty deep, as many of the spectators who could jam themselves about the scene stood to watch the last act of the great Jones drama of 1930 and lustily cheered the quiet, stocky young man who has knocked the statistics of golf groggy.

In his unprecedented sweep through the British and American tournaments this year, Jones today registered his fifth triumph in the United States amateur and his thirteenth national championship victory within the period of the last eight years. These achievements also stand alone as records. The only man who had ever won so many as four American amateur crowns is Jerome D. Travers, and no other man, Briton or American, has piled up so staggering a grand total of victories as Jones.

As he accepted the championship cup, Jones paid tribute to his opponents, to the galleries and to the Merion Club, where in 1916 he first played in the amateur tournament and where, in 1924, he won his first amateur championship. He now has won five of the last seven.

Will he continue to play or rest on his laurels? These questions buzzed among spectators as well as the experts after it was all over. Jones himself furnished the answer, so far as it may be given.

"I expect to continue to play golf but just when and where, I cannot say now," he told the Associated Press. "I have no definite plans, either to retire or as to when and where I may continue in competition. I might play next year and lay off in 1932. I might stay out of the battle next season and feel like another tournament the following year. That's all I can say about it now."

The significance of Jones' victory furnished much more excitement and interest than the final round match itself.

That Bobby would win was accepted as a foregone conclusion, almost from the start of the tournament. He won the medal in the qualifying play with a record-equaling score, 142, and he overwhelmed five successive opponents. His golf was not always "Jones golf," in the machine-like perfection it is thought of, but it was much too good for any one else to match.

Jones was never "down" to any of his five opponents in match play. Except for perhaps two or three lapses in his putting, he was never far enough "off" his game to cause the slightest concern to his intimate followers or alter the conviction that this was his tournament. Alone of the favorites who entered it, he swept along without the slightest interruption and with few challenges to his supremacy.

Homans, in the first final of his career, offered scant opposition, although his courageous finish extended the match farther than it seemed possible after Bobby assumed a seven-hole lead in the first eighteen.

The bespectacled New Jersey youth won exactly three holes out of the twenty-nine. Two of these were on birdies which he scored at the 213-yard seventh and at the 170-yard twenty-seventh. The third was the result of a stymie that Jones failed to negotiate on the seventh hole.

Jones shot his best golf on the inward nine of the morning round. He covered the nine in 33 strokes, one under par, sinking putts of 25 and six feet at the eleventh and fifteenth holes to offset a lapse on the seventh. These were the only good-sized putts he holed in the entire match but from tee to green his play was much superior to that of his opponent. The Georgian covered the first eighteen holes in 72, two over par, to Homans' 79. Bobby was four over par for the remaining eleven holes and so was Homans.

The answer was that Jones did not need to put on the pressure. He drove frequently with his spoon and he played for the greens, rather than for the pin, "safety first" golf that was good enough to win but not spectacular. Throughout, King Bobby gave the impression of just enjoying a good workout, while his opponent beat himself.

ROCK OF AGES

BY
Bill Cunningham

(BOSTON POST) APRIL 1, 1931.

T HIS PIECE IS WRITTEN by a fellow who couldn't be more dazed if he'd been belted between the eyes with a poleaxe, and these keys that have rattled on so blithely so many times and in so many sharps and flats about the famous "Fighting Irish" and the colorful figure who drove them are sticking and stammering and are all but mute, for the words, for some reason, won't seem to come through.

Rock dead?

He can't be. Guys like him don't die.

And yet out there on the Row the news-kids are yelling with a horrible—it almost seems a gloating—insistence, "Knute Rockne killed. Famous Notre Dame coach dies in airplane crash." Their high treble yells, riding a ghastly obbligato to the guttural thunder of a busy city street, sail even up to these windows and keep insisting it's true. Not even closing the windows can drown out that cry.

"Knute Rockne dead. Famous football coach killed out in Kansas," fainter, it's true. But there. Chiseling away through the cracks at the ear-drums. Dinning away at a brain that still can't believe. The telephone is ringing with folks asking if it's really true. Joe Gargan, Tack Hardwick, a cop with a broad Irish brogue, a school kid, a woman, a priest, a city official.

Over in the wire room some of the boys are standing silently and a little self-consciously around the teletype machines as in their cooly impersonal click-clickety-clack they hammer out the flat and workmanlike statement "Kansas City, March 31 (AP)—Knute Rockne, famous football coach of Notre Dame University, and seven others were killed when a Transcontinental & Western air passenger and air mail plane crashed in flames today..." but why go any further? There it is. It must be true. They don't take chances on stories such as that.

The entire football world is stunned, and this particular and small and suddenly humble-feeling member of it feels especially stricken—just why he can't explain except that in the past year he had come to know Rockne personally and intimately, had spent many enjoyable hours with him in California and Florida where he left him no more than three weeks ago. An autographed photograph of the famous builder of famous machines hangs there upon the wall smiling down as if it all were a joke. That picture came only last week, and a personal letter from him lies there unanswered, a warm, kidding, enthusiastic, truly typical letter to which I was planning to reply this very night. It has to do with a series of feature football articles we were to collaborate upon for a national magazine. They were to be smashed loose in slam-bang fashion in the fall.

But those stories will never be written now, for they were to be Rock's music set to my kind of words. And instead of answering his letter, it becomes my miserable duty to try to pay tribute to one of the most amazing careers in the history of the gridiron, and to say farewell to a friend who's beyond the power of hearing it.

Rockne, famous as he was as a coach, wasn't so much a coach as a builder of manhood, physically and spiritually. His life story is an old-fashioned Alger tale combined with a Frank Merriwell thriller. A highly educated and thoroughly cultured gentleman at the end, he had achieved that end over a pretty rocky road. Things weren't smoothed out for this immigrant kid from far Norway. He had to go it alone at a precocious age, and he had all the battles, the disappointments, the trials and temptations of a kid who's tossed upon his own. An indomitable will, a clear vision, a clean mind and a healthy body carried him through as it had many a youngster before him and as it will many another who will still come along.

He told this reporter that the foundation of what later became nationally famous as his "Notre Dame system" was laid on a Monday afternoon, back in 1914, when the Notre Dame team, he was assisting to coach, returned from a sound licking by Yale. Harper, the head coach, called him to one side and said, "I now know there's something wrong with our basic formations and I'm going to change to a little backfield shift Old Man Stagg at Chicago once taught me."

"I looked at it," said Rock, "and saw that if my ends were to cooperate with this shift to any extent they'd have to do a little shifting of their own. So I figured out one, and that's what we've been nursing ever since. If I had to describe it, I'd say it's a system of shifting backs and flexing ends."

Harper, somewhat ailing in health, retired to farm life in 1917 and recommended Rockne as his successor. Notre Dame confirmed Harper's recommendation and made Rockne not only the head coach but the graduate manager of athletics.

Then started, in earnest, the great Notre Dame era.

Headlined by brilliant stars such as the tragic George Gipp and the fleet Johnny Morhardt, the swift elevens from

South Bend began to range and to rout the best teams in all parts of the nation. Keen, they were. Hard hitting. Smoothly drilled. Splendidly conditioned. They established themselves as a traveling team. They became the greatest box-office attraction in the history of football. Unable to accommodate the throngs that clamored to see them, on their own small home field, they became annual features and fixtures in the biggest and most famous stadia in the nation.

Although always headlined with some star or stars whose names rang across the frosty Saturdays, the Notre Dame teams of Rockne's construction were really so smoothly fitted and so interdependent that picking a star in the usual sense of the word was impossible. The great team of 1924 was an example. That was the year of the famous "Four Horsemen." But you took the four, or you left them alone. It was impossible to choose between Miller, Layden, Stuhldreher and Crowley. Taken together, they were the class of the land, but no one outshone any other.

His great teams charged along. Even in lean years, and occasionally he had one, Rockne's elevens always provided clean, thrilling football that would bring any crowd to its feet. Their great annual spectacle with the Army became one of the real extravaganzas of the recurring autumns, and proof of its appeal was clearly given last December when the game solidly jammed the great Soldier Field in Chicago on one of the worst days of the year.

Rockne's last two teams were veritable gridiron marvels. They barged bravely and successfully through the two toughest schedules ever handed to any eleven athletes. Driven faultlessly by a typical Rockne quarterback, Frank Carideo, they clearly established their supremacy over the teams of every section and the great 1930 team, largely starless, but in the same breath composed of perhaps a score of stars, capped a glorious season of wins in the South, East and West, with a punitive expedition into far California, where it masterfully flattened the powerful Southern California eleven, called by Coastal folk the greatest team in the history of West Coast football and believed by them to be the strongest team the game of football ever knew anywhere.

Through all his career, Rockne kept growing in stature, finances and fame. His system has been copied all over the nation, even such a fundamentalist as Yale now aspiring to its maneuvers. Some sixty of his players are now football teachers. He was a very real head of a very real organization. Other coaches, some of them famous before he was born, and identified with the game for thrice his span of years, freely recognized him as perhaps the keenest among them. Some of them scoffed at what they considered looser governing bonds which gave him an advantage, but none ever quibbled over the fact that whatever the bonds, Rockne was a wizard with a megaphone in his hands.

Rockne's salary at Notre Dame was only $10,000, but he was making close to ten times that at the time of his death. This revenue came from magazine articles, motion pictures, radio speeches, addresses, and football schools. If his life had been spared and his health had stayed with him, he quite probably would have been football's first millionaire, for he was capitalizing his fame and his personality to the fullest, but legitimately, cleanly and with dignity.

He was a living dynamo. Every word, every motion of his was energy personified. Even in his last years, when crippled for a while with thrombosis, he never lost his punch. His voice never was free from that driving, ringing, inspiring vigor that used literally to lift his football teams out of themselves when things were going wrong and send them

back to play an inspired brand of the game as he wanted it
played and taught it.

Rockne was dramatic. He was visionary. He knew his
human nature. He was witty. He was keen. He knew how
to appeal or how to drive. He could take a high tempered,
sensitive and already mishandled star such as Brill of his
1930 team, and change him into a smooth, loyal and co-
operative unit. He gave his players a chance. He shot square
with them. There never was one who hated or feared him.
They stand tonight all over this nation, heartbroken and
distraught wherever they are. Each of them feels a personal
sense of bereavement. Rock was more than their coach. He
was their father, their friend. That, at least, he leaves behind,
and it is much.

I can't write his epitaph, but I can offer the following bit
of testimony. It's the only story I brought back from Hollywood and didn't write and it wasn't written because...well,
because it just isn't the sort of story that a fellow feels like
writing; but it shows so clearly, if automatically, what Rock
did to the lives of the boys that he taught, that I don't think
he'd object to its being told now. It, in its way, is his epitaph.

One of the big movie moguls won a large sum of money
on the Notre Dame victory out there. He thought he'd
show his appreciation by throwing a party for the members
of the Notre Dame team. The boys were told that they were
being invited to a big party in Hollywood, and, naturally,
they accepted, without asking much about the plans.

But the plans, as it happened, were unusual, to say the
least. Instead of a reception with the movie stars (or some
such), the host hired for the evening a sumptuous residence
far removed from any neighbors. He stocked it with a truck
load of the highest and hardest liquor, ordered suitable food,
and then, as the pièce de resistance, through an agent who

specializes in "party girls," he had a couple of dozen of the best looking and best dressed of this species assembled and quietly carted out to the address.

When the fleet of cars he'd sent in finally ferried the football players out from the Los Angeles Biltmore—the coaches were all going to another affair—he led them aside and said in an undertone: "Now, boys, this party's on me. I'm paying the bills, and the sky is the limit. Nobody's going to know what you're doing. There are the girls, there is the grog. Go ahead and have a good time for yourselves. We'll come back with the cars about 2 or 3 o'clock, with stretchers enough to carry you if necessary. Nobody will ever know what took place out here. It's just a little secret between you and me. This is the night you break training, and here's the chance to break it in a large way. Just have a good time. That's all I ask."

Then he and his aides went away.

At about 2:30 in the morning they came back with the cars—and walked in upon anything else but what they expected to find. For one thing there wasn't a woman to be seen in the place. They'd all left after a half hour or so, for the boys had completely ignored them. Barring one or two bottles of beer, not one drop of the liquor had been touched. Not a cork had been drawn from the whiskey or gin bottles. A little of the food had been nibbled and a few cigarettes had been smoked, but the first few cigarettes don't taste very good after you haven't had any for three or four months.

Here were the football players, some asleep in chairs or on couches, some few playing cards, three or four reading newspapers, other lolled around the radio—all bored, tired, sleepy and anxious to get back to the hotel.

This was the great Notre Dame football club, the hard-boiled, wise-cracking, hard-driving hellions of the 1930 gridiron, the personification, one supposes, of the redder-blooded flaming youth the college humor magazines blab about, yet so ingrained in them was clean living, right mindedness and decency that they weren't even tempted to take part in this orgy. Those temptations may come later, and may be succumbed to, yet it's the lessons, the teachings of one's youth, that stick with one longest and that always keep coming back.

And that's what Rockne taught his boys, taught them to the extent that here with football all over, and training for a while at an end, they couldn't or didn't care to forget his words for yet a while.

Only a football coach, maybe, but a football coach who can leave an imprint such as that has been a very real sort of clergyman.

Rock dead?

That poor broken body of his may be stilled forever out yonder, but the soul of the man, and the ring of his voice and the things he stood for and lived for and taught the boys who stood around him, live and will live, for they were clean and fine and such things don't die.

They really are his epitaph.

BROOKLYN CLUBHOUSE

BY
Quentin Reynolds

(NEW YORK WORLD-TELEGRAM)
APRIL 27, 1931.

I SHOULD OUGHT to have known better. I went to Ebbets Field yesterday, and the game was called off on account of the rain, and it wasn't raining violets, either. So I met a feller by the name of Mac, and he says, "Come over to the Plumbers' and Mechanics' Bridge and Whist Club, and there is a feller there who will give you a story for the paper."

"What!" I sez. "Play cards on Sunday?"

"You never seen chicken in chicken pot pie or eggs in eggplants, did you?" Mac says. "Well, you never saw a card game in the Plumbers' and Mechanics' Bridge and Whist Club."

So I went over there, and it turned out to be a place where you say "Two up" and you get two long ones and if you say "Two down" you get two short ones. Very tasty, too. So this feller introduces me to Barney, who runs the place.

"I am pleased to make your acquaintance," he says. "I think I seen you somewhere before. Your face is familiar, but I can't place the body."

Mac bursts out laughing. "Ain't he a riot? He certainly is a wit!"

"Yes," Barney says modestly. "I am a guy that is full of

laughs, and sometimes when people go out of here they are almost dying laughing. They say, 'That feller certainly is a card.'

"Now lots of times on rainy days I help the newspaper boys out with stories. Like, for instance, a feller named Robinson come in here after the St. Louises had clipped the Dodgers three in a row. I tell him to just say:—'The Cards is stacked against us.'...How's that, hey?...Then once when we lost four straight I tell a feller named Kase to say:—'Clean out the cellar, the Dodgers is coming.'

"I am always thinking of things like that, and, in fact, I should have been a sports writer, but it woulda broke my mother's heart, so I am now in the rum business, which is at least honest."

A gentleman at the end of the mahogany was making a great deal of noise singing a song called "Sweet Analine," or something like that. Barney got sore. "Stop that nerse," he growls, "or I will inject you outa the joint.

"Getting back to the Dodgers," he says, "the trouble with them is they don't live right. I hear they go to bed early and do setting up exercises every morning.

"Them Dodgers are too tense. They are all tightened up like a cop on his night off. They should unlax a bit.

"The last time they win the pennant I usta know a lot of them. After the game they would come in here and have a few. I remember one big guy who played for them. The first time he comes in here I say, 'What do you want?'

"'Three beers and a gin rickey,' he growls, and right away I knew he was a real ball player. He had a couple of more rounds like that, and the next day he hits five for five and gets himself a fifty-clam bonus."

Barney was frankly disgusted. "What do them Dodgers do now on their off days? They play bridge or they play ping pong, the big pansies. They ought to be out raising a little hell. It would do them good and they would get all that tenseness out of their systems....What? You gotta?....Well, so long and the next time you come in we will discuss the Yankees."

DERBY DAY

BY

Bill Corum

(NEW YORK EVENING JOURNAL)

Louisville, Ky., May 18, 1931.

LOOKING BACKWARD at the Kentucky Derby.... Rambling old Churchill Downs, with its spire like a church, close packed with 50,000 sportsmen and sportswomen from South and East and West and 5,000 gatecrashers from over the fence.... Flowers in bloom and Kentucky girls in party dress, for, as Irvin Cobb says, the Derby is their coming-out party....

The sun so bright that old-timers viewed it with suspicious eyes and wondered if it really could be a Derby Day with the sun shining.... Long lines at the mutuel windows, so, contrary to reports, somebody must have money still.... Derby breakfasts, and what once were called mint juleps in frosted cut-glass bowls.... Old Colonel "Stonewall" Jackson, the authorized and protected tout, bowing and scraping inside the main gate and handing out his infallible tips. Infallible, that is, until after the race.

A Vice President, Governors, Senators and Mayors and George (Bringing Up Father) McManus being knighted a Kentucky Colonel with the assistance of Bugs Baer and Rube Goldberg, so that he could join 10,000 other Kentucky Colonels on the front lawn.... Fried chicken and old hickory ham in baskets on the backstretch. . . . Colored horse swipes in stable colors, crooning to their darlings as they walked them round and round. . . . A little darky gal darting through the ten-deep crowd along the rails, saying: "Where is the horses? I done been here fo' hours, and I ain't seen no hosses yit." Flags flying and canned music and a small time, strictly private fight or two. . . . And then the race of races.

It was exactly 5 o'clock by your watch, if you still had it, when the bugle called them to the post. (Blow softly bugle o'er the Downs this day, for there are not enough bright Kentucky Derbies in the life of any one man.) There was that hush that comes with tenseness and expectancy, and then out of the little shoot that leads under the stands came the lead pony with his hunter-coated rider. This is the one your girl friend, seeing her first race, frequently wants to bet on, because he looks so cute.

Then as the Knebelkamp and Morris colt, Spanish Play, poked his nose through the crowd packed around the gate the first bars of "My Old Kentucky Home," played in slow time over the giant amplifiers.

The sun shines bright in my . . .

Charles Fisher's Dixiana Farm Sweep All, with the string-bean Italian booter, Frankie Coltiletti, in the solferino, buff blouse and scarlet cap, came next. He looked a good colt and he was to run like one.

. . . in my old Kentucky home.

Then the first of the three Greentrees, Anchors Aweigh, the devil horse. A spitting, biting, rearing son of Man o' War, who hasn't found out that the war is over. Already he had lathered himself with sweat just thinking up mean things to do at the barrier until his normally brown coat was black as ebony.

'Tis summer, the darkies are gay.

The Mongol came next, a son of Sir Martin, under the famous cherry and white hoops of the late John E. Madden. Not much colt, The Mongol, but it brought back memories to see those colors again. Mr. Madden, at near 70, practising sprinting starts between his barns at Saratoga, Mr. Madden matching pennies with a newsboy, Mr. Madden sending those great fat turkeys from Hamburg Place to his friends at Christmas time.

The corn top's ripe and the meadow's in the bloom.

The Kentuckians were singing it now, their voices more than a little husky, what with the corn liquor and the feeling they always put into the song. And Walter J. Salmon's Ladder, the flashiest looking animal in the field, was curveting by, his head pulled sideways and his bright chestnut coat a-gleam.

And the birds make music all the day.

"Ah." A ripple of applause not much louder than a sigh rang along the rails and up into the stands. A great bay colt had come bounding onto the track and danced his way into a slow gallop, the little boy on his back pulled stiff-armed to keep him from breaking into a full run. Your Derby crowd does not have to be told when it sees a race horse and it was seeing one. "Here I am," he seems to say. "Look me over, Big Red from Red Bank (N. J.), and right ready to run."

So weep no more, My Lady, weep no more today.

How Twenty Grand, the long-legged son of St. Germans-Bonus, did run to win the fifty-seventh Derby and break Old Rosebud's record is yesterday's story now. He came from last at the clubhouse turn to mow them down by ones and twos and threes at will and to win galloping, with little Charley Kurtsinger laughing back at the field.

He likes to laugh, this tow-headed German lad, with the steady eyes and wide grin, who was born just back of the hill from the Downs and who sneaked under the fence to watch the filly Regret win her Derby. Little did he dream that Spring day as he glued himself to the infield fence that one day he would ride a direct descendant of Regret's, through the mare Remembrance, down that shrieking lane of humanity, his red cap bobbing like a small buoy over the shoulders of one of the greatest race horses the Kentucky Derby ever has known.

That elderly gentleman who came chasing through the infield to the finish line, tossing his hat in the air as he came, was "The Flying Dutchman's" daddy, and he kept right on chasing him through the clubhouse and the jockey room while the cops tagged along in vain pursuit. There was no catching the Kurtsingers Saturday. And his daddy was once a race rider, too. That is to say, he rode two races, lost them both, and quit the turf when he got beaten a head in the second one.

Charley's mother was there, too, and a brother and three sisters and Lord knows how many uncles and aunts and cousins.

"Why," said Charley, "they had a big crowd at this Derby if just my folks were here."

We'll sing one song for the old Kentucky home . . .

And then, if maybe you were wondering why there were tears in the eyes of young Jimmy Rowe, as he went out to meet what may prove to be the best horse we have seen since Man o' War, I think I can tell you.

Fifty years before to the day, Jimmy Rowe's father had stood in the same circle to greet his first Derby winner, a little horse called Hindoo. And young Jimmy Rowe loved and admired his father, who was perhaps America's premier horseman. So there are heartbreaks as well as hoofbeats in a Derby. I guess that's why it is the greatest race of all.

For the old Kentucky home far away.

The Age of Reason

The extravagant, ebullient treatment that typified sports-writing of the 1920's vanished abruptly before breadlines and bankruptcies and bank holidays that were the evidences of a social revolution in the 1930's. A sense of the fitness of things tempered the writing that appeared with increasing frequency on the sport pages.

For the first time, the men who reported sport began to suggest that some of the heroes had feet, as well as heads, of clay. Restraint brought mature objectivity and critical examination of methods and motives. The boys no longer were naive and they were not given to supporting promotions merely for the sake of boosting the business. Their growing prestige gave them a feeling of responsibility and they commenced to expose rascals and denounce skulduggery.

Better pay and play in the paper brought more intelligent, well-rounded writers into the field. The overlapping of seasons and the expanding popularity of all sports gradually eliminated the specialists who were equipped to cover only one game. Budgets that were reduced during the depression no longer could afford the luxury of one-shot experts who went into hiding after their seasons were completed.

Smaller staffs called for men who could go from baseball to football to boxing or track or basketball, with a side excursion into other fields, without drawing a deep breath. The reporting of technical aspects of the several games did not suffer from this constant rotation of assignments. Indeed, *the readers were fed more precise and illuminating information than ever before.*

Stories were shorter and demanded sounder craftsmanship since all the elements of reporting—news, features, human-interest, authoritative comment and trend-charting—now were incorporated in one concise piece. The man who padded his copy with ringing, elaborate phrases that often collapsed under the sheer weight of words no longer was regarded as the fellow to be followed. The leaders were the men who wrote simply and compactly and did not neglect to include in their leads the winner of the ball game.

Perhaps the most important trend to appear during the Age of Reason was the gradual swing toward professional sport. The backbone of the sport pages always had been major-league baseball, boxing and racing, but during the 1920's college football made claims on space that pushed practically all other news out of the sport section. A forthright appraisal of the ideals and alleged lily-white purity of college teams turned many men to the out-and-out pros, with their refreshing frankness and higher caliber of performance.

A companion trend in the craft itself had come to accept competence as the only worth-while pay-off.

THE EDITOR

BOOS FOR THE PRESIDENT

BY

Joe Williams

(NEW YORK WORLD-TELEGRAM)

Philadelphia, October 6, 1931.

IT IS THE THIRD GAME of the World Series between the Athletics and the St. Louis Cardinals. A bright, flinty sun beats down on the thousands in the stands. The two rival pitchers, Grove and Grimes, are sharpening their control. From the high, swaying press box they look dwarfish. The illusion grows they are throwing cotton balls. You are so far removed from the ground all sound is blotted out.

The minutes tick by and presently a squad of bluecoats assembles in front of the Athletics' dugout. You know what this means. The story was in the morning newspapers. The President of the United States is about to arrive.

There is a break in the crowd to the left of the Athletics' dugout and the President's party, headed by two uniformed Army men, come on the field. It is easy to identify Mr. Herbert Hoover, his squat, square figure being so familiar. A gray-haired woman walks by his side, his wife. She is in a burgundy ensemble, gay orchids nod from her tailored coat.

The crowd back of the dugout recognizes the President and there is a pattering of palms and Mr. Hoover waves a gray, soft hat at mechanical intervals, and smiles his greetings. An official box has been set aside for the visitors from

Washington. Grove and Grimes, who have paused in deference to the President's entrance, go back to their mysteriously silent labors.

And then something happens. Some one boos. Or it may be a whole section which surrenders to this spontaneous, angry impulse. In any event, the boos rise from the stands and break with unmistakable vehemence around your ears. They grow in volume and pretty soon it seems almost everybody in the park is booing. Booing what? It doesn't take long to get the answer. They are booing the President of the United States.

By now the boos have changed to a chant. From thousands of voices come the cry: "We want beer. We want beer." It has the swing and resonance of a college cheer at a football game. It is a shocking manifestation of bad manners and lack of respect. Many in the stands sense this and begin to applaud, but the applause is light and the ugly overtones drown it out.

All the while you keep your eyes on Mr. Hoover. If he is surprised and resentful he gives no sign. He sits in his box with his hands folded across his stomach and looks straight out on the field where the umpires are beginning to group together at the plate. Mrs. Hoover seems to be studying a scorecard.

Once the game is started the rabble of the crowd fades and everybody in the park, including the Hoovers, presumably, concentrates on the vitally American issue of the respective strength of the American and National Leagues. But somehow, sitting up in the press box, it is hard to get your mind on the game.

This must be the first time a President ever has been booed in public, and at a ball game, of all places. There is something about a ball game that is supposed to make everybody kin and it's a high honor to sit in on a ball game where the President becomes a fan, just as you and I. Why, then, this brutal reception?

Well, these are dark days, you tell yourself. Unemployment is vast, yet not so bitter and pressing that these thousands can't find money enough to buy World Series tickets, many of which must have been bought at scalpers' prices. "We want beer!" That cry is, at least, understandable, even if the moment and place are not fitting. Prohibition has proved an evil, vicious thing and Mr. Hoover is lined up on the side of the drys.

You go on thinking out loud. Mr. Hoover is our leader and if the country has fallen on hard times perhaps it's only natural that the citizenry should single him out as a target. But the demonstration is so extraordinary, and you like to believe it is so un-American, you feel shaky and a little frightened. What if this mob mood should be translated into realistic action?

Your sympathies, meanwhile, mount for the Hoovers and you find yourself abstractedly following the game. The Cardinals get to Grove for two runs in the second and two more in the fourth. It is evident the Athletics' fireballer hasn't his customary swift ball and you get the impression he looks tired and is pitching with an effort. On the other hand, the burly, surly, unshaven Grimes is pitching shutout ball, enjoying one of his superlative afternoons on the mound.

The eighth inning is over and the National League champions are out in front, 4—0, when a voice crackles sharply through the amplifiers...."Silence. Silence, please." The President and his party are leaving the park. The voice asks for courtesy. Everybody is to remain seated, too.

But the voice is ignored. As the President, holding the arm of Mrs. Hoover, walks slowly past the Athletics' dugout and through the entrance which will lead him to his special train, the booing breaks out anew and rocks the stands and when the booing does stop it gives way to the chant, "We want beer. We want beer."

We can only imagine how Mr. Hoover, a real sportsman, who had taken a day off to relax at a ball game, a privilege at the command of even the most obscure citizen, must have felt as the train sped him back to his awesome duties in a troubled and distressed Washington.

(Note: Mr. Hoover has since disclosed to Mr. Williams the reason why he left this ball game before it ended. During the playing of the seventh inning, two telegrams were delivered to him in his box. One revealed America had gone off the gold standard; the other announced the death of a very close personal friend.

"Under the circumstances," Mr. Hoover said, "I decided I had no business watching a ball game."

Incidentally, the humiliation Mr. Hoover suffered at this game has had no chilling effect on his enthusiasm for baseball. He is to be seen often in the major parks of the nation.)

TEAM BOBBING

BY
Edward J. Neil

(ASSOCIATED PRESS)

———————

Lake Placid, N. Y., February 2, 1932.

THEY TOOK ME DOWN the most dangerous mile and a half in the entire sports world today, gave me thrills enough to last a lifetime and then before my eyes laid the picture of destruction that might well have come to me from less capable hands.

It was 7 o'clock in the morning, deadly cold on the top of Mount Van Hoevenberg, and the bobsledders of eight nations, men who can't have nerves, laughed and chatted in a polyglot of French, German, Swiss, Rumanian, Belgian, Italian, Austrian and English.

At their feet lay the Frankenstein contraptions known as bobsleds, 500 pounds of steel and oak. In the air was a fine mist of snow. We were at the start of the Olympic bob slide, the mile and a half of glare ice twisting through twenty-five awesome bends and hairpin curves down the mountainside, the racing strip that in two days has sent eight Germans to the hospital.

They watch the starter with his red flag and suddenly he gets word from a telephone strung along the slide that all is clear.

"Get ready," he yells. "To the mark. Harry Homberger's Red Devils."

Harry—they call him Hank—winks.

"You ask for it. Let's go."

He's just a pleasant kid, twenty-six years old, but a civil engineer from Saranac Lake, the fellow who built this slide. He is a pilot, four lives and a steering wheel in his grasp.

They say he's the greatest bobsled driver in the history of the sport—dark, keen-eyed, quiet. He is the Albie Booth of bobsleds, 158 pounds, but his shoulders are the widest in the crew. His world record is 1:52 for one and a half miles.

Hank climbs behind the wheel, we settle on the sled, bracing feet, gripping the straps on the side with hands shielded in padded gloves. I was No. 3, sandwiched in between huge Percy Bryant and the brakeman, Ed Horton, who yanks the steel jaws that clutch at the ice when we need to slow down.

Solemnly the men of other nations who can't hope to equal Homberger's skill shake our hands. They do that before each run; they act as though they never expected to see you again.

Particularly does Fritz Grau, German captain, make it a point to slap our backs. So did Albert Brehme, Hellmuth Hoppmann, the jovial Rudolph Krotki, the German team masseur who takes Max Ludwig's place for the day. An hour later they were all in a hospital.

Hank turns for a last word. "It's not so fast today," he says, "but I'll do my best to give you a thrill."

One heave and we're off. The foreigners dash for places around the telephone. Each station calls off our progress. I've watched them stand there tense, silent, seeming to be praying there'll be no shout: "They've jumped a bank!" That means you've smashed through a curve going a mile a minute and your body is hurtling down a mountainside studded with rocks and trees and ice. I saw that, too, later.

Swiftly we pick up speed on the first straight drop. We're shooting down what looks like a culvert of solid ice with the top half cut off. The steel runners begin to sing. The wind tears at your hunched head. Forty, fifty, sixty miles an hour.

"Lean," screamed Horton in my ear.

Up into my face came a dazzling wall of white ice. I leaned hard. We sweep up to the top. The runners slide, catch. We hurtle down again. That was the turn called Eyrie.

Now it's sixty again and going up, and one after another come the blinding banks, ten, twenty, thirty feet high. Desperately I leaned. This way, that way, gasping for breath, helpless, straining. The wind is blinding. Tears stream from your eyes. You think you can't hold on another second. You fight, surge, and then you're out of the curve and flying down a straightaway, seventy miles an hour, and you get a breath.

Then something begins to happen to your nervous system. The curves are getting steeper. You're taking them eagerly. Suddenly you begin to tingle; every nerve in your body feels as though some one were playing on it with the bow of a fiddle. Exultation sweeps up from your toes, reaches your throat. Back goes your head and you howl with the sheer joy of it.

You're ready now for the serious part. "Whiteface," a vertical semi-circle of ice thirty-five feet high at seventy miles an hour. The sky suddenly turned to a sheet of ice over your head, the track a streak of blue under one elbow.

"Shady Corner," again at seventy, a thud as you fly into the wall, smash off again, and just when you think you're gone, another straightaway, another breath.

Then the final test, a final surge of every drop of blood through your veins, the apex of sporting thrills and the end of many a bobsled career—"zigzag"—a whip to the left, a leap of five feet, all four runners off the ground, to straighten out, a whip to the right, one last burst and you're at the finish—limp, exhausted.

"Slow," said Hank, "about two minutes."

"Yes," said Horton, "I wish I'd brought my gun. I saw a rabbit I could have got when we were going through Shady."

We started back up the mountain. Almost to Shady we heard another bob screaming down the course. We jumped behind the track peering through the snow up the twisted ice ribbon. We could see Shady up the bend.

A bob flew into the turn at seventy miles an hour, swerved, runners shrieked. The sled swept up the incline, smashed through the top, four bodies hurled through the air, into a deep ravine below. It was our friends, the Germans, Grau, Brehme, Hoppmann and Krotki.

We raced up the slide, helped carry the battered, blood-soaked unconscious forms to the ambulances.

"That's the way it goes," Homberger sighed. Twenty minutes later they're racing down again.

THE MUSCULAR MUSE

BY

John Kieran

(NEW YORK TIMES) MARCH 12, 1933.

———————

JOHN T. MCGOVERN, called Terry in amateur and inter-collegiate athletic circles, recently wrote a book entitled "Diogenes Discovers Us," and in it he included a glowing chapter on the late Hobey Baker of Princeton as a great athlete, sportsman and soldier. This aroused Mr. William Van Dyke Belden, old Princetonian, who would take nothing away from the memory of Hobey Baker but who will always insist that his classmate, the great Johnny Poe, was the "beau ideal" of high adventure, the dashing athlete, the gay challenger, the courageous competitor and the gallant soldier.

In either case it's "Oranje Boven," the motto that is carved in stone over the open fireplace in Osborn Field House, where the Princeton athletes and coaches gather before the crackling logs to take their ease and talk of "moving accidents by flood and field." "Oranje Boven," as will be pointed out to any curious visitor by that former athlete and erudite scholar, Dr. J. Duncan Spaeth, means "the Orange above" or perhaps "Orange on high," or words to that effect.

It so happens that this "strange device" is a connecting link between the careers of Hobey Baker and Johnny Poe and the strange case of a great all-around athlete and soldier of something more than a century ago. "Oranje Boven" is taken from the banner of the House of Orange, and when the troops of Holland won some advantage over Napoleon's battalions this noted all-around athlete made some note of it in a diary he was keeping, and twice, at least, quoted the words that are carved over the fireplace at Princeton, "Oranje Boven."

He was an Englishman, this all-around athlete of old days, and he came of a titled family. One of his ancestors followed Richard Coeur de Lion to Palestine. On the maternal side he could trace the branches of his family tree as high as royalty, the Stuarts, and his ancestral home, Newstead Abbey, was presented to one of his forefathers by Henry VIII.

He was born Jan. 22, 1788, and seventeen years later he was the third best batter in the annual Harrow vs. Eton cricket match, cricket being one of his minor athletic activities. By the time he was graduated from Cambridge he was famous for his feats by land and water. He was one of the best swimmers of his era. He was an oarsman and a skilled skipper at the tiller of a sailboat. He was a crack shot with rifle and pistol.

He was ready to meet all comers on his ancestral lawn with single-stick, broadsword, saber or rapier. He was enthusiastic about boxing. He sparred for hours at a time with the great John Jackson, the professional. He sponsored and even fomented bare-knuckle fights between professional bruisers of those days. He attended all big bouts. He raised and raced greyhounds.

He supported, trained and backed one Dogherty in a finish fight with Tom Belcher, to the sorrow of himself and the aforesaid Dogherty. He dined often at the tavern kept by Tom Cribb, the old champion, and there cooked up arrangements for all sorts of contests, amateur or professional. As long as it was sport, he was in on it.

It must be admitted that he got himself into a number of rows, one way or another, and was regarded by conservative citizens as a harum-scarum, hot-headed fellow whose style of living was closer to riotous than righteous. He was no tee-totaler, and after swimming races in the lake on his own estate or sparring bouts on the ancestral turf he and his companions and competitors would dine in state in the great refectory at Newstead Abbey and linger late over the choice wines from the ancestral cellar.

One of the quaint customs of the place on such evenings was the passing from hand to hand of the burgundy in a cup fashioned from a human skull. He admitted that he was living not only beyond his means but beyond his expectations, and once in London his bed was sold out from under him for debt. He was such a fierce fighter that he drove most of his enemies to flight and, as a consequence, he was forced to fight with his friends and relatives, just to keep his hand in. He flared up on the slightest pretext, but perhaps he came by his hot temper naturally enough. According to historians, his mother died in a fit of rage brought on by reading an upholsterer's bill.

There was some relief felt throughout England when he decided to go abroad. He had tried his hereditary seat in the House of Lords, and, after a short stay, found it un-comfortable for a fellow of his belligerent disposition. He had defeated all his friends at swimming and shooting. Nobody would spar with him any more except John Jackson, who was paid to do it. He did write one hopeful note to Jackson. It ran:

"Dear Jack: I have to request you to call on Louch at Brompton and inquire what the devil he meant by sending me such an insolent letter at Brighton." But Louch was a disappointment. He apologized profusely.

So there was nothing to do but go abroad and take a chance on meeting adventure. At the age of 21 he started on his travels, swimming for two hours in the Tagus and later setting an Italian record by swimming all around the island of Lido, then through the Grand Canal of Venice from end to end and back to the bay again, being 4 hours and 20 minutes without touching bottom. He also challenged an officer of the garrison at Malta to a pistol duel, but the officer excused himself.

He swam the Hellespont, Sestos to Abydos, in 1 hour and 5 minutes, a new record at that time. He traveled through Albania, then a wild country. He went back to Italy and fought on the side of the people against the constabulary and the government. He lived there for years, getting into delightful rows, but finally he went to Greece to aid that country in its fight for freedom against the Turks.

He was almost captured by the Turks on the way, and his greatest worry was that the Turks would get the money he was carrying with him to help the Greeks. He raised, equipped and commanded a regiment of Suliotes, who revolted in camp. He reached the fighting front at Missolonghi, and there, in the mud and the rain, he caught a fatal illness and died April 19, 1824. A flaming spirit was quenched forever. He had a great many fine qualities and possibly a few faults. Among other things, he was addicted to writing poetry. His name was George Gordon Lord Byron.

THE BUTCHER BOY

BY

Richards Vidmer

(NEW YORK HERALD TRIBUNE) JUNE 15, 1934.

THE BAER WENT OVER the mountain and brought the heavyweight championship of the world back to the United States in his right hand.

With audacious confidence, smiling surety and a sledge-hammer punch developed slaughtering cattle, Max Baer whittled Primo Carnera, the man, down to the size of a Singer midget in the Madison Square Garden Bowl last night, toyed with him like a mongoose teasing a cobra, and made his final strike in 2:16 of the eleventh round after scoring his eleventh knockdown.

The curly-headed Californian kept 60,000 spectators quivering with excitement throughout ten rounds before he hammered his victim into such helplessness that Arthur Donovan, the referee, stopped the bout, leaving Baer, who hadn't fought in a year, performed in night clubs and motion pictures before he started training, and clowned his way through a month of preparation, champion of the world, while Carnera, defending his title for the third time in twelve months, was a battered, bleeding hulk, hollow-eyed and dazed.

From the start to the finish the great throng was kept in a state bordering on hysteria with pounding hearts and palpitating pulses, but there wasn't a doubt from the first minute to the last that Baer could drop his opponent just as he used to drop cattle in the slaughter house—decisively, with one blow—any time he wanted.

Baer looked like Dempsey, the killer of Toledo, the butcher of Boyle's Thirty Acres, the fury that fought Firpo, in the first round. With his lips drawn tight across his white teeth, a snarl twisting his face with rage, he tore in, ripped rights to the head and lefts to the body and battered Carnera's crown into a mass of scrap iron.

The towering Italian buckled at the knees, sank to the canvas and came up again glassy-eyed with surprise. Mercilessly, unrelenting, Baer followed him across the ring and beat him down into the resin again. Carnera was bleeding from the mouth as he staggered to his feet, but this only served as a red flag that stirred more fury in Baer's broad breast.

The Italian, who weighed 263¼ pounds to Baer's 210, was in full retreat now, moving backward as rapidly as his heavy legs and huge feet would carry him. There was fear in his expression and his hands were held before him as though warding off the attack of a wild man.

And Baer kept after him. When the welcome bell brought a moment's respite to the stumbling giant, Baer strutted slowly to his corner, his head held high, his lips parted in something between a sneer and a smile. But when he came out from his corner again he was still the savage.

Three times in the second round he bowled Carnera across the canvas with those destructive right-hand punches and each time as he fell Carnera reached out a desperate hand and clutched the nearest object, which, of course, was Baer.

Three times the two went sprawling on the padded mats of the ring while the crowd, viewing more action than it has seen in any battle since the Firpo-Dempsey slugging match, howled hysterically. Dignified men holding high positions, women in dinner gowns, bums and dirty-faced kids alike were on their feet, cheering wildly, slapping each other on the back, hungry with the prehistoric urge for the kill.

But with his victim helpless and hopeless, Baer had other business. He had his stuff to strut. Fundamentally a show-off, he swaggered about the ring, laughing at his opponent, making him look foolish. For the next seven rounds he posed and pranced.

In those seven sessions Baer smiled and used both hands to hoist his trunks while Carnera was throwing his most murderous punches. They never landed. Baer danced nimbly out of reach almost before they were started. Through these seven rounds Baer sneered at the ineffectiveness of Carnera's blows, disdaining even to block half of them but taking them on the chin, the chest or the head.

Through those seven stretches of three minutes each Baer never had a doubt or a fear. He knew he could finish his man when he pleased, but it pleased him to wait a while. For one thing, there was the declaration of Bill Brown, Boxing Commissioner, to consider. Brown had said he wasn't in shape and wanted to postpone the fight a month, or call it off altogether.

Baer couldn't have been in better condition. He wasn't even breathing deeply at the end of eleven rounds.

Then there was the feminine trade to please. He must have given a thought to the ladies. He always has. So he wanted to be on view more than a few minutes.

Apparently he had fixed the tenth round as the time to go to work in earnest, for he rushed from his corner before the last echoes of the bell had reached the spectators on the brink of the Bowl, and with a terrific right that would have dropped an ox or an elephant, he knocked Carnera clear across the ring. The Italian spun like a top as he covered the twenty-four-foot span, landing against the ropes.

There he hung for a moment like a crumpled bit of old laundry. It looked like the finish, but although the Italian may lack speed, science and sock, he has a heart, a great heart, in fact, that carried him across the expanse of Europe, penniless, wandering aimlessly and finally lifted him to the championship of the world. He still had that heart last night and it brought him back time and time again, back to the inevitable, back to the slaughter.

Altogether he was knocked down eleven times, but he finished on his feet, perhaps not like a champion, but at least like an ex-champion.

So he came back off the ropes, reeling, groggy, uncertain of what time it was, what town he was in, or his name perhaps, knowing only that he was in a fight and that his title was at stake.

He came back and twice more he was sent down. The smiling, suave Baer of the night clubs was the Baer of the jungles now. There was murder in his eye and no pity in his heart. He had strutted like a pouter pigeon, he had proved his supremacy, he had tossed Bill Brown's sneer back in his official face and now he was ready for the kill.

Through the three minutes of that tenth round he battered Carnera's huge bulk about as though it were a gunny sack stuffed with last week's papers. The Italian was defenseless and in deep distress, struggling to his feet with increasing effort and uncertainty after each battering and finally the bell sounded, saving him for another session.

But the next session was the last. Baer charged like a man from the jungles, using his padded right fist as a war club. Twice he beat Carnera down and the fading champion was too dazed by that time even to take a count and recover what senses he could. Both times he was up on his feet again after the referee had reached the toll of two, but after his second staggering ascent from the dust of defeat the referee interceded in the name of mercy.

Later Donovan said that Carnera beat him to it; that the Italian said he had had enough before the referee could reach the same decision. Carnera denied that he had quit, but it made little difference. Carnera had proved his gameness and Baer had demonstrated his right to the title, a clear claim for the first time since Gene Tunney retired and threw the heavyweight crown on the open market.

There have been pretenders, and for a time Max Schmeling, the German, held the heights, though he gained them on a foul. Then came Jack Sharkey, who wore the royal robe of ruler for a year, but he took it off Schmeling's back through a questionable decision. And finally there was Carnera, who knocked out Sharkey, but who could say that he had beaten a real champion?

And now, at last, there is Max Baer, butcher boy from Livermore, California, conceited and confident, ready to laugh at a joke or smile at a pretty girl, young, boyish, fun-loving and sometimes foolish.

O'DEA OF WISCONSIN

BY

Bill Leiser

(SAN FRANCISCO CHRONICLE)
SEPTEMBER 19, 1934.

———

THEY SAID HE HAD moved on to the next world—this man who crashed through with football records never surpassed or equaled in the gridiron history of America and then vanished as completely and mysteriously as Aladdin's Genii.

It was suggested in the Literary Digest of March that he must be resting in the unknown soldier's grave.

But Patrick John O'Dea, football's long lost immortal, is very much alive.

Out of the past he came smiling to sit across the dinner table last night. I could hardly believe it. This man, who once punted the length of the field in the air, this greatest drop kicker and placement kicker the world ever knew, this man who did Red Grange runs as a mere side line to a more spectacular game.

They said I would never meet him. Of him the Literary Digest, March 17, reported: "In 1917 when the Australian army was passing through San Francisco, where he was practicing law, (he) joined the Anzacs without informing even his brother, thus leaving the country as unostentatiously as he came. He has not been heard of since. Andy (his brother) is certain he is an unknown soldier."

He was the man who could curve a long punted football as a pitcher curves his throws. He could punt 85 yards against your "great" 60-yarders today. The record says he once lifted the football 110 yards in the wind. In an impossible 20-mile cross-field gale he place kicked half the length of the grid-iron, straight through the bars. He once sidestepped Gil Dobie on the run to drop kick 55 yards for a score. There has been no one like him, before or since, in the game.

And he was supposed to have moved on.

Yet there he sat grinning across the table last night, as healthy a specimen as I have seen in my time. He didn't go to war. He didn't disappear into thin air. He merely took up new work in his own way. And, up in Westwood, off in the northeast corner of California they will be surprised to learn this morning that the Red River statistician they have known for 15 years as Charles J. Mitchell is actually the long lost Pat O'Dea, one of the greatest athletes of all time.

Everyone who understands anything at all of the history of football knows of Pat O'Dea, the Australian, who came to America in 1896 and, for four years on the University of Wisconsin varsity, displayed a ravishing, kicking, smothering type of football that America never knew before and may never know again.

What's in the record books alone will keep his name alive as long as the game is played. There were heroes, great ones, before 1896, and there have been heroes of the gridiron since 1900, but, to those who saw Midwest football at the end of the last century, the names of Jim Thorpe and Red Grange, even, mean little alongside of Wisconsin's Pat O'Dea.

It was his fame that drove him out of sight. He was in San Francisco, in 1917, well known, too well known, per-haps, everywhere. Always he had to talk football. Always he was helping athletes—he even helped the Stanford crew of 1914. But always he was the man who had been great on the football field, and almost never the man who could talk of new work to be done. He didn't like living in what were to him "mere student days of the past."

With the war, his income from the home land was knocked down to nothing. He had an opportunity to start in a new field, off where no one knew him—off where he could be just himself and not the man who had kicked footballs for Wisconsin, so off he went to become Charles J. Mitchell of the Red River Lumber Company of Westwood, and he has been there ever since.

No one knew him there. He simply moved in as a stranger. For 15 years now, Charles J. Mitchell, a secretary-manager of the Westwood Auto Club (and Chamber of Commerce), a director of the Lassen Volcanic Park Association, a leader in the fight for good new roads that are being obtained, and roads open in winter, in that beautiful section, and a statistician for Red River lumber, has been the kind of fighting, astute, well-liked progressive citizen that makes small towns into bigger cities.

"Probably I was wrong," says the very live and smiling Pat. "Mrs. Mitchell, that is, Mrs. O'Dea, always thought I was. But I wanted to get away from what seemed to me to be all in the past. As Pat O'Dea, I seemed very much just an ex-Wisconsin football player.

"I was very happy as Mitchell for a while. Mitchell was my mother's name and Charley that of a cousin I like. Later, I often found it rather unpleasant not to be the man I actually am. So, if you want to write that I'm going to be Pat O'Dea again, for the rest of my life, write it.

"Perhaps I should never have been anything else."

So there he is, his old identity as one of the biggest of all athletes buried behind a 15-year-old Charles Mitchell off among 5000 citizens of Westwood, now come back to life again.

He's the kind of man who, perhaps as you and I, simply can't force a real smile before a camera, but what a swell smile he has. And what a stimulating person with whom to talk. And how he can tell you about football.

And what a life he has had, and is still having.

Almost cut down by sharks, as a boy, when he saved a young girl from drowning.

Transferred from the "polite" Australian game to the rough American football of the nineties he adapted himself to become the most spectacular and greatest star of his time.

Almost burned to death, in hot water, with his athletic career barely through.

Then driven by fame to comparative obscurity, and vanishing with a world believing him in an unknown soldier's grave and now coming back as the old Pat O'Dea.

But first, about that football. You don't have to ask him to learn what he did in football. The record books show a Pat O'Dea who outdid Red Grange before Red Grange was born.

Let me pick, here and there, from the old clips, just to give an idea of who was Pat O'Dea.

Against Pop Warner's champion Carlisle Indians, 1896, post season, a night game, and Pat O'Dea's debut. He sent a 50-yard "punted forward pass" to Judge Ike Carroll who, from an "onside" start, was eligible to and able to fall on the ball at the goal and roll over for the score. The Indians, who never saw the football because it went high over the girders holding the lights, refused to believe what had happened.

Against Minnesota, 1897, his first game against the team that had been treating Wisconsin badly. Got cornered, let the ball loose on the run and drop kicked 40 yards through the bars. Dad Moulton, later a Stanford track coach, then a trainer, dropped his water bucket in amazement on the side line. A flabbergasted Minnesota team, from that moment on, was kicked to death, 39 to 0.

Against Chicago, a "championship game," dropped over two 40-yard field goals and punted Chicago to submission, 28 to 0, much as Joe Paglia punted California into helplessness last year.

Against Beloit, 1897, a team that was tough, but one in which O'Dea was supposed to make the team do the work. Team couldn't do it, so O'Dea dropped over two drop kicks, only to get a bawling out from Coach Phil King. (Score, 10 to 0, field goals counting 5 points each in those days.)

Against Northwestern, 1898, a team supposed to whale the tar out of Wisconsin. O'Dea played with famous "kindergarten" team of those days, which included only one veteran besides Pat. O'Dea had disagreement with alumni representatives, who wanted to bring in more help. Said to have been nettled going into game. Ran two plays, dropped back, took two steps, and let the old drop go 63 yards through the bars, the world record. The ball went over the tops of the uprights, and 20 yards on to hit the fence surrounding the field. The game at the finish, 48 to 0!

Against Beloit, 1899, opening game, and supposed to be mean. O'Dea kicked four field goals and returned a kickoff 90 yards to the goal.

Against Illinois, 1899, another tough one. Twenty-mile gale blowing across the field. Back on his 55-yard stripe, O'Dea prepared for a place kick.

"What are you doing?" asked the referee. (It was after a fair catch).

"What do you think?" asked O'Dea.

"I think you're crazy, if you're trying to score in this wind."

Bill Juneau held the ball. Pat lined up so as to kick almost for the right-hand corner of the field. One step and he kicked, with the crowd spellbound. The football sailed directly for the corner for a time, then finally, as the wind caught it, it swerved back to the left, and floated smack through the middle of the uprights on the goal line, 55 yards away—the most impossible stunt ever performed.

Against Yale, 1899, lost, 6 to 0. Asked why Wisconsin lost, O'Dea said because he had missed his man, Richardson of Yale, who made the only score on a long run. Press of the day said two greatest sportsmen of all time were Sir Tom Lipton and Pat O'Dea, men who could take it when they lost. Press also talked of O'Dea's "best punting ever seen," and weeks later reported information that O'Dea's center, with an arm in a cast, couldn't pass the ball back 10 yards that day—and also that O'Dea played the game with a broken bone which pierced the skin of a finger on his right hand when he "missed his man."

Against Michigan, 1899, with press commenting freely on proposition that Michigan must stop O'Dea. O'Dea gave them a 35-yard drop kick score to start with, and a long curve punt, which the Michigan safety dropped, allowing Wisconsin man to pick up for touchdown, all in first half. Later, O'Dea was forced out of the only college game in which he did not play the full 60 minutes. Michigan center, as quoted in the old clips, said, "We could have won if we had gotten O'Dea out sooner."

Against Minnesota, 1899. Two plays, then O'Dea carrying the ball. O'Dea cornered by none other than Gil Dobie. O'Dea bluffed a run and Dobie prepared to block, and O'Dea, sidestepping, drop kicked over Dobie, 55 yards through the air, through the bars.

That's just a part of it. But you get the idea.

Once, in a tight spot, his little halfback, Paul Trat, had the ball and was in a tangle when a score was needed. O'Dea picked Trat up out of the jam and carried Trat, football and all, over the goal. No, he wasn't so big. A little over six feet, weight 170 pounds.

Why, O'Dea was supposed to have signals with his ends. He would inform the ends of which way the punted ball would curve after it started down the field. The ends, therefore, had that much advantage on the safety man, who didn't have the information.

I asked Pat O'Dea if it were true that a punted football could be curved?

"Certainly," he answered. He explained how. But I couldn't repeat in detail.

Oh, yes, O'Dea was a hurdle champ, a crack sprinter and a crew stroke besides. But I haven't space for that.

As for punting, 75 yards was a cinch for him, any time. He sent the ball just high enough to allow ends to get under it. If his first punt went too far for the ends, the next went much higher. He gave them all they could take, though they never could take all he could give.

Therefore, often, he punted for the goal line, and if the ball went over, in those days, the rival team had to kickoff in return from its 25-yard line. That would be a signal for a Wisconsin fair catch, and an O'Dea drop kick for points if points were in demand.

That is, if I read my old prints correctly.

I asked Pat if youngsters today could be taught to curve punts either way.

"Surely," he answered.

"I coached at Notre Dame just after I left Wisconsin. Red Salmon learned quickly. He was examined frequently by rivals, who sometimes insisted that it was really I who was in the game kicking. He had red hair and some tried to tear it off, thinking to expose O'Dea with a wig. He kicked as well as I could."

Yet Mr. Pat O'Dea believes that it would be entirely possible to teach a half dozen youngsters on each squad to kick as well as he did, or at least, nearly as well.

He learned, you see, in the Australian game, in which they punt forward passes as well as Americans throw them.

He has had a most unusual life.

He was almost cut to pieces by sharks, when he saved a young girl from drowning, when he was 16 years old, at Fort Phillip Bay in Australia. (He has the Royal Humane Society certificate for that.)

He almost burned to death of hot water when he once stunned his head in a bath tub. For days there was doubt and once reporters were waiting in the hall for the last word from the doctor. "What are they there for?" asked the deathly sick O'Dea.

"To learn when you're going."

"Go out and make them a bet that they're wasting their time," said Pat. They were.

And now, because of disappearance, he has been suggested as an unknown soldier.

His disappearance was natural enough. Almost every other man who has enjoyed tremendous fame has felt the urge, at times, to get away from it. Pat O'Dea did.

It wasn't exactly the "usual" thing. But there never has

been anything usual about Pat O'Dea since, as a boy, he played on amateur Australian game teams before 100,000 persons.

Many in San Francisco will know him, and he'll be seeing them again. Frank Guerena, little coxswain of Stanford's old crew, will know him, for O'Dea helped that crew a great deal.

Former Columbia Park boys will know Pat because, 25 years ago, when they wanted to go to Australia, he taught them the Australian kicking game, and they went, and split even on their tour.

Fifteen years ago fame drove him away, and changed his name.

Now he's back, Patrick John O'Dea, no longer football's long lost immortal, but a very vigorous, pleasant, smart young fellow, 55 years old, who has new work to be done and who's going to be his old self from here on out while he does it.

William H. Taylor

Full recognition of the outstanding reporting to be found on the sport pages finally came in 1935, and it came from the highest and most respected source. The coveted Pulitzer Prize was awarded that year to William H. Taylor for his coverage of the America's Cup yacht races in the New York Herald Tribune.

The citation of the award read: "A distinguished example of a reporter's work during the year, the test being strict accuracy, terseness, the preference being given to articles that acknowledged the accomplishment of some public good commanding attention and respect."

Taylor's descriptions of the six races in the series were notable for clear, straightforward explanation of a highly technical sport and for adroit, objective treatment of incidents that strained diplomatic ties between America and England. Taylor cut through the hoopla, hysteria and hokum that attended the races and won the top prize in his profession by the simple expedient of telling the readers what, when, where and how things happened.

The article that follows is Taylor's account of the last race in the series and includes the first half of the story as it appeared in the paper. That which has been omitted contained a formal analysis of the race pretty baffling to a landlubber.

Graduated from Dartmouth in the Class of 1923, Taylor comes naturally by his intimate knowledge of seamanship. A native of New Bedford, Mass., his forebears were among those hardy New Englanders who went down to the sea in *ships. Taylor still is a valuable member of the Herald Trib-une staff.*

THE EDITOR

AMERICA'S CUP

BY

William H. Taylor

(NEW YORK HERALD TRIBUNE)

———————————

Newport, R. I., September 25, 1934.

RAINBOW, ABLY SAILED by Harold S. Vanderbilt and his crew, completed her defense of the America's cup with a 55-second victory over the fifteenth challenger for the trophy, T. O. M. Sopwith's *Endeavour,* off here today. The trophy, which the New York Yacht Club has held for eighty-three years, will stay in this country for a while longer, at least, and the Royal Yacht Squadron, which was represented here by *Endeavour* and which originally put up the historic trophy eighty-three years ago returns empty-handed again.

The race today, sixth of the series, went to a better-sailed boat over a probably faster boat, but it was not until long after the race was finished that the decision was affirmed. Both Vanderbilt and Sopwith went over the starting line of today's race with protest flags flying, and finished the same way. At 8:30 tonight the second of the two protests was withdrawn.

The series was in a fair way to set a new high on inter-

national squabbles over the racing rules, and but for the
withdrawals of today's protests, first by Sopwith and then
by Vanderbilt, would have done so. Perhaps the stir aroused
by the protests has obscured the fact that Vanderbilt and
his crew defended the cup with a slower boat against what
for many skippers and crews would have proved overwhelming opposition. *Endeavour* sailed twenty of the thirty miles
of today's triangular race 4 minutes faster than *Rainbow,* but
it was the challenging skipper's mistakes on the windward
leg that cost the Squadron at least another chance tomorrow
at the cup.

As to the protests, and their solutions, they haven't been
as violent as may have appeared to non-yachtsmen. The
refusal of the race committee to hear Sopwith's protest on
last Saturday's race has created an unfavorable impression
among the general public, but actually it may have been a
blessing in disguise for the challenger. Sopwith's subsequent
comments added fuel to the fire, and he and Vanderbilt
went out to race today with chips on their shoulders, as
their handling of their boats before the start showed very
clearly.

As might have been expected under the circumstances,
each felt, by the time the race started, that he had been
fouled by the other, although few if any of those who
watched the proceedings shared in this belief. So up went the
protest flags, and up they stayed until after the finish. The
cool of the evening brought a change of heart, however.
Vanderbilt's protest had already been delivered to the
committee boat, when about 8 o'clock a messenger
brought a note from Sopwith saying that "in view of
the result of today's race," he withdrew his protest against
Rainbow.

A few minutes later along came a message from Vanderbilt

saying in the fewest possible words that he withdrew his protest against *Endeavour*.

The news came as no great surprise, for a couple of hours earlier word had mysteriously filtered through from *Vita*, Sopwith's yacht, that he was going to withdraw the protest. Obviously if he withdrew it didn't make any difference whether Vanderbilt protested or not, as he had won the race anyhow and a pushing of the protest would only have been one rather unpleasant item to add to the archives of the New York Yacht Club.

So the series was settled, and one by one motors began to rumble as yachts slid out of the harbor in the moonlight and headed for New York, Boston and other points. The impression here is that the challengers are going away from Newport pretty mad at the whole America's Cup business, although perhaps not as mad as they went away the last time the Royal Yacht Squadron challenged in 1895, when the famous "Dunraven controversy" arose. But the majority of even the British yachtsmen here will admit that their challenger didn't by any stretch of the imagination prove title to the America's Cup.

Endeavour, designed by Charles E. Nicholson, is acknowledged among American yachtsmen to be the fastest Class J sloop that ever raced for the America's Cup—not excepting *Rainbow*, or even *Yankee*, which did not race for the cup because *Rainbow* beat her in the trials. *Endeavour's* part amateur crew was not as smart as the crack forecastle crowd of *Rainbow*, but it was at least as good as the professional crew of *Shamrock V*, four years ago, and did rather better than expected, by and large.

Where *Endeavour* fell down fundamentally was in her racing strategy and helmsmanship, and this Sopwith, who sailed the boat and was in full command, will have to take on his own shoulders, a fact which he will probably be the first to admit when the smoke of battle clears away. His statement to the press today confirms this belief. Sopwith has had comparatively few years of yachting experience, and it will take a man riper in the knowledge of racing yachts to beat Mike Vanderbilt, Sherman Hoyt, Frank Paine, Jack Parkington, Starling Burgess and Zenas Bliss, who make up *Rainbow's* afterguard, with such a professional crew as that headed by Captain George Monsell and Harry Klifve, mate, to help them.

Some of the American yachtsmen at the series—men to whom a fine yacht is something to love and admire—have been really bitter at Sopwith for not winning the cup. The reason for this feeling was well expressed by one yachtsman who remarked today, "A man who'll murder a fine yacht like that doesn't deserve to win anything."

They are no bitterer, however, than Sopwith, judging by his remark tonight against the race committee, which seem to be the sacrificial offering of the series. Edmund Lang, E. Vail Stebbins and Clinton MacKenzie have put in a long summer of hard work and have done everything possible, since the challenge first came over here last fall, to insure fair and even racing. Last Sunday they were called upon to make a decision that was bound to be unpleasant no matter how it turned out.

They handled that situation as they felt was the fairest way to handle it, and they have been criticized ever since by hordes of people who did not happen to have the complete knowledge of the situation which they had and which, incidentally, they haven't passed along to anybody else, even yet. If they ever do, even Sopwith may feel quite differently toward them.

A late evening rumor concerning the fate of the *Endeavour*

has been rolling around town to the effect that Sopwith had agreed to sell her to Gerard Lambert, owner of *Vanitie*, for $100,000. This has not been confirmed, nor has a conflicting rumor to the effect that Lambert plans to buy *Yankee*, *Rainbow's* defeated rival of the trial series. Lambert has done a great deal for Sopwith, in taking out *Vanitie* to act as *Endeavour's* sparring partner for several weeks before the races and in other ways, and he could probably buy the British sloop if he wanted her.

On the other hand, *Endeavour* wouldn't be eligible as a defender in case the America's Cup has to be defended again shortly, because she is British built. *Yankee* would. It is anybody's guess, as is the rumor, that C. R. Fairey, Sopwith's racing rival in England and present owner of the *Shamrock V*, might challenge for the cup within a year or two.

The race today gave another demonstration of the fact that *Endeavour* is a fast boat slowly sailed. She beat *Rainbow* 1 minute 8 seconds reaching out to the first mark of the triangle, and she covered the last ten miles, running home under spinnakers, 1 minute 52 seconds faster than *Rainbow*, but in between on the second ten-mile leg Sopwith threw the race away by carrying the wrong headsails at first and by breaking one of the cardinal principles of match-race procedure, which is to keep your opponent covered when you are ahead of him.

Westbrook Pegler

The most controversial writer in America today is West-
brook Pegler, arch-enemy of hypocrisy in high places and
skulduggery in Labor, with a capital L. He got that way,
made his first muscles, beating the brains out of sport pho-
nies with his trenchant typewriter.

Pegler covered all major sporting events for many years
and, in fact, was writing a daily sport column for the Chicago Tribune syndicate when he went to the Scripps-Howard chain as a general commentator and hell-raiser. Fight
promoters, baseball owners and football coaches gave three
loud, fervent cheers when he moved to the other side of the
street and directed his acidulous attention to presidents and
kings, congressmen and cabinet members, racketeers and assorted no-goods.

Regardless of personal opinion concerning Pegler's attitude, philosophy and technique, everyone must agree on one
point: The guy can write. The following pieces are purest
Pegler and an explanation for using two of his articles seems
to be in order.

To appreciate fully "The Cast" and "The Harpoon," you
should know a story that does not take too long in the telling. The Nazis hollered bloody murder and made diplomatic representations to the State Department when "The
Cast" appeared. The State Department got in touch with the
Scripps-Howard people who, in turn, asked Pegler to apolo-
gize for his outburst.

Pegler wrote his apology, "The Harpoon," two days later.

The Nazis made no protest. They were very happy to forget the whole thing.

THE EDITOR

CASTING THE HARPOON

BY

Westbrook Pegler

(NEW YORK WORLD-TELEGRAM)

THE CAST

Garmisch-Partenkirchen, Germany, February 17, 1936.

EVERYTHING IS SAID to happen for the best, and whatever anyone may think of the propriety of our taking part in the political, military and sporting activities here in Garmisch, Thursday's experience should show a net profit to the United States.

Such shoving around as the populace received at the hands of the young strong-armed squad of Hitler bodyguards appropriately, though ingenuously, named Blackguards, was never seen in the United States, even in the heydey of Jimmy Walker or Huey P. Long.

American athletes and casual correspondents, journalists of all nations sent to cover the program of sports known as the winter Olympics, saw a perfect demonstration of military dictatorship, and there were those among the throng who agreed that if this is what Huey was promoting in Louisiana they'll be glad to have none of the same.

The Dictator held ten thousand people in the grandstand of the rink where the figure skating took place, although he was ready to take his leave, and before the event they paved his way with such idolatrous care that it made no difference whether anyone else reached the scene or not.

Thousands of people were herded this way and that in the snow who had bought tickets or were trying to buy tickets to see the sport event and thousands were shunted off and away from the inclosure by long cordons of officious, beefy young Nazis in various kinds of uniforms whose only duty was to flatter and accommodate the house painter who became the head man of the third Reich. It was a magnificent display of strong-arm authority wholly corroborating the old tradition that the German people's favorite sport is to be shoved around by men in uniform.

The road approaching the stadium was held clear by a double cordon of troops in brown uniforms who are supposed not to be soldiers but a civilian labor corps, although they dress alike, with a swastika worn on the left arm, and perform deeds with shovels instead of guns.

At the head of the line near the stadium the Black Guards took their stand. They are a special corps, like the King's Life Guard in England, except that they're all young, athletic, tall and of charming demeanor. They wear fine black uniforms, which flatter the youthful figure of a man, and wear on the left sleeve in silver embroidery the name "Adolf Hitler." Today they were wearing black skin hats and the very atmosphere was vibrant with protection and a sense of the importance of the leader's presence.

Your correspondent has seen in his time such men as Edison, Ford, Shaw, Einstein, Mussolini, Clemenceau and

Eugene Debs, and therefore might have been a trifle slow to take spark. It seemed a secondary experience, not to say an anti-climax, to witness Adolf Hitler, but to the German government which had invited the athletes of the world to Garmisch in the name of sport and human brotherhood it was a tremendous affair.

The Olympics were of secondary importance, if any. This was the Dictator's day, and it's a good thing for the Americans present that this was so, because they have nothing important to learn from the athletes but much to learn about absolute authority in government.

You must picture this town. Ten thousand swastikas stir faintly in the light winter wind along the streets of Garmisch-Partenkirchen. The flag is the color of blood, with a white circle containing an ancient device in black. The swastika flies from every house and store and some homes are adorned with long ribbons of little pennants strung together from window to window, fifty or a hundred swastikas in a row.

Soldiers are everywhere in Garmisch-Partenkirchen, where the athletes of many nations are competing on ice and snow and in the brotherhood of sports. There are soldiers in the old German field gray, soldiers of the labor corps in brown and special soldiers of the bodyguard in black and silver. All the soldiers wear the swastika, and it's seen again from the red postoffice trucks and the army transports, which go tearing through the streets off into the mountains splashing melted slush out of the narrow footway.

This motor transport gives a strange suggestion of war in the little mountain resort where sportsmen are drawn together in a great demonstration of friendship. When the United States held winter Olympics at Lake Placid the only armed force in sight was a small detachment of New York

State Police, with service pistols and cartridge belts, and they were there only to regulate traffic.

I do not know why there are so many troops and so much army transport at a great demonstration of international friendship in Garmisch and I hesitate to inquire unless that be construed as an effort to obtain military information. I was not interested in military affairs but only in sport and the great international Olympic ideal of friendship through chivalrous competition conducted in a spirit of comradeship.

I know the ideal by heart, having heard it many times in speeches and read it in statements by Mr. Avery Brundage, president of the American Athletic Union, who brought American teams over to this armed camp, and by other idealists in the Olympic organization who join Mr. Brundage in the enjoyment of official courtesies and flattery delivered in the elegant style of the Old World.

We ought to treat Mr. Brundage's vanity better at home. Perhaps an official dinner at the White House would equalize some of the honor which the Germans have shown him in their campaign to overpower the boycott movement in America and procure the participation of American athletes, who are not very important in sports but the most important political factor in the present tournament.

The big army trucks which roar up the hills are painted in camouflage loaded with soldiers. The little officers' cars built on the design of the old-fashioned lowneck hack are camouflaged, too, and the scene is strongly reminiscent of the zone behind the front when divisions were being rushed to the sector of the next offensive.

Up to this time no artillery has been seen. I take it that the brotherhood games of the winter Olympics run under the auspices of Nazi sportsmanship are only infantry action up to this writing. But they may be saving their heavy stuff tanks and bombers for the summer program.

Well, I'm glad I was here for this particular day and I insist that as matters turned out it was a good thing to send an American team. If they didn't learn their lessons this afternoon they're beyond teaching. At home we've never found it necessary to mobilize an army for a sport event, and even Huey himself when he went on tour with his football team carried only a few selected gunmen whose function was strictly retributive in the end.

THE HARPOON

Garmisch-Partenkirchen, Germany, February 19, 1936.

It is going to be pretty hard to do this, but right is right, as President Harding said, and I feel that I have done the Nazis a serious injustice, so this is my apology.

Two days ago these dispatches reported that the quaint little Bavarian town of Garmisch-Partenkirchen has the appearance of an army headquarters a few miles behind the Western Front during an important troop movement. That was wrong, and I can only plead that I was honestly mistaken and the victim of my own ignorance.

Those weren't troops at all but merely peace-loving German workmen in their native dress, and those weren't army lorries which went growling through the streets squirting the slush onto the sidewalks but delivery wagons carrying beer and wieners and kraut to the humble homes of the mountaineers in the folds of the hills. It is a relief to know this and a pleasure to be able to report that, after all, the

Germans did not conduct their winter Olympics in an atmosphere of war, which would have been very injurious to the Olympic ideal of peace through sporting competition.

My information comes from a kindly Bavarian cobbler in a long black overcoat who was standing in a cordon of cobblers along the main street Sunday afternoon during Adolf Hitler's visit to town to pronounce over the closing ceremonies the benison of a great protector of the world's peace.

"Are you a soldier?" I often inquired, for I had been told that in Germany strangers often mistake for soldiers people who have nothing to do with the military establishment.

"Why me?" he asked. "No, I'm a cobbler. All of us in the black costume are cobblers."

"Then why do you dress in military uniform?" I persisted.

"That's where you are wrong," said my cobbler friend. "This isn't a military uniform. It's a shoemaker's uniform, and this big clothes stabber in the scabbard at my side, which may look like a bayonet to you, is merely a little knife which we use when we cobble."

"But," I asked, "why do you march in military formation through the streets of international friendship?"

The cobbler controlled his impatience and explained that for hundreds of years the cobblers of Bavaria had worn the same distinctive costume, which looks military to the uninitiated. And why, then, do they march like troops and form imposing cordons around the streets to hold back the crowds during the Olympic Games?

The answer is that they don't really march at all. They just walk in step in columns of fours, because they like to walk that way. And it is an old custom of theirs to form cordons of military appearance along the curbs and just stand there by the hour for pleasure.

"But what about those other troops in the brown uniforms?"

"Troops?" said my friend. "Those are not troops. Those are gardeners who have always worn brown suits, which seem to be military but aren't. Just peace-loving gardeners is what they are, and those blades which you see hanging from their belts are not bayonets, either, but pruning knives. It is an old Bavarian tradition.

"They, too, like to go for long walks in columns of fours and drill with spades, as soldiers sometimes drill with rifles, but they are not soldiers, I assure you, my friend. They are just kind-hearted gardeners who wouldn't hurt a potato bug. It is interesting to see them strike spades when they come to the end of a stroll in columns of fours. To some people unacquainted with our local customs they may seem to be performing a military drill with their spades, but nothing could be further from the truth.

"I hope it never comes to the attention of our Herr 'Putz' Hanfstaengel, of the Foreign Propaganda Department, that you mistook our cobblers and gardeners for soldiers on the scene of the Olympic Games, because if there is anything that annoys him it is to see Germany accused of militarism in foreign papers."

Thus far two of my military corps had been explained away as harmless and altogether peaceful workmen, but I thought I had him when I mentioned the men in the gray uniforms, also with scabbards at their sides, who seemed to be regular infantry. He laughed uproariously at this.

"Oh, those!" he said. "Those aren't infantry. How could you make that mistake? Those are plasterers, and those tin hats which you undoubtedly mistook for shrapnel helmets are an ancient tradition of Bavarian plasterers. Sometimes the plaster falls down, and it would knock them for a lot of loops if they didn't wear something for protection. Wait till I tell the foreman of the plasterers—I suppose you have been calling him the general—that you mistook his boys for soldiers. He will laugh himself dizzy."

Still, there were other men all dressed alike in blue gray, with wings embroidered on their clothing. Undoubtedly those would be soldiers of the aviation branch, wouldn't they? But my friend the peace-loving cobbler in the black suit, which looked very military but wasn't, enjoyed another pleasant hysteric over that one, too. Those, he said, were poultry farmers, and the wings on their collars merely represented the harmless fowl in their barnyards.

It is not easy to be proven wrong in a serious matter. I had seen as many as 5,000, perhaps even 10,000, men in apparel which seemed to be that of soldiers, and had recklessly accused the peace-loving Nazi regime of converting the winter Olympics into a military demonstration, which would have been a grave breach of manners. My troops had been explained into gentle civilians, and the marching to which I had referred had turned out to be nothing but an habitual method of going for nice long walks.

The motor trucks still seemed questionable, however, for they were painted in camouflage like the lorries used in the war.

"Yes, I know," my friend the cobbler explained, "but we have painted our motor trucks in eccentric designs and colors for hundreds of years. It makes them look nicer."

A foreman of the cobblers came by at the moment, and my friend put his hand to his cap in a gesture which resembled a military salute. I asked him about this, but he said he was only shading his eyes.

The Nazi Press Bureau released the other day a quotation from a dispatch to *The New York Times* insisting that anyone reporting the presence of troops at the Olympic Games was a liar. I guess that's me, but the mistake was natural, as you can see, and I hope pardonable. When thousands of men seem to march but don't in clothing and tin hats which seem to be military uniforms but aren't, and carry harmless utensils which appear to be bayonets, any stranger is likely to make the same mistake.

OLYMPIAN HEIGHTS

BY

J. P. Abramson

(NEW YORK HERALD TRIBUNE)

Berlin, Aug. 5, 1936.

AMID PELTING RAIN, America maintained its stunning victory percentage procession, unparalleled in the post-war era, by sweeping again all three track and field championships decided within the packed inclosure of Reich Sportsfeld this fifth day of the Olympic games, shattering Olympic records in all events as Great Britain scored its first triumph by winning the 50-kilometer walk in record time.

Jesse Owens, the Ohio State flyer, concluded his awe-inspiring deeds by sprinting the fastest 200 meters ever run around one turn, gaining his third title in three days and annihilating his own one-day-old Olympic record by four-tenths of a second with a clocking of 0:20.7. In so doing he becomes the first Olympic triple winner since Paavo Nurmi, the Flying Finn, completed a triple in the 1924 games, and the first American to fashion three victories in thirty-two years.

For the second time in these games the throng saw American Negroes finish one-two in a sprint, this time Matthew Robinson, of California, chasing his countryman home, four yards behind, with the Hollander, Martin Osendarp, third;

Paul Haenni, of Switzerland, fourth; Lee Orr, of Canada, fifth and Wijand van Beveren, of Holland, sixth.

Kenneth Carpenter and Gordon (Slinger) Dunn, the giant Californians, added another one-two unexpectedly, in the discus throw, beating back the challenge of the world record holder, Germany's Willie Schroeder, who placed fifth.

None of the several 170-footers in the international field could reach that mark during the stress of Olympic competition, but Carpenter, always marvelously consistent, whirled the Grecian plate 165 feet 9-16 inches. He broke John Anderson's Olympic record by more than three feet on his next to last throw, after barely qualifying for the final on his last effort.

The German populace, dismayed by the turn of events that gave Americans the oak tree and laurel in this event, tried in vain to spur their favorite on, tens of thousands chanting in unison to Schroeder: "Take your discus in your hand, throw it for your Fatherland."

The most dramatic moment of all remained for the bitter end. Delayed by the afternoon storm and completed after nightfall in an eerie light of the Olympic torch and a battery of floodlights, the pole vault developed into the heralded duel between America and Japan, repeating the battle of Los Angeles.

In awful conditions that challenged the mettle of competitors to the full, Earle Meadows, slim, dark-haired Texan from the University of Southern California, emerged supreme with the Olympic title for sub-stratosphere flight of 14 feet 2 15-16 inches.

He grazed the cross-piece with his arm while descending on his second try at that height, landing with a shock in the raisin-packed sandpit while the bar teetered for a moment on its pegs and stayed aloft.

Two Japanese vaulters, Shuhei Nishida and Sueo Oye, and Meadows' classmate, Bill Sefton, who remained in the fight at this height, couldn't match Meadows after five hours of intense struggle, continued two hours after the last track event. The vaulting was made harder for the athletes because the International Amateur Athletic Federation refused to heed the protests of Americans and Japanese to provide the sawdust landing bed to which they were accustomed.

Forty or fifty thousand of the sellout crowd remained standing in the wet stands to see it through. They had read in the German press this morning that the whistling proscribed here was an accepted American manner of cheering. So they alternated with a siren-like blast of whistling for the Americans and a thunder of hand clapping and cheers for the Nipponese.

Nishida and Oye tied for second place in the vault-off and declined to continue, settling the second-place tie between themselves, with Nishida getting the runner-up prize, Oye placing third and Sefton fourth, all tied at 13 feet 11¼ inches. Sefton, in the morning rain before 90,000 spectators, had barely qualified, clearing 12 feet 6 inches on his last try. Bill Graber placed fifth and eleven others tied for sixth.

The afternoon trials in other events saw the American mile trio, Glenn Cunningham, Gene Venzke and Archie San Romani, qualify for the twelve-man final in the 1500-meter run tomorrow, along with the defending champion, Italy's Luigi Beccali, and the New Zealander, Jack Lovelock, as England's pride, Stanley Wooderson, a 4:10 miler who has beaten Lovelock consistently for two years, but handicapped by a muscle pulled today, failed to qualify.

Cunningham, running easily, took the fastest heat in a tie with Eric Ny, of Sweden, in 3:54.8. Venzke, pocketed in the backstretch, came on from fifth place in the straightaway to lead Jerry Cornes, of England, and Lovelock in the slowest time, but San Romani provided the fireworks in the final trial.

Last of the eleven in the heat for half the distance and apparently going nowhere, ninth with a lap to go and seventh on the last turn, the little Kansan rocketed home in second place on the strength of a blinding 55-second lap. The American contingent almost had heart failure from this performance. Wooderson slowed up in the last sixty yards, finishing ninth.

All three American high hurdlers won their first heats, Forrest (Spec) Towns at 0:14.5, Fritz Pollard Jr. next, with the Englishman, Donald Finlay, in 0:14.7 and Roy Staley, also a winner. Towns, unbeaten all year, is rated as a sure thing in tomorrow's final with Italy almost a sole foreign threat.

Americans were nowhere in the fifty-kilo walk, which started and finished in the stadium and took the contenders on a sightseeing trip around Gruenwald Forest and along Lake Havel. England's Harold Hector Whitlock, taking the lead at the twentieth mile, won with plenty to spare in 4:30:41.4, beating the record and retaining the title for Albion. The Swiss, Arthur-Tell Schwab, was second, Bubenko, of Latvia, was third, and the first American to finish was Albert L. Mangin, of Lowell, Mass., who placed twenty-first.

There is no denying that this monopolistic demonstration of the omnipotent Americans is not being received with the greatest joy here. Europeans generally are tired of the unending American victories through the Olympic years and one can not blame them. America now has won eight of the twelve men's titles decided, Germany has taken two and Finland and England one each. There are eleven more men's track and field events and Americans are favored to win five, and perhaps six, if our milers can outrun Lovelock and Beccali tomorrow.

In six of the eight American men's victories, Olympic records have been made. Rain and cold have affected them less than all the others, for they have done as well as they could have done in perfect weather.

There has hardly been weather here that Owens would have chosen, for Negroes generally go best in intense heat. His performances have been unbelievable. In four straight days he has made fourteen consecutive appearances, running four heats each in the 100 and 200 meters and jumping six times, breaking Olympic records a total of nine times, equalling them twice.

In the century, he returned 0:10.3, 0:10.2, 0:10.4 and 0:10.3 against a world record of 0:10.3. In the 200-meter final, he returned 0:21.1 twice, 0:21.3 and 0:21.7 against the Olympic record of 0:21.2. He bettered Olympic records in all five of his measured leaps. The world is, or should be, willing to concede that never has it seen a sprinter-jumper like him.

He won his semi-final easily, as always, while Robinson tied his best mark of 0:21.1 in the other semi-final as Bobby Packard, the Georgia freshman, ran fourth and was eliminated. In the final a mean cross-wind swirled about under a black canopy of clouds and rain descended as Owens broke the tape in majestic style. Running in the third lane of the staggered start, he rushed to the front immediately, whirled into the straightaway more than a yard in front of the field and widened the gap with every stride, running stronger than ever when many thought he would begin to show the strain of his heroic efforts in four days.

Robinson closed strongly in the last fifty yards to beat Osendarp for the place by two yards, clocked in 0:21.1. No sprinter ever had broken 0:21 flat around a turn until Owens did it today. He may have been helped or not by the swirling wind—it was difficult to say—but he ran on a heavy track.

Dunn led in the discus throw from his first heave until Carpenter pulled up in the late stages to beat him, sending the Italian, Giorgio Oberwager, coached by the American, Boyd Comstock, into third place.

Sixteen vaulters cleared 13 feet 1 inch, but only the three Americans and the two Japanese cleared 13 feet 7¾ inches, Sefton making it on his last leap. At the next height, close to fourteen feet, Sefton and Nishida cleared on their first tries, Meadows and Oye on their second while Graber, urged on by his teammates, narrowly failed in a darkness in which he could not see the bar clearly.

Bundled in blankets between vaults, the four carried on in mounting excitement. After Meadows went over he had the agonizing suspense of waiting to see whether any one would match him. All three of his rivals almost made it, knocking down the bar on their descent with their arms or bodies.

Chancellor Adolf Hitler again was a spectator today, with Crown Prince Umberto of Italy as his guest, both sitting through the early showers in raincoats.

YANKEE DOODLE WENT TO TOWN

Sid Mercer

(NEW YORK AMERICAN) NOVEMBER 4, 1936.

THE SPIRIT OF THE old Irish-American Athletic Club lived again for a brief but vivid moment the other night at Dinty Moore's.

Some world renowned survivors of that famous organization gathered informally to fight over again the battles of Celtic Park and Travers Island and the Olympic wars of the last thirty years.

They were a stalwart band, those Irish-Americans. Their club flourished from the turn of the century until the World War—years of keen rivalry on track and field between the Irish and the New York A. C.

As a fitting climax Walter C. Kelly, the "Virginia Judge," told the story of the sensational finish of the 1908 Olympic Marathon in London.

He spoke—shall we say, feelingly?—with his hand on the shoulder of Johnny Hayes, the winner of that race. We first heard the Kelly version many years ago but it grows better as the retrospect deepens.

Near the head of the table sat Matt McGrath, a fine figure of a man. Matt is now a deputy police inspector in New York. Your glance, roaming down the table, took in Big Jim Rosenberger, who won great honors as a sprinter 25

219

years ago; silver-thatched Dick Remer, champion and Olympic walker; Abel Kiviat, former champion miler; Hayes, and Mel Sheppard, a distinguished gray-haired veteran. Sheppard was America's great middle distance man. He brought home three championships from the 1908 Olympics.

After the "red mike and violets"—corned beef and cabbage to you—and some lilting Irish songs by Morton Downey, the boys were in the proper mood for the entrance of Kelly. And the "Judge" was in the mood, too. He fell upon the neck of Johnny Hayes and presently they got him up to tell the story.

"I haven't seen this little guy in ten years," he said, his arm around Johnny's shoulders. "He gave me one of the greatest thrills of my life.

"I was playing vaudeville in England in 1908, and on the day of the Olympic Marathon in London, I was the box guest of Sir Thomas Lipton and Lord Dewar, God rest their souls. We sat not more than twenty feet from the royal box at Shepards Bush Stadium.

"The stadium held 90,000, 60,000 of them Britishers. The American crowd numbered about 4,000, mostly college boys from Yale and Harvard. The runners started from Windsor Castle. England had twelve entries. Nobody had heard of Hayes. They announced the runners were nearing the stadium. Dorando, of Italy, leading and Mike Heffernan, of South Africa, second. No mention was made of Hayes.

"Dorando staggered in under the stadium ramp. He still had 385 yards to go. The first foul was committed when he turned the wrong way and an English policeman turned him back. He went 60 or 70 yards and collapsed.

"Then up through the ramp came a little fellow trotting like a coach dog. Who was he? Two Britishers back of me put their binoculars on him. 'I cawn't recognize him,' said one. "'Ere, 'arry, you take the glasses,' 'arry peered a moment and then smote his forehead and exclaimed: 'God's truth, it's a Yankee.'

"I began to root and one of the men behind me fetched me a whack over the shoulders with his binoculars.

"'Sit down, you bloody Yankee,' he commanded.

"'Sit down yourself, you so-and-so,' I yelled. 'Where are your Englishmen? They ought to be in. Washington taught you Britishers how to run.' He sat down.

"Men ran out on the track and surrounded Dorando. They got him up and he ran about 100 yards and again collapsed. By this time the identity of the American runner had been discovered.

"'It's Hyes,' those Englishmen moaned.

"Dorando was carried across the finish line. Then came Hayes with his coach dogtrot, Heffernan and Forshaw, of St. Louis. Johnny went off the track with 60,000 Britishers booing him. But as he passed the American section, those college boys were singing 'It's A Grand Old Flag' and you could hear them above the roar of the crowd in its unsportsmanlike demonstration. I felt proud of my country then.

"Well, England was sunk that night. On the way home I put on an English accent and asked a newsboy who had won.

"'I 'ates to tell you, sir,' he said, 'but it was a bleddy Yenkee by the name o' Hyes.'"

Johnny interrupted the Judge at this point. "Do you remember that night along the Strand? Dorando was reported dying in a hospital, and you were reported cleaning up English waiters at the Savoy."

"Do I remember," roared Kelly. "I had three good men with me to help settle those arguments. They were Ralph Rose, the big shot-putter; Kid McCoy and Jimmy Britt. We were arrested three times that night."

MARATHON

BY
Austen Lake

(BOSTON AMERICAN) APRIL 19, 1938.

THE HUMAN PICTURE of today's B.A.A. Marathon is not the broad panorama of front runners as they go twitching and squirming away from the herd of untalented hacks. It is the milling, ant-heap scene just before the race when 200 leather-skinned men overflow the frame farmhouse at Hopkinton and climb into their race-lingerie for the long drudge—the most laborsome form of athletic endeavor known to man. No sport scene on earth is like it.

There is the commingled stench of perspiration, the sick sweet of rubbing oils and kitchen smells, as unstandardized people from an opium dream harness themselves for the horrors. Solid, earthbound types most of them, men who might have modeled for Millet's painting, "The Man With the Hoe." Skins of every shade, from licorice black to whiskey brown to skimmed milk. All shapes from scrawny runt to classic Greek. Kids with peach fuzz cheeks. Bald and silver-topped elders. Fat boys with watermelon middles, skinny ones with pipe-rail legs.

Yes, the real scene of the Marathon is the gypsy carnival in the Tebeau barnyard, where relatives and friends of the athletic artisans crowd like anchovies in a pâté-tin, plain-faced folk with high hopes in their eyes and wearing holiday homespuns and unaccustomed starch. Wholesome people near to nature—a posthole digger, a brick mason, roofers, moulders, carpenters; awkward types who behave with shy courtesy and are come with mild-mannered wives and fresh-scrubbed children.

There is a social rating even here in sport's most plebeian event. The veteran road horses like Clarence DeMar, Dave Komonen, Johnny Kelley and Gerard Cote—high rankers of former Marathons—move apart from the pack, herding with athletic equals and ignoring the unknowns or viewing them bleakly—royalty regarding the steaming masses.

On the grassy knoll outside the frame dwelling where B.A.A. officials register the athletes and listen for heart-leaks gather the assorted oddities of the race, cousins to the rubber-skinned circus people—men like Johnny "Cigar" Conners and Bill "Tobacco" Enos who flatfoot the 25 miles puffing stogies and making faces at the crowd. Or Peter Foley, the 86-year-old granddad who starts at sun-up and finishes by moonlight. Or 65-year-old Al Monteverdi and a swarm of perennial failures who possess none of the athletic graces save a restless itch to make their bones go.

It has been going on for 42 years, the biggest and freest sport spectacle on earth and watched by half a million spectators who line the way between Lucky Rock manor and Exeter Street to catch brief glimpses of the runners' convulsions and hear the pompous honk of official motor cars.

The most human side of the scene is the roadside start at Hopkinton at the instant the pack comes clawing and clattering along the bush-bordered lane, wedged like hysterical sheep. Then for a few miles the unknown hacks sprint to the front and go sailing away as though making history. And always some shaggy type pulls far to the front, enjoying his moment of bogus glory and prompting the

crowd at Framingham Center to thumb their programs to
identify his number.

For here is the secret of the Marathon's charm, the annual
big moment in the lives of plain people, a momentary escape
from obscurity, a social leg-up in their communities and a
remote, wispy chance for celebrity. They thirst for a flash
of glamour in lives that are filled with year-round simplici-
ties, dreaming that some chancy freak of form will drive
their creaky shins home to a sprig of laurel, one of the silver
medals or, at least, a plate of ice cream.

Trailing the processions, far in the rear, come the Red
Cross ambulances with Dr. Walter Kendall and his lady
aides, whose job is to hoist the stomach-sick athletes aboard
and snap ammonia crackers under the nostrils or dose them
with "eagle-soup." For always several dozens of Marathon
addicts turn up for the race and hoof only a few miles before
turning tourist and seeing the rest of the race from the
tailboard.

But many others, like Clovis Bourdelais of Brockton and
Martin Silver of Medford, plod along behind the leaders
like a comet-tail of disembodied spirits, seeing faces swim
past and listening to the pound of their pulses. These are
the gallant, unsung heroes of the mad cavalcade, men who
swallow their gas bubbles and stagger in after the event is
done.

They are symbols of plain American life and the Marathon
is a thumbnail measure of human hope. The few front
runners reap glory and the prizes. The inferior breeds
bounce a few spendthrift steps and become passengers for
the rest of the journey. And the great body of undistin-
guished but resolute plodders keep churning away, clutching
their ribs below the heart and surviving on wind, courage
and determination.

The refreshment cars stay up ahead, handing out lemon halves, dousing the leaders with jugs of water and leaving the rear-running hacks to lick dry lips and swab their burning eye-sockets with their own knuckles. And long after the police escort has conducted the Johnny Kelleys, the Gerard Cotes, the Mel Porters, the Les Pawsons and the vanguard into Exeter Street and the hallelujah howls and camera flashes are over, the unknown artisans will wobble home with nothing for their day but nervous palsy, numb knees and skinned heels. Stout Fellas!

HOCKEY HOOLIGAN

BY
Edward Burns

(CHICAGO TRIBUNE) JANUARY 8, 1939.

THE LIFE STORY OF Johnny Gottselig, veteran left forward of the world champion Blackhawks, properly may be divided into two chapters. One may be called a press agent's version, or "My Boyhood in Darkest Russia," and the other the less dramatic or more factual which might be called, "My Life as I Have Lived It."

Johnny currently rates a life story more than ever before. He led all scorers in the Stanley cup series last spring and in the first half of this regular season has been constantly at the top of the list of the National Hockey League's leading scorers.

Having no desire to hold out on any of the Old Subscribers, Taxpayers, or just plain hockey fans, we propose here to give you a touch of Russia then veer, with great dexterity, to Canada, the United States, and Chicago.

Johnny and the Blackhawk press agent, Joseph C. Farrell, who has outlived an even dozen Blackhawk managers as an employe of Maj. Frederic McLaughlin, owner of the Hawks, are here at our deskside, Johnny wearing a rather honest mien and Mr. Farrell with two magnificent Russian wolfhounds which he says are just a couple of the pack of fifty which Johnny keeps in his room in a west side hotel—he's that crazy about anything that springs from his native Russia.

We now are about to interview Gottselig:

We: Were you really born in Russia, Johnny?

John: Yes, sir, 25 or 31 or 32 years ago.

We: Where in Russia, Johnny?

John: Near Odessa, but I never can remember whether there are two dees or two esses in Odessa, so I always say I was born in Omsk.

[At this point Press Agent Farrell is beaming widely. It was indeed he who found out there is a town in Russia named Omsk.]

We: What is your real name, Johnny?

John: Ianovich Nicholai Lipescu Gottsoff.

We: Ah, just a touch of the Rumanian. Well, anyhow, Ianovich, tell us something of your life in Russia.

John: Vell, you zee it was dees way——

We: Just leave the Russian accent to Farrell, John. Give it to us in straight Canadian and we'll supply the color later.

John: Well, my father, whose name was Alexovich, was one of the original Vodka boatmen.

[With this reply Johnny shot a quick glance at Press Agent Farrell, who grinned his approval.]

We: How did you happen to take up hockey, Johnny?

Johnny: Well, it was late in the fall and I was sitting one evening on the front steppes watching the Czar's soldiers march by. I tell you it was maddening. Boots! Boots! Boots! sliding up and down again. The monotonous roll of the Czar's doldrums sickened me. I was very, very unhappy, for that day I had been fishing and the caviars weren't biting.

We: You were about to tell us about how you happened to take up hockey in a section which has plenty of ice but no hockey, Johnny.

John: After I had come in with no caviars on my string I went into our Russian bath and, after shoveling coal and peat to one side, washed out a samovar, or sprinkling can, which had been placed there by my dear aunt, Petrushka. I can see Aunt Petrushka now—her clear blue eyes, sparkling with kindness, yet reflecting a shadow of the suffering suffered that time she went to Siberia to work in a comb factory.

We: Very interesting, Johnny. But about the hockey start.

John: After I had finished my bath I slipped on my little silken cossack, pulled on my little leather droshkies with the red tops and the hobnailed soles, and then, noticing that I still had on no pantaloons, I wrapped a balalaika about me and went out to sit on the front steppes.

We: Which, Johnny, brings you to exactly where you were just thirty-seven minutes ago. Now, please, about the hockey start. If you don't snap into it faster you're going back to the rink and find you are working for another new manager.

[With this crack the Russian wolfhounds which Farrell was holding became restless and enmeshed the Hawk press agent in a hopeless tangle of leashes.]

John [ignoring Farrell's plight]: I sat on the front steppes until I saw my father approaching. At first, I could not make out what he was carrying, but he was carrying something. As he got nearer I perceived it was an ikon, or broken oar, from his Vodka boat. The way pappy's whiskers were bristling I thought at first he was sore about something.

We: For goodness' sake, what happened then, Johnny?

John: Well, as my old man came up to the steppes where I was sitting dressed in my little silken cos——

We: What did the old man do with that broken oar?

John: He tossed it to me, saying in purest Russian of the Romanoffs, 'Here, son, be whittling out from this a hockey stick.' So every day I whittled and whittled, some days longer than others. At last the stick was finished. The rest is an old,

old story. How a Russian coffee taster heard about the little boy in darkest Russia who practiced and practiced for 20 years with no one to practice with. How that old coffee sipper, Boris, cabled Maj. McLaughlin about me. Need I now repeat how the major signed me and how I have played only for him during my entire major league career?

[The dogs still are playing hell with Farrell and now Gottselig is trying to help him. Which gives us a chance to set down some lines on that second chapter.]

John Gottselig's father, Albert, of Baden, Germany, and his mother, a Weber from Bayern, Germany, "took up land" in a German settlement near Odessa, called Klosterdorf. They tried to make a living out of a vineyard but later learned of a more promising frontier, in Regina, Sask. So two months after their son John was born, they left Russia and set sail for Canada. For more than 30 years the Gottselig home has been in Regina, where Johnny, like all the kids in Regina, grew up with a hockey stick in his hand. Johnny's mother lives in Regina, and he writes her regularly, in German. And in the summer time they live under one roof and converse in German only.

We: And now, Mr. Farrell, don't you think it's about time for you to get them rushing woof hounds out of here?

THE DARK HORSEMAN

BY

Frank Graham

(NEW YORK SUN) MAY 6, 1939.

THE SKY HAD CLEARED and the sun was shining in the paddock at Jamaica. The vans were bringing in the horses that are stabled at Belmont and Aqueduct. Early arrivals were walking about and in the open windows of the jockeys' house the jocks sat talking and looking out and listening to the radio that blared just behind them.

"Did you hear about it?" a man asked.

"Yes," another man said. "I went looking for a priest but I couldn't find one and when I got back he was dead."

"I was there," somebody else said. "I was there when the doctor put that thing on him and said he was gone."

"Too bad," the first man said. "I knew Charlie Carroll when he was with Pittsburgh Phil."

"Is the horse going to run?" somebody asked.

"Yes. That's what I heard."

In the receiving barn Charlie Carroll, who was about seventy years old and had been on the turf since he was a kid, had taken the bandages off his horse, Rosarian, which was entered in the first race, and had slumped over, dead. Bad heart the doctor said.

Hadn't anybody told Charlie his heart was bad?

"Sure. He knew it. A doctor told him to go away some place and take it easy."

Go away some place and take it easy? A man who had been on the turf for fifty years? Who remembered Bennings and Sheepshead Bay and Coney Island and Morris Park and old Washington Park in Chicago? Who had seen all the great horses for fifty years and known all the great figures on the race track? who had been a stable boy and a rubber and a betting commissioner? And had owned and trained horses? Go away some place and take it easy? When the horses were running at Jamaica...and he had the horse Rosarian in the first race? Where could he go...away from the roar of the crowd and the beat of the horses' hoofs as they came down the stretch?

Nowhere, of course. And since he had to die some time, where was he to die but in the barn at Jamaica, taking the bandages off Rosarian?

And would the horse run? Well, why not? Nobody seemed to know who would scratch him if he was going to be scratched. And it was a cinch that Charlie would have wanted him to run. Weren't the weights and the conditions right? A mile, a fast track and 122 pounds in a claiming race for four-year-olds and upward. Top weight, sure. But he could carry that weight and win that one.

Around the jockey room somebody wanted to know if Eddie DeCamillis, who had the mount on Rosarian, knew that Charlie Carroll had died.

"Sure he knows it. Everybody on the race track knows it by now."

And how did he feel about it? Was he superstitious?

"Maybe he is. I don't know. But I know how he feels about it. He thinks he can't blow the race."

Rosarian opened at 8 to 1. The word had gone around.

Charlie Carroll was dead. The horse was running for a dead man. Some of the players, being superstitious, took the tip. Others, being superstitious, stayed away from it. Went to Ritorno or Balios or Alarming or Credence or Que Gato. Rosarian closed at 5 to 1.

Now they were at the post...Now they were away... Credence was on top...Rosarian was second passing the club house...Around the turn and into the back stretch... And now Rosarian was on top. Rosarian and DeCamillis, riding in the colors of a dead man...Brown, green hoops, green sleeves, green cap...Now they were in the stretch... Alarming, on the rail, closed up on Rosarian...Canoe, on the outside, was coming fast...But Rosarian fought off the challenge and roared under the wire in front.

"Did you hear," a man on the club house lawn said to the woman with him, "that his owner dropped dead just before the race?"

"No," the woman said. "That's too bad....I wish I'd known it. I would have had a bet on him."

In the paddock the sun was shining and the horses for the second race were being saddled. Men walked about or stood in groups, talking. Talking about the second race, a five-furlong dash for maiden fillies, two years old. About Pirate Ship and Goose Girl and Firette and Updo. About the Kentucky Derby. And somebody said:

"See that fellow over there? That's Joe Notter. He rode Regret, the only filly that ever won the Derby. That was in 1915."

Men stood along the rail by the shed under which the horses are saddled and talked about Charlie Carroll. "Too bad. . . . I knew him when he—" . . . "I remember the time..."

Over in the receiving barn they were cooling Rosarian

out and getting ready to put him in the van. In the jockeys' house, Terry Farley took the silks from DeCamillis and hung them up ... Brown, green hoops, green sleeves, brown hoops on sleeves, green cap.

DOYLE THE MAGNIFICENT

BY

Dan Parker

(NEW YORK DAILY MIRROR) JULY 12, 1939.

WHEN TWO FIGHTERS have knocked out the same opponent the logical thing for a promoter to do is match them with each other. England, therefore, has the battle of the aeons in its perfidious lap. Last Fall, a handsome Irish pugilist named Doyle (pronounced Dile) knocked out a beautiful Irish singer named John Aloysius Doyle (pronounced Derl) by aiming at one Eddie Phillips (whom he was fighting, not Dile) a polthogue of such terrific velocity and elliptical trajectory that it landed on the cleft of his own chin, tore his medulla oblongata loose from the pericranium, cured him of chronic dandruff and knocked out four impacted wisdom teeth. The same Doyle was lulled into the land of the banshees with a single punch Monday night in London by Eddie Phillips, one of England's best sixth-raters. Both Phillips and Doyle having scored a knockout over Doyle, it is now reasonable to expect that they will be matched in the Battle of the Ages.

In fact it is always safe to assume that Doyle will be matched again in London. He's one Irishman who seems to be able to handle the traditional enemies of his forefathers. Such is the power of his Blarney and the hypnotic quality of his quavering tenor voice (pronounced vice or verce or vice

versa) that he has but to screech a few bars of "Little Old
Town in the Old County Down," flash his perfect set of
teeth, turn on his County Cork smile and, sure there's no
resistin' the spalpeen, bad cess to him!

Doyle may be the worst fighter in the world and the second
worst singer, but no one tops him as a con man. He's been
kidding the English that he's a fighter for a half-dozen years
now, and they are no nearer tumbling than they were the
night they first laid eyes on his magnificent physique. 'Twas
Dile and no one else who drew most of that crowd of 65,000
to the White City for Monday night's bout. Fancy an Irishman beating the English at the favorite sport of their
statesmen—duplicity!

It seems incredible that Doyle could go on kidding the
English like he does but the records prove it. Monday night's
alleged fight was Doyle's 20th. Of these 20, ten ended in the
first round. Of course, Jack me bye "won" six of them, but
what's to stop a fellow from drawing his own conclusions
in the light of later developments? Seven more of Doyle's
brutal battles ended in the second round with Jack winning
five of them. Once, the blighter went four rounds but that
was in this country after his one-round invisible punch
victory over Phil (Tomato) Donato met with skepticism to
which Doyle wasn't accustomed. This bloodless (but not
waterless) battle was with Jack Redmond, who is not to be
confused with the bog-wallowing Pat Redmond, a County
Down man who was often down but never out. Jack's purpose in going four rounds on this occasion was to prove he
could "travel the route." He almost knocked himself out in
the third and Redmond developed knots in his muscles from
pulling his punches.

Every time Jack has been put on the spot, he has been put
on his back. Probably his first on-the-level bout was with

Jack Peterson for the British heavyweight title and he fouled out in the second round when the going got a bit too rough. He had his choice of stopping the fight and singing "Kathleen Mavourneen" or fouling out and he wasn't in good voice that night.

His bout with Buddy Baer here was on the up and up and Jack wound up on the down and down. The next time he ventured into the ring, he was disqualified for fouling on the first round. He not only stayed 12 rounds with that paragon of the art of stepping on his own feet, Kingfish Levinsky, but actually won the decision.

"I'll knock out Louis next," cried Jack after this bout. "Lave me at him."

The Eddie Phillips bout last September in which Jack knocked himself out should have ended Doyle's boxing career, particularly since he brought himself to by taking a good whiff of perfumed smelling salts. But it seems the English merely regarded this as another of Jack's charming drolleries which enhanced his drawing power. Coming on top of his self-inflicted knockout, the one-punch defeat he suffered at the hands of Phillips should put him in a position where he can demand 80 per cent of the gate and have a deputy do his fighting for him the next time. Maybe that last idea is the solution of the Derl problem.

BROTHER ACT

BY
Jack Miley

(NEW YORK POST) NOVEMBER 18, 1939.

WELL, IT WAS The Kid's Last Fight, all right. Jackie Conn last night announced his retirement from the ring at the age of seventeen. Or rather, brother Billy announced it for him. For poor little Jackie, after being flattened in a round at the Garden, was lying in Polyclinic Hospital with a possible brain concussion and a bad case of hysterics.

"From now on there's only one fighter in the Conn family," declared Billy, as they half-carried the sobbing Jackie into the Garden dressing room the two boys shared, "and it is I!"

Jackie flopped on a rubbing table and wept as if his heart was broken, which it probably was. Billy, who was waiting to face Gus Lesnevich in a fifteen-rounder he won with the greatest of ease, rumpled Jackie's wet hair and consoled him:

"Now, listen, Jackie, you're through, see? You're hanging up your gloves, right this minute. I'm not going to have guys like that Mutt Wormer knocking you out. If anybody's going to lick you, I'll do it myself.

"But I won't have total strangers coming along and punching the hell out of you. If anybody lifts a hand to you, I'll slap him silly. But that's only if it is out of the ring—for you're not going in any more rings. I'm not going to have you disgracing me by getting yourself stiffened by some bum every time I'm waiting to do a little fighting myself. How does that look, huh? Ain't you got any regard for my feelings?

"I'm sitting here in the dressing room a minute ago. The door's open. I'm wondering how I'm going to do with my guy—that Gus. A couple of fellows come by. They've just seen you fight. One says to the other:

"'Who was that fat little punk who just got his lumps?'

"And the other bird says, 'Why, that's Jackie Conn—Billy Conn's brother!'

"Then the first guy says, 'Billy Conn's brother, huh? Geez, if Billy Conn's anything like him, he must be a pip!'

"How do you think I felt? I ran out into the hall, but they'd gone. I'd popped 'em, sure. They can't talk that way about you—not me, either!"

Jackie's shoulders shook. Tears the size of Cape Cod oysters coursed down his round little baby face. His snub nose sniffled. He ranted: "This is awful! That bum Wormer can't do this to me. He can't knock me out!"

"He can't, huh?" snickered Billy. "Well, he just did! Now, lissen, champ, get those duds off and get under that shower!" Still crying, Jackie did. But there was a terrific commotion in the shower room a moment later. The youngster, in a fit of hysteria, was banging his head against a tile wall.

When they fished him out, Jackie was worse than ever. He pounded a door with his fists, he kicked chairs and stools out of his way, and he yelled at the top of his lungs:

"I'm NOT through fighting! I WILL come back! You CAN'T make me quit, I tell you. I'll lick YOU some day, Billy, if it's the last thing I EVER do!"

"That's what he thinks," whispered Billy, "but he's all washed up right now. Maybe I shouldn't have let him try to be a fighter in the first place. But he talked me into it, the little devil!

"But I'm not listening to him any more. And if he argues with me, I'll throw him over my knee and fan his pants for him. Why kid ourselves? Jackie's just a baby! And this racket is too tough for babies.

"If Jackie keeps on the way he's going, he'll be punch drunk by the time he's eighteen. And my Ma will give me hell!"

As Jackie was dressing, he kept shouting his defiance of those who would try to regulate his life. Neither brother Billy nor Johnny Ray, who manages the Conn boys, would make him go back to school or get a job in those Pittsburgh steel mills, he shrieked.

Presently Dr. William Walker, Boxing Commission physician, came into the room. He suggested Jackie go across Fiftieth Street to Polyclinic Hospital and rest there for the night. The lad had worked himself into an hysterical condition and a sedative would help him sleep it off. Jackie had given his head a pretty bad wallop, too, and maybe he'd hurt himself.

Jackie didn't want to go. Even if Billy hadn't been too sympathetic with him, he still wanted to remain and see his brother box. But everybody present persuaded him this was the wisest thing to do.

So out the door and into the night went the poor little Conn boy, flanked by two husky cops in uniform, who'd been told to go along and see that he didn't change his mind.

"Gu-gu-goo'bye, Billy," Jackie gulped as he paused at the threshold. Then he came back and shook his brother's hand.

"I hu-hu-hope you win, bu-bu-Billy," he whispered.

And thus ended the career of a fighting man, Jackie Conn, seventeen.

73—0

BY

Arthur J. Daley

(NEW YORK TIMES)

Washington, December 8, 1940.

THE WEATHER WAS PERFECT. So were the Bears. In the most fearsome display of power ever seen on any gridiron, the Monsters of the Midway won the Ed Thorp Memorial Trophy, which is symbolic of the world football championship, before 36,034 stunned and deriding fans in Griffith Stadium this balmy afternoon.

It being a Sunday, the Washington Humane Society had the day off. So the Bears had nothing to combat in the playoff except the Redskins, who were pretty feeble opposition indeed. Hence it was that the Chicago Bears scalped the Capital Indians, 73 to 0, the highest score in the history of the National Football League.

This was simply dreadful. The only question before the house was whether the Bears could score more points when they were on the offensive or when Washington was on the offensive. It was a fairly close competition, Chicago with the ball outscoring the Redskins with the ball, seven touchdowns to four.

Before fifty-six seconds had passed the Bears had a tally. Then, when the second half began, they cut that time down, registering another marker in fifty-four seconds. It probably is just as well that the football rules permit only two halves to a game or else George Halas's young men would have been down to fractions of seconds.

There never was anything quite like this. Three weeks ago the Redskins edged out the Bears, 7 to 3. Today it was something else again. Chicago was a perfect football team that played football of such exquisite class that Washington could not have won with a brick wall instead of a line and howitzers instead of backs. The Bears would have battered down everything.

By the time the second half began the Redskins showed a marked improvement. Their defense against points after touchdown had reached such perfection that four out of seven were missed. Washington was the unlucky outfit today. It had the misfortune to have to face a team that could have beaten the other nine elevens in the league just as badly.

This was football at its very best. The Bears had the timing for their quick-opening plays down to the hundredth of a second. They riddled the Redskins at will with the overwhelming power of their ground game, rocked them with their infrequent passes and smothered them with their defensive power. The blocking was fiendishly accurate and it almost was a physical impossibility for them to make a mistake.

The Bears registered three touchdowns in the first period, one in the second, four in the third and three in the last. Halas used every eligible man on his squad, thirty-three of them, and fifteen had a share of the scoring. It even reached such a stage that the Bears passed for one point after touchdown by way of variety and by way of adding to Washington's humiliation.

Halas used Sid Luckman, an Old Blue from Columbia, as

his first-half quarterback, and no field general ever called plays more artistically or engineered a touchdown parade in more letter-perfect fashion. But the Lion sat out the second half and still the mastodons from the Midwest rolled.

Ray Flaherty's young men were physically in the game, but that was all. After Bill Osmanski had romped 68 yards for the first touchdown, the 'Skins reached the Bear 26, only to have Bob Masterson's 32-yard field goal effort fail. That was a blow from which George Preston Marshall's lads never recovered. Had they scored, it might have been different.

But when they missed they wound up with a minus 10 yards for their first seven passes and went speedily downhill the rest of the way. After a while that descent began to resemble a snowball on the way, picking up power and speed as it heads toward the valley.

The first touchdown was a 75-yard zip to a score. George McAfee picked up 7 yards and then Osmanski, cutting inside Washington's right tackle, went 68 yards more. The tip-off on the Bears came when George Wilson erased two men with the same block to clear the way for the counter.

Then the Bears rolled 80 yards in seventeen plays, the pay-off being Luckman's quarterback sneak from the six-inch line. A moment later Joe Maniaci, the old Fordham Flash, streaked 42 yards for another counter. Jack Manders, Bob Snyder and Phil Martinovich added the extra points and it was 21 to 0.

Redskin fans who had watched their heroes win their first seven games of the league season could not believe their eyes. Yet even they were to become convinced that they were watching one of the greatest football teams of all time in action, a team that had everything.

The Bears reached the 16 in the second quarter and fumbled. Washington made a gesture by going 63 yards to the 18 on ten successive passes, only to lose the ball on downs. The Chicagoans went 56 more to the 24 but Martinovich failed on a field goal try.

Ray Nolting boomed through with one of the eight Bear pass interceptions and the victors were off to the races. Ground plays advanced only 26 yards, so Luckman flipped a 30-yarder to Ken Kavanaugh in the end zone, the freshman from Louisiana State plucking the ball from the grasp of two defenders for another counter. Snyder converted.

The third quarter saw the Redskins give up the ghost. They attempted a pass from the 19, but Hampton Pool, an end, intercepted Sammy Baugh's lateral flick to Jimmy Johnston on the 16 for a marker. Then the Capital crew tried a fourth-down pass from their 33. It was batted down.

So the Bears took over. Nolting gained 10 yards. But he was just warming up. On the next play he burst 23 yards through the middle, feinted Baugh into the middle of the Potomac on the 8 and went across standing up. Dick Plasman missed the conversion, which promptly labelled him an absolute outcast.

Washington took over again and McAfee intercepted a Roy Zimmerman pass for 35 yards of gorgeous broken-field running for a touchdown. It then was Joe Stydahar's turn and he split the bars with a placement.

The Redskins made an effort to score, reaching the 16 only to lose the ball on downs. When the Bears punted Washington assumed the offensive on its 37. A bad pass from center was recovered on the 21 and Zimmerman's pass was intercepted by Bulldog Turner on the 30. He scored, thanks to a block by Pool. Maniaci's placement was blocked and it was 54 to 0.

The league's champions rumbled 74 yards for their next touchdown in the fourth quarter, Harry Clark going 42 yards on a double reverse for the tally. On this he feinted Frank Filchock into Chesapeake Bay. Gary Famiglietti was elected as the point converter, but failed.

The hapless Redskins later saw Filchock fumble in the shadow of his goal posts. Jack Torrance, the reformed shot-put world record-holder, fell on the ball on the 2. He almost crushed the air out of the ball when his 300 pounds landed on it. So Famiglietti burst across on a quick opener. The crusher was a Saul Sherman-Maniaci pass in the end zone for the extra point.

The last touchdown resulted from a 52-yard drive that was culminated by a 1-yard dance by Clark through the middle. He crossed standing up. A Snyder-Maniaci conversion pass missed. And Maniaci intercepted again just as the Redskins gave promise of threatening.

There was no Redskin hero outside of Flaherty, who had to sit on the bench and absorb it all, too much a beating for so fine a gentleman and coach. The Bears had thirty-three heroes. Luckman, Nolting, McAfee, Osmanski and Maniaci in the backfield were outstanding. So were Lee Artoe, Stydahar, Danny Fortmann, Turner and Plasman in the line.

The day was gorgeous. The crowd was representative, with high government officials scattered throughout the stands. Everything was under the control of the Magnificent Marshall, except the Bears.

At the end the Redskin band played "Should Auld Acquaintance Be Forgot?" If said acquaintance is the Chicago Bears, it should be forgot immediately. At the moment the Bears are the greatest football team of all time.

RACKETY RACKET

BY

Tom O'Reilly

(PM) JUNE 23, 1940.

T HIS IS A TALE that has needed telling for many years if only because it belongs to the great sporting lore of America. It concerns the truth as to why football was abolished at one of the most respected institutions in this land—Sing Sing. There has been no football at Sing Sing since 1934.

At that time, it was announced that Warden Lewis E. Lawes banned the game because he felt that the attending crowds were too disturbing an influence on the Sing Sing routine and attracted entirely too much attention to his charges. There was also something about one of the players who didn't quit running in the end zone.

That is true as far as it goes but it is not complete. Football lost face at Sing Sing because of an attempt at one of the most outrageous betting coups in gridiron history—an affair that rocked the old institution from front gate to solitary cells, causing fights, minor riots and near murder.

As you know, when football was introduced at Sing Sing, in 1930, the players had little talent. Coached by Notre Dame's perfectly named prison preceptor, John Law, Sing Sing's eleven was shellacked by such semi-pro outfits as the Danbury Trojans, the New Rochelle Bulldogs and, saddest

of all, the Port Jervis Police. While lacking in talent, however, the players were earnest and the police reporters, wittily
calling them Caged Tigers, Black Sheep, Zebras, etc., said
they had plenty of time to learn, with quotes around the
word time.

This was true. Practicing faithfully the year round, Sing
Sing's team soon became a power in its district. In fact, by
1934, it was so good that it outclassed all its opposition. This
proved to be a curse in disguise. Since Sing Sing is filled with
gentlemen devoted to taking chances, it was only natural that
football provided them with plenty of sport.

Every week during the season it became customary to bet
money, tobacco, shoes and even food on the games. By 1934,
however, the team's excellence made it impossible to bet on
mere victory or defeat. Any man wishing to back Sing Sing
had to give away 21 points. In other words, if Sing Sing won
by only 20 points supporters of the team lost their money,
tobacco, etc.

Sing Sing was hot that season, beating everybody by scores
ranging from 27—0 to 40—0, until the big game with the
Port Jervis Police. Then an unforeseen thing occurred. Coach
John Law, happy in the knowledge of his team's superiority,
announced that he would not be on hand for the game with
the Cops.

In addition to master-minding the Sing Sing games on
Sundays, he was acting also as a Fordham scout, for his old
Notre Dame pal, Jim Crowley, on Saturdays. On the Satur-
day before the Sing Sing-Police game he had to scout N. Y.
U., in Georgia. Naturally he would be unable to return to
Sing Sing in time for the game next day. He told his men,
confidently, "You know what to do. Go ahead and do it."
They did.

The members of the starting eleven quickly got together

and selected secret agents to go through the prison quietly
betting against Sing Sing's chances of winning by 21 points.
They were so delighted at the idea that they gave nice odds
and didn't even inform the members of the second team,
who were among the biggest bettors.

Well, when the great day arrived and the game started it
became apparent, quickly, that the Cops were no match
for the home team. Within 2 minutes of the start, a large
and loose-hipped lifer galloped 40 yards for a touchdown.
Following a kick-off and punt he did it again. On both occasions, Sing Sing's kicker easily scored the points after
touchdown. In the second period, Sing Sing scored on
straight line plunges.

Then, with the score at 20—0, the usually consistent place-
kicker booted one far wide of the mark. Other strange things
followed. No matter how hard Sing Sing tried, it didn't seem
able to hold the ball near the goal line. It would march 50
yards to the goal and then fumble. Invariably the Cops recovered. This happened twice and nobody thought anything
about it. When it occurred for the fifth time, however, substitutes began to trot out on the field. But the regulars waved
them back and refused to leave the game.

In the meantime Coach Law got a break in Georgia. Ed
Huntsinger, who was with him, met an old Army pal who
was flying a transport plane and obligingly offered to give
them a lift back to New York. As it turned out Law arrived
at Sing Sing between the halves.

There was an argument of gigantic proportions going on
in the dressing room when he entered. On his appearance
it stopped abruptly and he swears that one of his Negro stars
nearly turned white. When told of the situation Law said
nothing. He sent his first team back into the game for the
second half. He watched them fumble once and then sent

in the second team. The substitutes played like madmen and walloped the Cops, 50—0. The double-crossers were double-crossed. The repercussions that followed caused trouble for months and finally football was queered forever.

IRISHMAN'S DREAM

BY

John P. Carmichael

(CHICAGO DAILY NEWS)

———————

New York, June 19, 1941.

IT'S AN OLD, old story. The gun wasn't loaded as Billy ("The Kid") Conn toyed with it. But suddenly it went off!

The Brown Bomber was just a dud, after all. The fuse had burned itself out and nothing had happened. So "Billy the Kid" went over to pick it up. Then it exploded!

So they picked Conn up off the floor instead and patched the powder marks on his handsome Irish face and took him away while the winner, and still champion—Joe Louis—walked to the center of the ring and permitted his hand to be raised in victory.

Yes, it's an old, old story. Don't play cards with strangers and don't mix it with Joe Louis. While upwards of 50,000 fans were seeking the exits from the Polo Grounds, where one of the greatest fights in history had just been staged, Billy Conn sat on a table in his dressing room and said: "I guess I got too much guts for my own good." Ruefully, he said it, and regretfully, perhaps, but he'd probably do it all over again. It's the Irish in him.

He was a 4-1 shot going into the ring. He was no worse than even money at the end of the 12th round and maybe even 5-6. Our score showed the rounds at six for each man. Around the ringside the counts varied from 7-5 in Conn's favor to 6-5-1 in favor of Louis. The challenger had withstood a terrific body beating which cost him five of the first seven frames, had bounced back to take four of the next five rounds, to outfight the champ in furious flurries and snap him back to his heels with slashing left hooks.

That title was close to resting on an Irishman's brow for the first time since Louis wrested it from Jim Braddock four years ago this month in Chicago. The 13th round opened. Two more to go and there was little to choose between the men. Then Conn struck out with a left hook. It missed. Inside that left, Louis swung a vicious right. It didn't miss. It landed with a crackling sound on Billy's jaw bone and the light of battle died in Conn's eyes. His head fell forward. Two right uppercuts sent it flying back. Three more rights and a left scored bull's-eyes. One more smash, still a right, and Conn fell with his face turned toward Louis, lying on his right side. At "10" he was barely on his knees and it was all over. 'Twas only an Irishman's dream, after all.

But it was a grand dream while it lasted. Conn's eyes never once fell before Joe's. His lips were parted in a wide smile that not even Louis could wipe off when there was nothing left to smile about. In the ninth round, Billy came flitting from his corner, his purple tights and body dripping the waters of rejuvenation over the canvas. He flung a left and a right at Joe's head and in his bravado, he barked at the titleholder:

"Come on, you've got a fight on your hands now, Joe."

His words were plainly audible at ringside and so were Joe's as he replied "I know it" without missing a counterpunch. Then they went to it, hammer and tongs, pounding away inside, going as long as 30 seconds, with their arms intertwined, flailing away at each other's stomachs, the challenge still in the set of Conn's chin and the answer written in the stubborn lines around Joe's murky eyes and tight mouth.

By the time the 12th heat rolled around, the Polo Grounds was an open-air asylum as thousands envisioned a new champion, a successor to Louis in the amazing recuperative powers of this 175-pound giant-killer. In that 13th Louis landed early with a right and left and re-opened a tiny meaningless cut under Conn's right eye. Just enough to start a trickle of blood again. But Billy was fighting in flurries now, husbanding his strength for a surge.

He launched one as Joe stepped back from a clutch. Conn swept in and pumped rights and lefts to Louis' head until the champ padded back on his heels in bewilderment. It was a savage thrust and when the bell rang, Conn was closer to the heavyweight crown than any man has been since Louis placed it on his own brow. Here, in the making, was the greatest upset since the first Schmeling-Louis fight. Conn's star was in ascendancy. It never shone brighter during the night. But it never shone again, either.

Conn took a sound lacing around the body in those early rounds and from time to time was forced to hang on for the bell, that he might go back to his corner for a much-needed breather. His handlers worked furiously on him during every rest-period, dousing him with water, rubbing his midriff and chafing his legs and arms and from each ministration he would spring to battle again as though the battered water bucket was the fountain of youth.

But Conn was beaten at his own game up to the time he was licked at the other guy's game. He was the master boxer, the man with the unbeatable left hand, the guy with the winged feet. But it was Louis who piled up points with his own left, who out-boxed Conn to take an early lead and stay in the fight, who went step for step with Conn all the way, although obviously tiring and unable to crash through in the second and third rounds when he had Conn in evident distress with ripping jolts to the body.

Louis admits today that Conn was the smartest, best boxer he ever met. He was told by Trainer Jack Blackburn as late as the 12th round that "you gotta knock him out, chappie, to win." At that moment it didn't look as if Joe could knock anybody out or even be sure he wouldn't be flattened himself. All night long he had been waiting for that sure-shot inside one of Conn's left hooks. He hadn't been able to find such an opening.

But it was there, right around the corner, when he needed it most and today Billy Conn is no longer a name, but a number: No. 18, in Louis' book of failures.

TENNIS BUM

BY

Bob Considine

(INTERNATIONAL NEWS SERVICE)
JULY 25, 1941.

CONFOUND THAT INFERNAL Frankie Parker for pat-balling me out of the Seabright tournament! Why don't he get out there and hit 'em on the nose, like I do? What's he trying to do, ruin me? Now I've got to get at least to the finals in the doubles or the committees up at Newport and Rye won't put me on the cuff. I simply gotta....

It wouldn't have been so bad, losing to Parker, if Beth and her old man hadn't come all the way in from Southampton, just to see the match. Brother, if you ask me, that's no way to get Beth—getting licked right in front of her ugly kisser. Why the blazes didn't she come around earlier in the week, when I was hot? First thing I know she'll be going for that new California kid...what's his name. Beth and her old man sure are suckers for tennis champs, thank God. If I can win at Newport in the singles, I think she'll marry me. Wow!—all those bucks.

Midge Trevor? I've got to get her out of my mind. Just like she's got to get me out of hers. What sense would there be in two tennis bums getting hitched? What would that equal? Nothing! She's in the same boat I'm in. Sure, she's pretty. Sure, people think she's got a lot of jack, to be play-

253

ing tennis at all the smart tournaments all year long. I guess there must be people who think I've got dough, too, doing the same thing. But forget Midge. We're just alike. I've got to get Beth, somehow, and she's got to get Freddie Cornelius III, the big simp. If she don't land him, she'll wind up like I will—if I don't land Beth. Phew!...what a mugg that Beth's got. But what bucks.

How about that sap on the Daily Mirror? He had a piece yesterday saying that the draft board officers should advance on Seabright and induct the whole crowd of us who have been playing in a tournament a week since last January. Haven't we got enough trouble, without having a guy like that inviting the draft board to come down here? I guess it's all Willie Kennedy's fault. Imagine a guy who has been around playing with us in all those tournaments suddenly just joining the Army. They didn't even come and get him. He just joined, like it was a club or something. But Willie always was a little tetched. I even saw him reach for the check one night when the people he was living on, during the National singles, took him to the Stork Club. Probably too much sun....

Well, now that Parker's knocked me out of the singles here I'd better go over to the club dining room and see if I'm still on the free list. I wish those things were more standardized. Some committees boot you right off the free list as soon as you lose in the singles. Some leave you on the list, and even let you keep your room and sign for things, even if you only stay in the mixed doubles. Some of these committees are rats. Some of them even act like I'm not doing them a favor by even playing in their stinking tournament.

I certainly won't enjoy my meal tonight, wondering whether it's free or not. Anyway, I'm going to squawk to the tournament manager about the service I'm getting here. Damnedest insolent waiters I ever saw. You know what one said to me last night, after I left him a dime for my dinner and Midge's? He said, "Can you spare it, brother?" How do you like that for insolence, the dirty Greek. He gets a salary, don't he? Besides, that's all the money I had, after being cleaned out by Bobby Riggs in that crap game, and Midge had spent all her money on a damn hair-do, to dazzle Freddie later on. I wonder if there's some way to improve my crap shooting, like I improved my forehand....

I oughta be able to get a ten-spot tomorrow from that cheap chiseler whose company's racquets I use. There's an ungrateful dog if I ever saw one. He thinks he's doing enough for me, just keeping me in free racquets and restringings. I'll fix him. If he don't cough up at least a tenner I'm going to hold his racquet behind me, the next time I get in one of those posed pictures at the net. That'll teach him to take better care of a fellow who's decent enough to hold up my racquet in such a way that everybody who sees the picture in the papers the next day can see what kind of bat I'm using.

Boy, I hope that guy from the slacks company comes through with a free pair for the finals of the doubles. I'll take a few pratt falls tomorrow during the doubles, to dirty up the ones he gave me last week in New York, so he'll get the hint and come through with a new pair. If he don't, then I'll have to wash out an old pair myself—like I used to when I was just coming up. Damn that Parker and his pat-ball! I wouldn't have to be worrying my head off about money from the racquet company and clean pants if I was still in the singles.

What the hell is happening to the world? The older guys tell me that 10 or 15 years ago the clubhouses were filled with rich blokes who considered it an honor to lose money to us amateur stars; you know, bridge and kinda polite bets where we got all the edge. I bet I would have done all right, if I had been playing during the Twenties. Now, it's tough. You gotta work to make a living out of amateur tennis. Even gals with kissers like Beth are hard to get. Maybe Willie Kennedy had something...but no, let him have his craziness about the Army.

I just gotta do good here at Seabright, from now in. I gotta win the doubles, so I get a bid from the Newport committee. God, I hope Riggs or somebody takes care of that Parker at Newport. That damn pat-ball of his will make me lose Beth ...make me lose everything I've got in the world. That's what it will do.

TROUBLE IN PARADISE

BY

Tom Meany

(PM)

Philadelphia, September 19, 1941.

THE DODGERS ARRIVED here today to learn that they had received a reprieve from the governor. There's no other way to explain their elation at learning that Boston had topped St. Louis in the Cards' final game against an Eastern team. Brooklyn came here resigned to finding itself in second place and discovered that Casey Stengel had pulled a miracle out at Sportsman's Park. Any time Manuel Salvo beats a pitcher like Mort Cooper it must be construed as a manifestation of divine blessing.

As matters stand now, both are tied in defeats and the Dodgers still have two games on the win side, only one of which St. Louis can make up. Furthermore the Dodgers play the Phils seven games and the Braves two to conclude their schedule, while the Cards are picking on the Pirates for four and the Cubs for six.

It was a blessing to Leo Durocher and his harried league leaders to discover this morning that the Cardinals had been beaten. Otherwise they probably would have blown their toppers. That their nerves were frayed to the breaking point was obvious to anyone who witnessed the disgraceful exhibition in Pittsburgh yesterday. Durocher and others are likely to pay through the nose with fines for their performance, and it is just as well that they still are in first place. It will make the fines easier to take.

The Dodgers really rallied like lions yesterday, then played like hoodlums, all in the same eighth inning. With two out in the eighth, and behind 4—0, the Flock made six straight hits against Johnny Lanning, including a smashing two-bagger by Cookie Lavagetto. That put the Dodgers ahead by a run and set the stage for the fireworks by which they eventually lost the game, 6—5, thus breaking even in the West.

Luke Hamlin, picked to pitch the ninth, was nailed for a slashing single to left by Vince DiMaggio, and Joe Medwick bobbled the ball, allowing Vince to take second. Hugh Casey, for the fourth time in five days, took the hill and started off with a masterly exhibition. He retired Garms on a fly to right, on which DiMaggio took third, and then made a sucker of pinch-hitter Van Robays with a curve that the latter tapped harmlessly to Reese.

With Lopez at bat, DiMaggio made a break for the plate, a phony start to upset Casey. It did. Hughey halted in the middle of his windup and palpably balked. Umpire Magerkurth called the play rightly and the storm was on.

Lopez, of course, called the balk as soon as it was committed and Magerkurth was instantly after him with his decision. Casey's explanation of halting his windup was that he did so only because Lopez had stepped out of the box and there was no one to pitch to. This could be so, but I was watching the play and Casey checked his windup when DiMaggio made his break, precisely as White did in the disputed balk play in the first game in St. Louis which was not allowed. The difference was that Hughey didn't deliver the ball to the plate.

Durocher, as you may imagine, stormed in great style,

which was excusable, perhaps, in view of the importance of the game. What followed wasn't. Casey got two strikes on Lopez and then threw a ball behind Al's head which rolled to the screen. He threw another and then another. At that juncture Magerkurth walked out to the mound to remonstrate with Casey and Durocher was off the bench again. This time his gesticulating protests were so vigorous that he was thumbed and deservedly so.

Lopez, remember, represented the winning run. Casey's fourth pitch was wide and Al walked. He scored when Alf Anderson, of all people, tripled to the rightfield corner. After the game, Coscarart, Franks, Camilli and Medwick assailed Magerkurth verbally under the stands, according to Mage's testimony.

The beefing in the Dodger clubhouse was a new high for the year in a clubhouse which has never been exactly docile in defeat. All were insistent that Casey had not balked, something of which you couldn't convince an unbiased spectator. Hugh, himself, explained the three throws to Lopez's skull by saying the ball had "got away" from him, which doesn't explain how he got two strikes on Al before he lost control.

It would seem that the simplest answer to it all is that the players lost their heads under the stress of the pennant drive. They can yammer all they want about Casey's balk not being such, but the point to remember is that Casey's balk didn't beat the Dodgers.

That only tied the score. What beat the Dodgers was the pass to Lopez, which consisted of three balls thrown so wide of the catcher and so far behind the batter that they rolled 127 feet behind the plate.

It wasn't a pleasant exhibition for any one who has grown enamored of the Dodgers as I have. They were so gallant when they tied the score, so raffish when they permitted their tempers to hand the game to Pittsburgh. Maybe if I had five or six thousand at stake, I might view it differently.

Well, it's all water under the bridge now, fellows. The governor came through with a pardon in the form of that win by Salvo over the Cards. Let's go get the Phillies—nice fellers, who never harmed anybody, and aren't going to start now, I hope.

FUN IN THE KITCHEN

BY

Caswell Adams

(NEW YORK HERALD TRIBUNE) MAY 12, 1942.

BOB PASTOR GOT THE BREAK of his life yesterday when it was learned that Billy Conn had broken his left hand on the granite head of his father-in-law, Jimmy Smith, at an Irish post-christening party in Pittsburgh early Sunday night. Because the shattering of Billy's metacarpal bone in his stabbing hand means that he will wear that weapon in a cast for at least six weeks, and this adornment will deprive him of his second crack at Joe Louis here in June, and shoot Pastor into his third try at the great Negro.

Conn arrived at LaGuardia Airport late in the afternoon, looking much worse than the morning after he fought Louis last June. He unfolded a tale of wild doings at the party after the christening of six-weeks-old David Phillip Conn, a tale that seems symbolical of all Irish celebrations and which just missed the tragic ending of that classic Irish ballad, "McSorley's Two Beautiful Twins," in which the Flynns and the Murphys fought so wildly that they turned over the bed "and smothered the two little twins."

Conn, his left hand in a cast, his right arm thoroughly swathed in bandages on account of a severe cut when one of his right-hand swings at his father-in-law went wild and through a kitchen window, and his face a mass of vicious

261

scratches, went immediately to Fort Wadsworth, S. I., where he is a private in the Army. Billy wasn't thinking much about his injuries as he took the ferry to the fort. But he evidently was worried over the military approach to the fight and the attendant publicity, not to mention the slight detail that some of the proceeds of the Louis-Conn battle, temporarily listed for June 24, were to have gone to the Army Emergency Relief Fund.

The repercussions of the family squabble at the christening will not only deprive Billy of a lucrative jab at Louis—evidently a lot less rough than Jimmy Smith, an old Pittsburgh infielder who once challenged the entire Brooklyn Dodger bench and received no response in 1920—but will shove Pastor into the big money.

Just before he left on his scary trip to the officers at Wadsworth, Conn gave a play-by-play account of the proceedings in the happy Smith homestead, following the baptism (under fire, as it turned out) of the Conn baby. It was mere expected embellishment on the widely circulated reports last year that Smith frowned on Conn as his daughter's choice for a life partner.

Seems that neither Conn nor Smith went to the christening. Conn stayed home with Art Rooney, the promoter who has put on fights and who owned the Pittsburgh Steelers, the professional football team there, and who once broke bookies at Saratoga. Smith lingered at his own home preparing the punch for the horde of relatives who would soon be back from St. Bede's Roman Catholic Church a few blocks away. Seems that Smith phoned Rooney to come over and chat and that Art did. Seems that Rooney soon called Billy and told him that his father-in-law would like to see him to bury the hatchet.

Conn tripped over to the festive Smith mansion and the

aunts and uncles and the baby soon arrived. A little later, according to Conn, his father-in-law asked him to come out into the kitchen and talk a bit, although Smith and Conn hadn't spoken a syllable to each other since Billy's engagement to Mary Louise Smith was announced last year.

"Then," said Billy, "as the rest of the family were talking and shaking hands, I went out into the kitchen.

"The old man started right away to bring up old sores. You know, grievances, and I said that I didn't come to argue and he started to holler. And I told him not to holler at me, that I wasn't deaf and I kept smiling through it all. Finally the yelling gets so loud that I asked him if he was trying to scare me and he shook his finger at me and I said I wasn't scared of any one and he said that he waited long enough to get me.

"Well, he punched me and then I punched him and right away I felt a funny feeling in my left hand after I hit Smith on top of the head and then I threw my right, but through the window and then we both went down on the floor, with him scratching at me and giving me this. And then the place was a madhouse, with every one coming in from the other room and...It's a hell of a thing that whenever you get in a fight your friends grab and hold you. Why don't they hold the other guy?"

Seems, faith, that Billy's shirt was ripped off his back in the encounter and that, according to Willie, his father-in-law tried to pull out his (Billy's) hair. One of the awed throng of reporters and photographers who greeted the arrival at the airport then said: "Did you belt him, Billy?" and Willie rubbed his sore right arm and said: "Once it started I wasn't just standing there. I think the old man deliberately planned this. He bothered me before the last fight with Louis and he's certainly kicked this one into the soup. And I think I split his head. And Milt Jaffe, you know, our pal, well he got so excited he fell downstairs and I think he broke his arm. And even Mary Louise got punched around."

Reports from the scene of battle had it that gore was all over the Smith household and the battle had ended when up drove Tommy Silverblatt, local florist, bearing a plant Billy had sent as a peace-offering to his mother-in-law. Tommy was commandeered by Mary Louise, who screamed that Billy was hurt and ordered Thomas to proceed at the risk of tires and waste of gasoline to Mercy Hospital, where Dr. Harold Kuehner attended to the wounds of the fighter and kept Conn overnight.

Mary Louise was in hiding at home yesterday. Jimmy Smith, who, if Pastor can't make it, may be in there with Louis in June, merely murmured: "Conn get hurt? Must have been in an accident." Mike Jacobs, to whom the costly belt on the head meant real money, laughed and said: "You could have called the turn on a thing like that happening at a christening. That's the way those things go." Jimmy Johnston, manager of Pastor, sent Smith a wreath of roses.

David Phillip Conn, the baby, was quiet as a mouse and didn't even say "Goo."

IT WAS ONLY MONEY

BY

Red Smith

(PHILADELPHIA RECORD) AUGUST 7, 1942.

---

*Weather clear, track fast, and the flowers nodding brightly in
the paddock gardens.... The sun shines down on the shim-
mering silks, shines on the shifting, glistening hides, shines on the
jostling crowd on the grandstand lawn, the leisurely crowd in the
clubhouse enclosure.... Weather clear, track fast, and the notes
of a bugle lingering in the air....*

IN THE RAMSHACKLE ruin of a house that serves as a stable
kitchen at Garden State Park, a man and a woman sat at
lunch. A little man in stained work clothes, with pinched,
wizened features and gray hair slicked back in the tight
pompadour the dandies affected in the days of the last war.

"Yes," he was saying quietly, "I made about a million dollars, I guess."

You can hear talk of millions anytime around a race
track. But when Buddy Ensor said it, you knew it was true.
Because it hasn't been too long to remember when the papers
carried stories comparing his annual earnings with those of
the President of the United States, and Buddy didn't get
the worst of the comparison.

Buddy Ensor may have been the greatest jockey that ever
pulled on silks. Some say he was. They say there was some-

thing about the touch of his hands that made a horse run better than it knew how.

He was a flashy little somebody then, a high roller, a razor-sharp dresser, and as fast a man with a century note as he ever was with a horse. You could brace him for a cup of coffee and he'd laugh and toss you a twenty.

He'd shoot craps with the stable swipes and break 'em all and then stake the game until, playing with his money, they'd clear him. And he'd laugh. What the hell, it was only money.

And today—well, today he's galloping horses for Dick Johnson, who trains for Henry A. Parr, 3d, and there's been many a day in between when he wasn't sure of tomorrow's breakfast.

"Or tonight's dinner," said Mrs. Ensor. "If Buddy had half the money that's owed him——"

Her husband shrugged. "I never expected to see it again when I lent it out. It slipped away easy. Once I blew $90,000 shooting crap with Nick the Greek in about two hours."

That wasn't bright. Nick couldn't ride horses with Ensor, so why should Buddy try to beat Nick at his game?

"No, it wasn't smart. But I thought my money would out-last his. I had $90,000 and he had about $40,000. But there was always plenty more. I was riding the best horses that ever looked through a bridle. Exterminator, Grey Lag, Cirrus——"

"I like to remember Cirrus," Mrs. Ensor said, "and that Brooklyn Handicap."

"I got $33,000 for winning that race," Buddy said. "One race. Harry Sinclair bet on the horse until they rubbed him off the slate, and he had a good chunk on for me.

"We were an entry in that race, Cirrus and Mad Hatter. Mad Hatter was supposed to set the pace and then I'd come on when he killed the others off. But Cirrus beat the gate about four lengths and Mad Hatter was off third.

"Earle Sande—he had Boniface—was watching Mad Hatter, figuring to move with him when my horse stopped. I just kep' stealing away and stealing away and I had about six lengths before Sande realized my horse wasn't going to stop.

"He took out after me then, and I showered down hard and I beat him just this much at the wire."

"Buddy was on the ground 10 years," Mrs. Ensor said, "and when he got back up again he won with his first mount. Horse called Nelson. I'll never forget that, either."

"No secret about why I was set down," the little guy said. "I just got too quick a temper and when a bad break comes along I get sore and I take a drink and—well, one drink never was any good with me.

"Like this spring when I was working for Doc Jones. We had a filly called On the Level, a full sister of Level Best, that could really run. But one day she got left at the post and Doc said, 'I can't take any more chances with her. I'm going to let you ride her in the Coaching Club Oaks.'

"I said, 'You're kidding,' but he took me to New York to get me a license. I got no license there, although I'm all right in Maryland and Florida. Well, the fellow we went to see, he hemmed and hawed and pretty soon I saw he wasn't going to okay my application and I blew up. I tore up that application and I walked out of there, and made a chump of myself again."

"I think Buddy should be punished when he does something wrong," Mrs. Ensor said. "But it's 10 years since they let him ride in New York. That's a pretty stiff punishment."

"Sure, just because I'm Buddy Ensor it's no reason I should get away with anything the other boys can't do. I'll take my punishment. But 10 years—. It's not as if I ever hurt anybody but myself.

"I could still make 106 pounds, even if I am a grandfather. Look at this picture here; that's my grand-daughter. She's five. Pretty kid, eh?

"I rode in Maryland last year, you know. Maryland, that's where I rode my first winner. Horse called Owaga, in the mud at Pimlico. I'll never forget it. I'm on top and all of a sudden I hear a sort of whooshing noise behind me and I can't figure it and I look around, and I'll be darned!

"The horse behind me is down and he's sliding along in the mud on his side, shoving his rider along in front of him so the kid looks like a little tug pulling a big liner. Funniest thing I ever saw.

"Well, I got some hope maybe I'll get a license here before this meeting closes. Mr. Tom Healey, the steward here, he's been the best friend a man ever had. He's gone to bat for me a hundred times and I owe him more than I could pay in two lifetimes."

"We've got a wedding anniversary on the 30th," Mrs. Ensor said. "Our 23d. I was just thinking, if Buddy could only have a mount that day. He rode three winners the day we were married. At Saratoga it was..."

Far away, the notes of a bugle shivered in the air. The horses were coming out for the first race. Weather clear, track fast....

THE PRINCE OF PITCHERS

BY

Lloyd Lewis

(CHICAGO DAILY NEWS) JANUARY 23, 1943.

WHEN THE BLEACHER GATES at Shibe Park in Philadelphia were thrown open on the morning of Oct. 24, 1911, I was in the mob that went whooping toward the front seats. I got one, partly because the right field crowd was smaller than the one in left, partly because most Philadelphians wanted to sit close to their worshipped Athletics, for the World Series at that moment stood two games to one for Connie Mack against John McGraw, and Philadelphia was loud and passionate in the confidence that now they would get revenge for the bitter dose—four games to one, three shut outs—the Giants had given them six years before.

Me, I wanted to get as close to the Giants as possible, and found a place at the rail close to the empty chairs which would that afternoon become the Giants' bull pen. My whole adolescence had been devoted, so far as baseball went—and it went a long way to an Indiana farm boy—to the Giants and to their kingly pitcher, "Big Six," the great, the incomparable Christy Mathewson. I hadn't had the courage to cut classes in the nearby college and go to the first game of the series at Shibe Park. But today I had. Things were desperate. Up in New York's Polo Grounds to start this, the World Series, Mathewson had won—2 to 1—giving but five hits and demonstrating that with 12 years of herculean toil behind him he was practically as invincible as when in 1905 he had shut out these same Athletics three times.

It had looked like 1905 over again; then, in the second game, the A's long, lean yokel third baseman J. Franklin Baker had suddenly and incredibly knocked a home run off Rube Marquard, the Giants' amazing young pitcher. Baker, who had hit only nine homers all season, had tagged the 22-year-old Giant and two runs had come in—and the final had stood 3 to 1.

The papers which I read, as the morning wore on, were still full of that home run and its aftermath.

From the start of the series the newspapers had been publishing syndicated articles signed by Giant and Athletic stars —the real start of the "ghost writers" whose spurious trade flourished so long but which the better papers in time eliminated. And in the article signed by Mathewson the day after Marquard's disaster it had been said that Rube had lost the game by failing to obey orders. The article rebuked the boy for throwing Baker the high outside pitch he liked, instead of the low fast one he didn't like and which McGraw had ordered.

The rebuke had been a sensation which grew in the third game when Baker had hit another homer off Mathewson himself, and had been the main wrecker of the great man's long sway over the A's. Up in the ninth inning of that third game Matty had kept command. Always when the Athletics had got men on bases he had turned on his magic. As he went to the bench at the end of the eighth, New York had risen and given him a tremendous ovation, for in 44 innings of World Series play, 1905 and 1911, he had allowed the Mackmen exactly one run—and the A's were hitters, indeed. Their season's average for 1911 had been .297.

Then in the ninth, Eddie Collins had gone out, and only two men had stood between Matty and his fifth series victory over his victims. Up had come Baker with the American League fans begging him to do to Matty what he had done to Marquard—and, incredible as it seemed, he had done this.

As home runs go, it hadn't been much more than a long fly that sailed into the convenient rightfield stand at the Polo Grounds, but it had gone far enough to tie the score and give Baker a nickname for life—"Home Run" Baker.

Snodgrass, the Giants' center fielder, one of the smartest and greatest of base runners, had ripped Baker's trousers almost off him, sliding into third in the first of the 10th inning. With McGraw snarling, railing, jeering from the coaching line, the Giants made no secret of their hatred of Baker. To them he was merely a lucky lout, a greenhorn who had by sheer accident homered off the two top pitchers of the season.

But Baker had hit again, a scratch single, in the 11th which had been part of the making of the run which had won, and Marquard in his "ghosted" article had quipped at Mathewson's advice.

All that was in everybody's mind—and mine—as on Oct. 24 the fourth game came up. The papers had had time to chew the sensation over and over, for it had rained for a week after the third game and now, with seven days' rest, Mathewson was to try again—this time in Shibe Park.

The long delay hadn't cooled excitement. The press box was still as crowded as at the opening game. This was the first World Series to be handled in the modern publicity fashion—the first to have as many as 50 telegraphers on the job—the first to wire the game by play-by-play to points as distant as Havana, Cuba—the first to which newspapers in the Far West and South sent their own writers. And though the A's now had a lead of two games to one, the threat of the Giants was still great enough to keep fever high.

It was a little after one o'clock when my long vigil ended. Onto the field came the Giants with their immemorial swagger, chips still on their shoulders—the cocky, ornery, defiant men of Muggsy McGraw—the rip-roaring demons who had that season of 1911 set a record of 347 stolen bases—a record which would stand for another 31 years without any other club ever coming nearer to it than the Senators' 288 in 1913.

And here at long last they were! I knew them from their pictures as, clad in dangerous black, they came strutting across toward their dugout. McGraw had dressed his men in black, back in 1905 when he had humbled the Athletics, and he was playing hunches now.

Muggsy was first—stocky, hard-eyed. Behind him came slim, handsome Snodgrass, striding as became a genius at getting hit by pitched balls and in scaring infielders with his flashing spikes. Then came swart, ominous Larry Doyle; lantern-jawed Art Fletcher; Buck Herzog, whose nose curved like a scimitar; lithe little Josh Devore; burly Otis Crandall; flat-faced, mahogany-colored Chief Meyers, the full-blooded Indian; Fred Merkle, all muscles even in his jaws, a lion-heart living down the most awful bonehead blunder ever made in baseball.

Then came Marquard, 6 feet 3, his sharp face and slit-like eyes smiling—his head tilting to the left at the top of a long wry neck—Marquard the meteoric! At 19 years of age he had been bought at a record price from Indianapolis and had immediately flopped two straight years for McGraw, becoming the nationally goatish "$11,000 lemon." Then, this 1911, he had flamed out, won 24 games, and become the "$11,000 beauty."

As the Giants began to toss the ball around, I couldn't see

my hero, the Mathewson whom I had come to see, the great one who from the time I was nine I had pretended I was, playing ball in the Indiana cow pasture, throwing his famous "fadeaway" which, for me, never came off. Then, suddenly, there he was, warming up and growling "Who am I working for, the Giants or the photographers," as the cameramen, not 20 feet from my popeyed head, begged him for poses.

I was let down for a minute. He didn't speak like a demi-god, but as I stared, he looked it, all the same. He held his head high, and his eye with slow, lordly contempt swept the Athletics as they warmed up across the field. He was 31, all bone and muscle and princely poise. Surely he would get those Athletics today and put the Giants back in the running. Surely his unique "fadeaway," the curve that broke backward, his speed, his snapping curve, his fabulous brain, couldn't be stopped. It had been luck that had beaten him in the last game. Now he'd get them.

My eye never left him till the bell rang and he strode, hard but easy, with the swing of the aristocrat, into the dugout and little Josh Devore went up to hit.

Josh singled, Doyle tripled, Snodgrass scored Larry with a long fly. Black figures were flying everywhere. The big copper-colored Chief Bender on Mack's mound was wobbling, and when the side was finally out he practically ran for the dugout. Later, we learned, he had run in to cut off bandages from his ribs, tape from a recent injury. After that he was to be unbeatable.

Up came the Athletics. Matty, as though in princely disdain, fanned the first two men. The third man, Eddie Collins, singled. Here came Baker, his sun-tanned face tense, his bat flailing—the air thick with one word from 25,000 throats, "Homer! Homer!"

Matty studied him as a scientist contemplates a beetle,

then struck him out! What I yelled, I don't know. All I remember is standing there bellowing and paying no heed to the wadded newspapers the Athletic fans around me threw. It was wonderful.

In the fourth, Baker came up to start it and doubled. Dannie Murphy doubled. Harry Davis doubled. Ira Thomas hit a sacrifice fly—three runs. It couldn't be. Up came Baker again in the fifth with Collins on first and another double boomed across the diamond. I saw Snodgrass eventually stop it, but he didn't really have it in his glove at all. It had stuck in my gullet.

Right in front of me an unthinkable thing happened. Hooks Wiltse, the southpaw, began warming up for the Giants. Was Matty knocked out? Another figure rose from the bull pen. Rube Marquard. He didn't warm up, he only strolled up and down, a great sardonic grin on his face. The fans around me were screaming at him, "You're even with Matty now, Rube! He won't tell you what to pitch anymore!" etc., etc. Rube smirked at them.

Matty got by without more scores, but in the seventh with a man on third Christy walked Baker on four intentional balls, and Shibe Park's walls waved in a cyclone of "boos." I wished I were dead.

The eighth. A pinch hitter went up for Mathewson. I was sorry I hadn't died in the seventh.

Finally it was all over.

I walked out through 25,000 of the most loathsome individuals ever created—all jeering at Mathewson, all howling Baker's virtues. I dragged my feet this way and that trying to escape the currents of fans. At the end of a dolorous mile I stopped at a saloon. I had never had a drink. Now was the time.

"Beer," I said, in the voice of Poe's raven.

"You ain't 21," the bartender rasped. Then he took a second look, saw that I was 100 years old, and splashed a great stein in front of me.

I took one swallow. It was bitter, just as bitter as everything else in the world. I laid down a nickel and walked out. Every step of the way downtown I kept telling myself that in my coffin, some day, there'd be only room for one thing besides myself—my hatred of the Athletics.

But what I started out to tell was about my greatest day in baseball. That came three years later, Oct. 9, 1914, when the lowly, despised Boston Braves wallowed, humbled, trampled, laughed at the lofty Athletics to the tune of 7 to 1. Hoarse and happy, I came out of Shibe Park, spent hours hunting that same saloon, but I couldn't find it. It had to be that one. What I wanted to do was to walk in all alone—find nobody else in there—order two beers, and when the bartender looked inquiringly at the extra one, say to him in a condescending voice, "Oh, that? That's for Mathewson."

INTELLIGENTSIA DE LA BOXE

BY
Stanley Woodward

(NEW YORK HERALD TRIBUNE)
FEBRUARY 3, 1944.

ROYAL CORTISSOZ was unavailable. Carlyle Burrows had other things to do. Therefore your agent went to cover one of the principal art exhibits of the current winter season, in the Jansen suite of the Waldorf-Astoria. This exhibit was unique in that no one looked at the pictures. The clientele stood around drinking Martinis and Manhattans, talking fights, submitting to radio broadcasts and newsreels, yet, withal, keeping their minds open in case any one should mention art.

It was the world premiere of Mickey Walker, the old battler, on painting canvas. He had been out of circulation ever since he quit the ginmill on Eighth Avenue which bears his name, but he was there among his paintings, his former managers, his historians and his fleegees.

Your agent timidly approached Mr. Walker and requested that he make a circuit of the fourteen exhibits and explain them. Unfortunately, the painter was summoned at that moment to appear in a newsreel, with a prop beret, a palette and a brush which one of the photographers had borrowed from a fellow artist who had been painting the elevator shaft.

Consequently we made the artistic tour alone, except for

Willard Mullin, "The World-Telegram" maestro, whose comments were designed to confuse rather than aid. As we walked around attempting to see the artistic light, Mr. Mullin poured a line of double-talk into our ear about the Siennese influence, the tonality, the depth, the color—in short, the entire flebiscence of the trocunda.

Disregarding the professional comments of Mr. Mullin, we shall now give our own impressions of the exhibit, as follows: the drinks were good; the editors of "Click," which fostered the show, were hospitable; the Kleig lights were bright, and the painting was just about what you'd think it would be.

The surprising thing was that Mickey could get hold of the gear a painter is supposed to handle and make anything that looked like anything: a house, a cow, a field of wheat or a seashore. Notwithstanding our pre-exhibit doubts, Mickey is capable of reproducing all these things, and more. Incidentally, he has put the old one-two in some of them.

Now to describe the high lights of our tour of the room: the newsreel photographers kept moving the pictures around so it is hard to list them as (1), (2), (3), (4), as is done at less well attended art exhibits. When we started, No. 1 was a prizefight scene in which one competitor was lying on his face, the other was rasing his hand in triumph. Blobs of faces surrounded the ring. Mickey said that each one was a study.

However, when we went back for a second look to be sure of this, the painting had been jerked into the other room for examination by Tony Galento, who had been outfitted with a monocle and was standing in a glare reciting art criticism that some one had given him on a piece of paper. Tony had studied the fifteen-word critique for an hour, but it took twenty minutes of unbroken photography to get him to come up with a resemblance of the original.

There was a boating scene in which all the boats were anchored with their sails up in bright moonlight. There was one called "The Bridge of Sighs" which was chiefly notable for the detail and lack of perspective which marked the masonry.

There was a hayfield fantasy in which two dames were handing marsh grass to a gent in a two-wheeled cart drawn by two vestal virgins in long shifts. There was a New York skyline at night with myriads of lights dubbed in, a picture of the old Walker homestead in Rumson, N. J., with each bush and flower in place. There was another which depicted a man carrying a bundle on a stick, just passing a stone and wood garage and setting out across a mass of brown and purple uncertainty.

The one that Mickey obviously liked best was called "Ghost Town." It represented the busted night club and pugilistic exploits of one Billy Duffy. It looked like the world's fair the day after. In the foreground was a sign with the names of some of those managed by Duffy, including Walker and "Canera."

Duffy himself was there and looked benignly on this effort and the others. Before the show was over a lot of other guys from the mob drifted in. However, Galento was the one the newsreels wanted and it was pretty uproarious when Tony got off his artistic criticism.

As Mr. Mullin was going out, with his co-artist, Alan Chidsey, your agent attempted to get a final impression from them. Mr. Mullin refused to be interviewed. Mr. Chidsey was more obliging. His comment follows:

"Boil me for an artichoke if that wasn't the damnedest art exhibit of history"——

FEET OF CLAY

BY
Dave Egan

(BOSTON DAILY RECORD)
FEBRUARY 17, 1944.

ROGERS HORNSBY, A MEMBER of baseball's Hall of Fame and a connoisseur of the superior mudder, has accepted a position as manager of the Vera Cruz team in the Mexican League, and the righteous brethren who operate major league baseball should hang their heads in shame.

There would be fierce resentment, I feel sure, if Man o' War were put to work pulling a vegetable wagon through his declining years, and the Society for the Prevention of Cruelty to Animals would take an immediate interest in the affair. But the baseball brethren will derive smug satisfaction from the fact that one of their immortals will play the patched-roof circuit, and one of their idols will gather the dust of sleepy Mexican towns. He sinned against their narrow code, and as a sinner should, he now gets his comeuppance.

His sin was that he was a robust horse-player, and did not care who knew it. So he was ridden on a rail out of the major leagues, not because he wagered on the steeds but because he had the common honesty to admit it and to ask, in a cold voice, whose business it was.

I could name you a highly respected umpire who in the

privacy of his hotel room wears thick-lensed glasses, the better to study the past performances in the racing sheets.

I could name you a prominent major leaguer who, under a convenient alias, owns and races a string of thoroughbreds.

I could name you squads and platoons and regiments of big-leaguers, from general managers down to substitute right fielders, who wager on the relative speed of the dobbins. But Hornsby, with his ruthless honesty, did not conceal it and would not deny it. So you may believe me when I tell you that hypocrisy pays large dividends in our national pastime, and that ordinary candor winds you up in Vera Cruz.

Your correspondent lately has been reading the life story of John Barrymore, by the brilliant Gene Fowler, and it strikes me that Hornsby is the Barrymore of baseball; that these two men, so diametrically different, are strangely alike. No more turbulent figures ever took such twisted routes to their individual halls of fame, and no two gentlemen ever got more action wherever they went.

The big guy with the ice-water eyes and the disarming dimple was appointed playing manager of the Cardinals in the midst of the 1925 season. In 1926, he led them to the first National League championship they ever had won. He parlayed that into a stirring victory over the Yankees in the World Series. So he asked for a boodle of money and the Cardinals, out of sheer gratitude for their first championship, promptly traded him to the Giants, in a pleasant little display of sportsmanship that led the customers to boycott the team.

The horses, however, had been running to form in the good year 1926, and Hornsby had the forethought to purchase more than 1000 shares of stock in the Cardinals at $45 the share. Now the momentous question arose, could a player on the Giants hold stock in the Cardinals? The answer, of course, was an emphatic no. So Hornsby hung on the neck of the Cardinals like unto an albatross until he sold them back the stock. Not, however, at $45 the share, but at $116 the share, to make a net profit of more than $75,000 from the tidy little deal.

He played in New York for one season, which seems to have been par for his particular course. Mr. Stoneham, president of the club, asked him one day whether or not it was true that he wagered on horses. His answer offended Mr. Stoneham deeply, with the result that he was traded to the Braves in return for Frank Hogan and Jimmy Welsh. The ordinary athlete, traded to the Braves, usually slips into obscurity and is forgotten by everybody except his next of kin, but Hornsby, somehow or other, succeeded only in stepping from the frying pan into the fire.

Here in Boston, he became manager as successor to the popular Jack Slattery and immediately was hailed on all sides as a Ku Kluxer. The truth was that he had married a Catholic girl, and was bringing up his children in the Catholic faith, but it made no difference then, and it makes little difference now. He was born to be a target, and brought up to be a stormy petrel, as one of the lads at the gym always puts it.

So he moved on to Chicago, and naturally became manager of the Cubs. There a genteel shakedown ensued, and Hornsby refused to be shaken. So a blood-thirsty bookmaker, in a laudable effort to ruin his career, sued him for something like $60,000. The case was thrown out of court, but Hornsby also was thrown out of Chicago, with the result that he found himself back in St. Louis as manager of the Browns.

The rest of the column could be written with ditto marks, if I were as lazy as some folks, mentioning no names and present company naturally excepted. Mr. Donald Barnes, owner of the club, one day asked him the usual question about betting on horses. The Rajah made the usual answer, and appended the usual so-what-if-I-do. So he was fired forthwith—fired out of the American League, fired out of the National League, fired out of the life he had known for a quarter of a century because he had not been a hypocrite, and had not played it smart, and had not told smooth lies.

This is not the usual picture of a baseball immortal, but it is the right picture of Hornsby, a great ball player and a great manager who did not drink and did not smoke and could not lie even when his career depended upon a successful lie. So now he is in Vera Cruz, which is a long way from Cooperstown as the crow flies, yet somehow or other, he is of taller stature and greater dignity than the righteous brethren who now rejoice that the mighty have fallen.